Scott Foresman

Assessment Handbook

Reading STREET

Grades K-1

Glenview, Illinois • Boston, Massachusetts • Chandler, Arizona • Upper Saddle River, New Jersey

ALWAYS LEARNING

PEARSON

The Pearson Promise

As the largest educational publishing company in the world, Pearson is committed to providing you with curriculum that not only meets the Common Core State Standards, but also supports your implementation of these standards with your students.

Pearson has aligned the Common Core State Standards to every grade level of *Scott Foresman Reading Street,* our premier educational curriculum.

We value your partnership highly and look forward to continuing our mission to provide educational materials that fully satisfy your classroom needs.

ISBN-13: 978-0-328-72632-5
ISBN-10:   0-328-72632-X
2 3 4 5 6 7 8 9 10 V016 21 20 19 18 17 16 15 14 13 12

Contents

Scott Foresman *Reading Street* Assessment

Some Questions and Answers

This *Assessment Handbook* will be a resource throughout the school year. The handbook presents an overview of the Scott Foresman *Reading Street* assessment program, and it provides numerous resources that you may use to best fit your assessment, instruction, and learning goals. In addition, the *Assessment Handbook* may be regarded as a professional development resource. Inside you will find:

- guidance for using a variety of diagnostic, entry-level, progress-monitoring, summative, and classroom-based assessments;

- suggestions for using writing to strengthen learning and to assess learning;

- proven methods and models for assessing, evaluating, and grading children's work;

- steps for designing quality assessments in all content areas; and

- instructional strategies for preparing children for state-required assessments.

Scott Foresman *Reading Street* assessments reflect current theories of teaching language and literacy and are aligned with solid classroom teaching practices. Formal and classroom-based assessments, combined with "assessable moments" during instruction, become a continuous cycle in which one is always informing and supporting the other, resulting in a seamless learning program for children.

Following are some commonly asked questions about the Scott Foresman *Reading Street* assessment program.

How was the Scott Foresman *Reading Street* assessment program developed?

The assessment components of Scott Foresman *Reading Street* were developed by a specialized testing organization, Questar Assessment, Incorporated. Scott Foresman authorial and editorial staff guided these development activities, specifying the purposes to be served by each component and their general coverage. In addition, Scott Foresman editorial teams critiqued and approved the test specifications and prototype test items for each program element that were developed by Questar. Finally, Scott Foresman reviewed and provided editorial feedback on all test content. However, the development of all materials was the responsibility of Questar Assessment staff.

Questar Assessment's development team, formerly Beck Evaluation & Testing Associates, Incorporated (BETA), is one of the country's most experienced assessment-development corporations. Over the past twenty years, Questar's test development team has provided standardized test content for a broad range of state and federal agencies in addition to most leading test and textbook publishers. Questar has played key roles in developing large-scale, high-stakes testing programs in over twenty-five states. Questar staff regularly assist state Departments of Education and federal agencies on matters of test development, implementation, and psychometrics, providing such consultation to over thirty-six state Departments of Education. Over the past decade, Questar has developed over 82,000 test items for use in large-scale assessment programs. Most of these programs include the assessment of elementary reading and other language arts skills.

All test items developed by Questar are written by experienced assessment-development professionals, all with extensive experience in creating test questions in the appropriate content areas and for the targeted grade levels. The development activities in support of Scott Foresman *Reading Street* were directed by Questar senior staff members, and all test items were written specifically for Scott Foresman *Reading Street*.

How will your program help prepare children for required state and national standardized tests?

In many ways! The Student Editions, Teacher's Editions, and Reader's and Writer's Notebooks are all carefully crafted to teach the knowledge, skills, and strategies children need in order to meet or exceed the standards in all their reading and writing tasks. Many Reader's and Writer's Notebook pages contain items that reflect common standardized test formats, allowing children repeated opportunities to become familiar with question patterns. In addition, the formal entry-level, progress-monitoring, and summative assessments are comprised of literal, inferential, and critical-analysis questions based on the question-answer framework used in instruction and are similar to question types on high-stakes tests used in school districts. Tips on instructional strategies designed to prepare children for state-required assessments are described in Chapter 1 of this handbook and in Chapter 6, where they are tailored for English language learners. With the preparation provided by Scott Foresman *Reading Street* materials, children will have experience with a variety of test-taking situations and learn a variety of test-taking skills.

How do I find out where children are at the beginning of the year?

Finding a starting point for each child can be difficult. Scott Foresman *Reading Street* makes it easier by providing test options and parent and learner surveys to help you get to know children's skills, abilities, and interests.

Entry-level assessments provide information about where to begin instruction for individual learners. The more you know about your children at the beginning of the year, the better equipped you are to maximize their learning experiences to ensure that they achieve continuous growth in writing, speaking, reading, and listening skills. The group-administered *Reading Street* Baseline Group Test gives you information about the instructional needs of your class and points you to program features that help you meet those needs. The Group Reading Assessment and Diagnostic Evaluation (GRADE) is a norm-referenced formal assessment that may help you to determine children's prerequisite skills and knowledge. The Developmental Reading Assessment (DRA) enables you to make a quick analysis of a child's independent reading level. Student surveys, such as the questionnaire Myself as a Learner, familiarize you with each child's reading attitudes and interests, while parent surveys, such as My Child as a Learner, give you insights into their literacy habits and behaviors when they are not in school. Chapter 2 of this handbook describes all of the entry-level formal and informal classroom-based assessment techniques and tools available to you through
Scott Foresman *Reading Street*. All entry-level and diagnostic assessment information helps you determine which content standards have been mastered, resulting in appropriate placement and planning for each child in your class.

How do I know that children are being tested on the right skills?

Scott Foresman *Reading Street* is founded on a carefully crafted scope and sequence of skills, based on the most current research and accepted practices in reading instruction, and systematically aligned with state language arts and reading standards.

This scope and sequence is the basis for both the instructional plan and for the depth and breadth of the Scott Foresman *Reading Street* assessment program. Target skills and strategies are taught in each lesson and then assessed in the Weekly Test. Each target skill is also assessed in the Unit Benchmark Test after it has been taught and reviewed multiple times. This systematic alignment of instruction and assessment ensures that children are being tested on what they are being taught, in the way they are being taught.

What is the best way to assess my class? How does your program provide what I need?

Accurate and ongoing assessment enables teachers to monitor children's progress toward achieving the standards, to evaluate classroom instruction, and to help children monitor their own learning. An effective assessment system incorporates a variety of assessment methods—both formal and informal—to help teachers meet those varied purposes.

Scott Foresman *Reading Street* provides a full complement of materials to meet your assessment requirements. For a formal assessment of unit skills and selections, you will find several different tests from which to choose. For classroom-based assessment, the *Assessment Handbook* contains surveys, observation forms, and reporting forms, as well as questioning and observation techniques you can adapt for your classroom needs. These informal strategies will assist you in making children's self-assessment, peer assessment, portfolios, and grading more efficient. Also, the Teacher's Editions provide tools for you to make both immediate and long-term decisions about the instructional needs of children in your classroom.

How does your program support assessment of my English language learners?

Scott Foresman *Reading Street* recognizes the unique challenges and rewards of teaching and assessing the progress of English language learners. Chapter 6 of the *Assessment Handbook* discusses research-based methods of assessing the strengths and needs of English language learners in your classroom. Scott Foresman *Reading Street* classroom-based assessments reflect those methods as they help teachers monitor progress in the basic reading and expression skills of alphabetic understanding, decoding, sight vocabulary, and grammar, along with measurement of the more complex skills of fluency, comprehension, and vocabulary. The chapter provides guidance on instructional strategies designed to prepare English language learners for standardized tests, including high-stakes tests, as well as advice on appropriate use of accommodations for Scott Foresman *Reading Street* formal assessments.

How will your program help me when I have to assign grades?

Because we know that grading is a major concern for many teachers, we devote an entire chapter (7) to record keeping and grading. We recognize that you will be using the Scott Foresman *Reading Street* tools to assess children's literacy skills and strategies at the beginning of the year and monitor progress throughout the year. You will be collecting large amounts of information about children. Access to this data informs sound decision-making relating to the focus of the curriculum, effectiveness of instruction, meaningful feedback to children and parents, and improved achievement, but it is often difficult to manage.

In Chapter 7, you will find guidance for keeping accurate, informative records and sharing details with children, parents, and others. Advice for implementing portfolios and grading is also provided; you will review how to design scoring rubrics, evaluate children's participation in class discussions and group activities, grade oral presentations, and assess individual or group writing.

Add to this the many formal testing opportunities, which are an integral part of the program, and you have an assessment program that gives you the information you need to meet your assessment requirements.

Program Assessment Overview

A variety of assessment instruments, used with fiction and nonfiction selections, allow you to

- determine children's strengths and needs
- monitor children's progress
- measure children's skill and strategy proficiencies
- evaluate the effectiveness of instruction

from the beginning of the school year to the end!

Baseline Group Tests

Weekly Tests

Fresh Reads for Fluency and Comprehension

Unit Benchmark Tests

End-of-Year Benchmark Tests

Assessment Handbook

Technology

Online
ASSESSMENT
ReadingStreet.com

Beginning of the Year

Entry-Level Assessments

Baseline Group Test

- Is administered as a placement test to your entire class
- Provides options for group and individual administration
- Identifies your below-level students requiring strategic intervention
- Identifies your on-level students
- Identifies your above-level students requiring challenge
- Helps you use Scott Foresman *Reading Street* features and components to focus instruction on students' needs
- Establishes baseline data

Assessment Handbook for Grades K–1

Informal, classroom-based assessment tools and techniques, including:

- Student and parent surveys
- Reading, writing, and oral-language teacher checklists
- Learner inventories and profiles

During the Year

Progress-Monitoring Assessments

Teacher's Edition and *First Stop*

- Ongoing assessment
- Success Predictor boxes
- Guiding Comprehension questions
- Reading fluency assessment
- Think Critically
- Look Back and Write scoring rubrics
- Writing model answers
- Spelling tests
- Weekly assessment for phonemic awareness, phonics, high-frequency words, and comprehension

Reader's and Writer's Notebook

- Provides practice pages for phonics, vocabulary, spelling, and comprehension skills
- Reading and writing logs
- Helps you identify children needing more instruction

Weekly Tests (Grade 1)

- Are multiple-choice tests administered on Day 5 of every week
- Measure children's understanding of each week's high-frequency words, word reading/phonics skills, and comprehension skills
- Help identify children who have mastered each week's words and skills and children who may need intervention

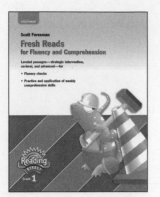

Fresh Reads for Fluency and Comprehension (Grade 1)

- Are multiple-choice and constructed-response tests administered throughout the year, each week after children have been taught the comprehension skill lesson

- Give children opportunities to practice the target and review comprehension skills of the week with new selections matched to their instructional reading levels

- Provide checks of oral reading fluency for first-grade children

Unit Benchmark Tests

- Are multiple-choice and constructed-response tests administered throughout the year, at the end of each six-week unit

- Measure children's abilities to apply target comprehension skills and other literacy skills taught during each unit

- Help you make instructional decisions for each child

- Provide feedback about the effectiveness of your instruction and help you plan instruction for the next unit

Assessment Handbook for Grades K–1

Informal, classroom-based assessment tools and techniques, including:

- Questioning strategies
- Teacher observation forms
- Fluency checks (Grade 1)
- Retelling and summarizing forms
- Work habits and skills conference records
- Parent observation form
- Student portfolios
- Reading and writing logs

Technology

- Online assessment and data management with diagnostic prescriptions

- Exam View: Test generator with alignment to statewide and district-wide standards and prescriptions

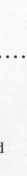

End of the Year

Summative Assessments

End-of-Year Benchmark Test

- Is a cumulative test administered at the end of each grade
- Provides three reading selections
- Tests comprehension skills, high-frequency words, phonics skills, written conventions (grammar, usage, and mechanics skills), and writing
- Combines multiple-choice and constructed response questions
- Provides an integrated approach to assessment

Assessment Handbook for Grades K–1

Informal, classroom-based assessment tools and techniques, including:

- Summary reports, forms, and checklists
- Student portfolios
- Cumulative folder forms
- Reading and writing logs
- Reading and writing assessment forms
- Guidance with grading

Technology

- Online assessment and data management with diagnostic prescriptions
- Exam View: Test generator with alignment to statewide and district-wide standards and prescriptions

Chapter 1

Assessment Literacy

Overview

Classroom teachers make an extraordinary number of decisions every hour of the school day. Four important decisions are:

1. What are the critical understandings and skills that I want children to know and be able to do upon completion of this lesson/unit/grade?

2. How will I know if the children have reached these expectations?

3. What will I do to support those who have not met these standards?

4. What will I do to support those who already have exceeded the standards?

The critical understandings and skills are the **learning targets,** usually based on school, district, and state curriculum standards. The second question is the focus of this introductory section of the handbook: ***How will I know? What evidence must I collect?*** Scott Foresman *Reading Street* Teacher's Editions and other program resources provide ongoing guidance for implementing intervention techniques for struggling readers and extending and enriching the curriculum for advanced learners.

Reading Street also offers valuable resources, strategies, and tools for collecting evidence of achievement and encourages educators to be wise about the subject of **assessment**—what it is, when to use it, how to do it, and why it is so important.

What Is Assessment Literacy?

Now, more than ever before, it is important for all teachers and administrators to be "literate" about educational assessment and evaluation. Why? Research tells us that the use of meaningful classroom assessment strategies and tools, such as questioning, observational methods, and student self-assessment, empowers educators, guides instruction, and improves learning.

Further, we cannot ignore that increased demands for accountability at the state and national levels, e.g., *Reading First, No Child Left Behind (NCLB),* and *Adequate Yearly Progress (AYP),* etc., have produced an unprecedented proliferation of testing, and children's test performance has become the accountability yardstick by which the effectiveness of schools, districts, states, and even teaching is measured and judged.

To be informed consumers and creators of assessment, individuals must:

- understand the power of assessment in promoting student achievement;

- become knowledgeable about the functions, strengths, and limitations of formal and informal assessment;

- maintain a balance of summative and formative assessments in their classrooms and schools;

- embrace standards of quality as they evaluate and create assessments; and

- use sound assessment practices to design and administer quality classroom-based assessments.

What Is Assessment?

The Latin root of the word "assess" means "to sit beside." This is a much gentler notion of this concept than most of us have, although "sitting beside" a child to confer about the development of a story in progress, to conduct a fluency check, or to observe a group discussion are valuable assessment techniques. What is assessment? *Assessment is simply the gathering and interpretation of evidence about student learning.* There are many methods for collecting information to determine if children have mastered the knowledge and skills, or the learning targets. We can use a variety of formal and informal or classroom-based measures to collect that evidence.

Summative and Formative Assessment

Summative assessments are formal assessment measures, most often regarded as tests or tasks presented to children in order to obtain conclusive evidence about their performance. Tasks are designed to provide samples of individual achievement and are administered, scored, and interpreted according to mostly prescribed conditions. These activities are regarded as **summative** because they come at the *end* of an instructional process and are used to determine placement or assign grades. Examples might be chapter tests, unit projects, culminating performances, and final examinations. (Airasian, 2000)

Standardized tests are summative assessments designed to be administered to large numbers of test-takers. The tests are administered at the same time each year, and testing conditions, such as precise directions, time allowances, and security procedures, are tightly controlled. Test questions are written, reviewed, and revised following tryouts by a representative sample of the population for which the instrument is designed.

Examples of standardized tests are commercially published tests, as well as state assessments, which are now used annually to measure student achievement of standards for reporting and accountability purposes, in compliance with federal *NCLB* legislation and other mandates. These tests are often called "high-stakes," because scores are made very public, and schools and districts are subject to sanctions and embarrassment if they do not make annual *AYP* goals. (Popham, 2004)

Dr. Richard Stiggins distinguishes between assessment *of* learning and assessment *for* learning. Assessments of learning are generally formal, summative assessments administered at the end of an instructional period. They answer the question, "How much have children learned as of a particular point in time?" (Stiggins, 2002)

Formative assessment is the process of systematically and continuously collecting evidence about children's learning and monitoring their progress. It is classroom-based assessment *for* learning that helps us *dig deeper* in order to ascertain exactly *how* individual children are making progress toward achievement of the learning targets. These assessments are called **formative** because they are influential in "forming" the process under way and are intended to guide and inform instruction.

Scott Foresman *Reading Street* offers a variety of formal and informal formative assessment techniques. While informal assessment tasks may not be the same type or depth for all children, and may not be recorded in a prescribed, standardized manner, they are not "informal" in the sense of "casual" or "random." Instead, use of informal assessments is the thoughtfully planned, intentional monitoring of learning embedded within the instructional process, rather than the evaluation of learning at the conclusion of the process.

Examples of formative assessment tools are teachers' questions, observations, checklists, portfolios, homework, student self-assessment, and teacher-child conferences, as well as weekly and unit tests.

Balancing Formative and Summative Assessment

Annually administered tests provide general feedback about children's performance related to broad content standards, or achievement targets. These tests are not designed to offer the immediate and ongoing information about achievement that teachers need to make critical instructional decisions. Even once-a-unit classroom tests do not provide sufficient information to improve teaching and increase learning. (Stiggins, 2004)

To establish and maintain productive, learning-centered classroom environments, teachers rely on a balance of informal assessments *for* learning and formal assessments *of* learning to guide their instruction. They use an array of formative and summative measures *derived from* and/or *aligned with* the content standards and based on their assessment purposes.

> "Balance continuous classroom assessment in support of learning with periodic assessments verifying learning."
> (Stiggins, 2004)

Why and when do we monitor progress with formative assessment?

- To diagnose children's strengths and needs

- To elicit prior knowledge for a concept or topic

- To provide frequent feedback to children that is descriptive and helpful, rather than judgmental, as in grades

- To motivate learners to increase effort as they experience incremental successes

- To build children's confidence in themselves as learners

- To help children take responsibility for their learning as they monitor their progress and adjust their goals

- To plan, modify, and regulate the pace of instruction to meet the needs of all children

- To communicate with parents and caregivers (e.g., learning expectations, children's progress in meeting learning targets, and methods of providing support at home)

Why do we obtain evidence with summative assessment?

- To report achievement of the reading and language arts content standards, the learning targets

- To document growth over time (e.g., unit-to-unit, year-to-year)

- To assign grades appropriately at the end of a unit, for a report card, etc.

- To validate judgments and decisions about children's achievement

- To recommend children for promotion and placement in special programs

- To gauge program effectiveness, note strengths, and identify gaps

- To examine comparative data across schools and districts in order to make programmatic decisions (e.g., establish school improvement priorities, improve curriculum alignment, establish a need for intervention programs, additional resources, etc.)

- To satisfy state and federal accountability mandates, such as AYP

- To inform the public (e.g., tax payers, business leaders, and legislators)

Evaluating Assessments for Quality

Most textbooks and instructional programs, including Scott Foresman *Reading Street*, have accompanying assessments for teachers to use. The formal and informal measures within *Reading Street* reflect the highest standards of quality and seamlessly align with the instructional program, yet teachers may wish to occasionally construct their own tests and performance assessments for other content areas and interdisciplinary studies.

> "…educators need to become sufficiently assessment literate so they can understand and, if necessary, help improve any accountability system that relies on unsuitable achievement tests."
> (Popham, 2004)

In order to implement fair and sound assessment, teachers are encouraged to consider the following standards for evaluating the quality of commercial assessments and designing their own classroom assessments to augment or replace the textbook measures.

Know Your Learning Targets

Statewide and district-wide curriculum statements embody the content knowledge and skills we want our children to have, and they are the basis for all of our testing.

- "Unpack" the content standards to identify the underlying knowledge, concepts, processes, skills, and dispositions (e.g., attitudes, values, habits of mind) that become the **learning targets.**

- Translate the targets into child-friendly language.

- Post the targets in the classroom for all to see.

- Discuss the targets with the children at the beginning of the instructional process (e.g., lesson, unit, marking period).

- Review them throughout the process so that children have clear, reachable targets to hit.

Determine the Match

Teachers must carefully scrutinize each test item to ensure that the assessment has **content validity**. To what extent does the assessment measure what it is used to measure? Does the content of the test or task represent a balanced and adequate sampling of the targeted knowledge and skills as they are taught in the classroom? In other words, a recall exercise in which children are to match vocabulary words with their definitions would not be a valid assessment of a vocabulary standard requiring children to use structural analysis and context clues to determine word meanings. Test questions and tasks should be "instructionally sensitive"; that is, they should clearly reflect the learning targets and require children to perform the behaviors as you have taught them.

Consider the Number of Tested Standards

An effective assessment measures only a modest number of important learning targets and measures them well, so that teachers and children are not overwhelmed by the length and complexity of the activity. (Popham, 2004) Assessments are meant to sample components of the learning that takes place in the classroom, so an appropriate test or task must also contain a sufficient number of items related to each sampled learning target. In this way, teachers can be confident that the results will identify target skill areas that have been thoroughly taught and those that need improvement.

Strive for Reliability and Fairness

Reliability: How trustworthy is this assessment? Can I rely on the scores? Will this assessment give me the same results about the same learning targets every time?

Scoring of selected-response tests is considered quite reliable, and two teachers scoring the same set of multiple-choice tests will probably get the same results, barring a small chance of human error.

Although constructed-response assessments may measure more meaningful learning targets, they are considered less reliable because extensive training is needed in order to achieve consistency in scoring. To increase reliability, many states and school districts develop scoring rubrics and train scorers in a thorough, systematic way. Panels of raters score a large number of papers and discuss their scores until they're consistent in their ratings. Some papers are chosen as anchor papers because the raters believe they exemplify score points on the rubric. These papers are then used to guide subsequent scoring sessions, and reliability is improved. This activity can be replicated at the building level as teachers of the same grade level collaborate to design and score performance assessments, such as end-of-unit projects and presentations.

Fairness: Do all children, including those with diverse cultural and linguistic backgrounds, have an equal chance to demonstrate what they know and can do? Have all of them had the same opportunity to learn the content? Are the directions clear? Is the environment comfortable?

Fairness in assessment is compromised when teachers assess knowledge and skills that have not been taught or use assessment formats that do not reflect *how* the learning targets have been taught (e.g., asking for opinions and reasons when the emphasis has been on recall of facts).

Designing Quality Classroom Assessments

Teachers can construct multi-purpose classroom assessments that reflect the standards of quality—validity, reliability, and fairness. Purposes include diagnosing children's strengths and needs; planning, monitoring progress, and adjusting instruction; and providing feedback to children, parents, and others regarding progress and proficiency. The following design questions are intended to guide educators as they plan and build their own assessments:

1. **What learning target(s) based on the statewide and district-wide curriculum standards will you assess?**

2. **For which formative or summative purpose(s) is this assessment being administered?**

   - To detect strengths and needs
   - To motivate learners
   - To assign grades
   - To check progress
   - To group for instruction
   - To collect additional evidence
   - To evaluate instruction
   - Other

3. **Who will use the results of this assessment?**

   - Students
   - Teacher(s)
   - Parent(s)
   - Principal
   - Community
   - Other

4. **What format will the assessment take?**

   It is important to select the format that most appropriately matches the target. For example, you wouldn't create a multiple-choice test to assess children's use of action verbs in their writing. Rather, you would assign a constructed-response activity asking them to incorporate action verbs in their text.

   Conversely, you wouldn't use a constructed-response format to assess children's identification of states and their capitals. An activity requiring them to match states and capitals would suffice for this purpose—assessing recall. Constructed responses are valuable because they help us seek insights into children's reasoning behind their answers or evidence that they can apply what they have learned. Possible assessment formats and examples of activities are listed in the table on page 23.

5. What criteria will you use to evaluate performance?

- How will you know it when you see it?

- What does hitting the target look like? What are the qualities?

- Is there one right answer or several possible answers?

- What will you accept as evidence that children have hit the target; that is, that they have acquired the knowledge and skills identified in the content standards?

6. What type of feedback will be provided to guide improvement?

How will results be communicated? How will you tell the story behind the numbers? Will you use a letter grade, a rubric score, written descriptive comments, a checklist, a point on a continuum of learning (such as an oral language behaviors' continuum), or another way?

The most valuable feedback is very specific and descriptive of how the performance hits (or does not hit) the target. Give concrete suggestions rather than vague comments or encouragement, such as "Nice work!" or "You can do better next time!" Share clear examples of successful work with children, and have them compare their work with the model. Allow children opportunities to revise their performances.

Transforming learning expectations into assessment tasks, assigning criteria, designing scoring procedures, and preparing feedback are challenging and time-consuming activities when they are attempted alone. It is a rewarding and collegial experience to collaborate with peers in articulating expectations, designing common assessments, analyzing student work, and selecting anchor/model performances. When educators work together to become assessment-literate, they empower each other with the ability to improve assessment practices and accountability systems in their school districts and states. More importantly, they increase learning for children.

Assessment Design Options

Possible Format	Examples of Tasks	Suggested Scoring/Feedback
Selected-Response	• Multiple-choice • Matching • True-false	One right answer; cut scores and percentages
Short Constructed-Response (written/oral)	• Fill-in-the-blank • Sentence completion • Graphic organizer • Brief response to prompt	One (or few) right answers; cut scores and percentages
Extended Constructed-Response (written/oral)	• Prompt-based narrative, descriptive, expository, and persuasive writing • Retellings • Position with support • Summaries	More than one right answer; scoring with checklists, descriptive criteria, standards, continuum, rubrics, comparative models
Performances	• Oral presentation • Demonstration • Discussion • Role play	More than one right answer; scoring with checklists, descriptive criteria, standards, continuum, rubrics, peer and self-evaluation, comparative models
Products	• Science project • Visual display • Model • Video • Poem, story, play • Log/journal • Portfolio	More than one right answer; scoring with checklists, descriptive criteria, standards, continuum, rubrics, comparative models
Processes	• Strategy applications (e.g., think-alouds, questioning) • Teacher-student conferences • Peer and group assessments • Student self-assessments • Interviews • Inventories • Observations • Book club participation • Surveys of reading or writing behaviors • Portfolio entry slips • Response logs • Reading/writing lists	No one right answer; it is not necessary to score; collect as additional evidence; provide descriptive feedback to children

What Is the Scott Foresman *Reading Street* Assessment System?

All assessments in the program reflect current theories of teaching language and literacy and are aligned with solid classroom teaching practices. Scott Foresman *Reading Street* offers a "seamless assessment system" at each grade. The formative and summative assessments, combined with "assessable moments" during instruction, become a continuous cycle where one is always informing the other, resulting in a seamless learning program for the children.

Fundamental to this cycle are clear, grade-appropriate, and important learning targets that are aligned with statewide and district-wide reading and language arts curriculum standards.

To prepare students for standardized tests, teachers should teach "the key ideas and processes contained in content standards in rich and engaging ways; by collecting evidence of student understanding of that content through robust local assessments, rather than one-shot standardized testing; and by using engaging and effective instructional strategies that help students explore core concepts through inquiry and problem solving."

(McTighe, Seif, & Wiggins, 2004)

- At the beginning of each school year, the cycle begins with the administration of entry-level assessments used for screening and diagnosis. They will help you establish a starting point for children and determine the amount of instructional support children will need in order to hit the targets. Informal tools will provide additional information about children's learning styles, confidence, and interests that will help you in designing effective instructional plans.

- During the school year, literacy achievement is checked daily and weekly through formative, progress-monitoring assessments—informal, such as teacher observations, running records, retellings, and conferencing, as well as formal assessments. For example, the Scott Foresman *Reading Street* Weekly Tests assess children's understanding of the skills taught during the week, and the Fresh Reads for Fluency and Comprehension give children opportunities to practice comprehension and build fluency with new selections matched to their instructional levels.

- The Unit Benchmark Tests and the End-of-Year Benchmark Test are formative and summative assessments designed to assess students' understanding of the targeted skills, strategies, and critical thinking skills taught throughout the unit and the school year.

What Are the Assessment Targets?

Reading

What are the reading targets? *Reading Street* emphasizes the reading skills that are described by the National Reading Panel. These reading skills are essential as children learn to become independent, strategic readers and writers.

Phonemic awareness is the ability to identify the separate sounds, or *phonemes*, that make up spoken words, and to alter and arrange sounds to create new words. It is a subset of phonological awareness, a broad term meaning the awareness of sounds in spoken language. Knowledge of phonemic awareness allows children to hear separate sounds, recognize a sound's position in a word, manipulate sounds, and understand the role sounds play in language. In Scott Foresman *Reading Street*, phonemic awareness instructional and assessment activities include isolating, blending, segmenting, deleting, adding, and substituting phonemes.

Phonics is the study of how letters represent sounds in written language, unlike phonemic awareness, which is strictly *oral*. Phonics instruction and assessment in *Reading Street* include:

- **Print awareness** Understanding the relationship between oral and written language, that written language carries meaning, and that print is read from left to right.

- **Alphabetic knowledge** Knowledge of the shapes, names, and sounds of letters.

- **Alphabetic principle** Understanding that there is a systematic relationship between sounds (phonemes) and letters (graphemes).

- **Decoding** The process of analyzing letter-sound patterns in words to ascertain meaning.

- **Knowledge of high-frequency words** Sometimes called "sight words," these are the words that appear most often in our written language. Because children need to know these words when they read stories and write sentences, the words are introduced before children have learned many letter-sound patterns. Many high-frequency words cannot be decoded easily because of irregular and uncommon letter-sound patterns. Others do conform to phonics rules but must be taught as whole words because children have not yet learned the letter-sound relationships within them.

Oral reading fluency is the ability to effortlessly, quickly, and accurately decode letters, words, sentences, and passages. Fluent readers are able to group words into meaningful grammatical units and read with proper expression. Fluency is an essential component of comprehension and is assessed regularly in Scott Foresman *Reading Street*.

> "Having a strong vocabulary is not only a school goal, it is a characteristic that allows us to participate actively in our world, and it is viewed by those we meet as the hallmark of an educated person." (Blachowicz, 2005)

Vocabulary acquisition and development contribute significantly to overall text comprehension. While extensive reading experiences with varied text types and opportunities for classroom discussion are known to increase word knowledge, *Reading Street* explicitly teaches and assesses vocabulary skills through the study of context clues, word structure, and dictionary/glossary use.

- Context clues from the words or phrases surrounding an unknown word help readers identify its meaning. Some words have multiple meanings and can only be understood through the context in which they are used. Context clues include synonyms, antonyms, definitions, explanations, descriptions, and examples that appear within the text surrounding an unfamiliar word.

- The study of word structure is the analysis of word-meaning elements to make meaning of the word as a whole. Such meaningful elements include word roots, prefixes, suffixes, and compound words. Syllabication generalizations and inflected endings, which change the tense, case, or singular-plural form of words, but do not affect meaning or part of speech, are also taught and assessed.

- Understanding what dictionaries/glossaries are and why, when, and how to use them helps to increase children's vocabularies. They become familiar with the organization and format of dictionaries and glossaries and are guided and assessed in their use of the components of an entry, including syllabication, pronunciation, part of speech, etymology, and definition.

Reading comprehension, the overarching goal of reading, is the active process of constructing meaning from text. It is a complex process in which readers apply their prior knowledge and experiences, use their understandings about text (types, structures, features, etc.), and intentionally employ an array of before-, during-, and after-reading strategies and skills in order to attain meaning. Effective readers combine their own experiences with their interpretation of the author's intent as they work to make sense of ideas in text.

In Scott Foresman *Reading Street*, children's use of targeted comprehension strategies and skills (e.g., identification of main idea and details, author's purpose, sequence, and inferences) is monitored continuously, starting in grade 1, on the Weekly Tests and Fresh Reads for Fluency and Comprehension. Children read a variety of engaging, culturally- and age-appropriate narrative and expository texts and respond to appropriate multiple-choice questions designed to assess how they use the comprehension skills in constructing meaning. There are three types of comprehension questions that correspond to the *In the Book* and *In My Head* categories of questions in the instructional program.

- **Literal** questions, which focus on ideas explicitly stated in the text, although *not necessarily* verbatim. In response to these items, children *recognize* and *identify* information which might be found in a single sentence or in two or more sentences of contiguous text.

- **Inferential** questions, which are based on the theme, key concepts, and major ideas of the passage and often require children to *interpret* information from across parts of the text and to *connect* knowledge from the text with their own general background knowledge.

- **Critical-analysis** questions, which are also inferential in nature and focus on important ideas in the selection. Yet they differ from inferential questions in that readers are required to stand apart from the text and *analyze, synthesize,* and/ or *evaluate* the quality, effectiveness, relevance, and consistency of the message, rhetorical features (tone, style, voice, etc.), author or character motivation, and the author's purpose or credibility. (The kindergarten and grade 1 assessments contain few of these advanced-level questions.)

Throughout the program, children are scaffolded and guided as they move from literal understanding, to inferential comprehension, and to critical analysis of text.

Writing

Targeted skills are based on the writing strategies and writing applications strands of state language arts standards. Skills include:

- Focus on the topic
- Demonstrating understanding of purpose
- Writing coherent sentences
- Interesting word choice and sentence variety
- Narrative, descriptive, and expository compositions
- Evaluation and revision of writing
- Penmanship

The Unit Benchmark Tests and End-of-Year Benchmark Test in grade 1 require responses to narrative, descriptive, and expository writing prompts.

Other informal writing assessments in *Reading Street* include:

- The Writing Behaviors Checklist, which provides information about children's awareness of basic writing concepts and their ability to communicate through writing.
- Written retellings demonstrate children's abilities to understand narrative and expository text elements and to recall and record information in writing.
- Teacher-child conferences provide insights about children's writing behaviors and strategies.
- Student portfolios, containing draft and final copies of work, give evidence of children's growth and progress in writing.
- Writing logs allow children to monitor their writing growth over time.
- Writing strategy assessments help teachers synthesize information about children's writing progress and use of writing strategies.

Writing Conventions

Targeted skills include:

- Sentence structure
- Grammar, including singular/plural constructions, contractions, subject-verb agreement, parts of speech, etc.
- Punctuation, capitalization, and spelling

Skills are assessed in the Unit and End-of-Year Benchmark Tests. The writing scoring rubrics assess sentence structure, fluency, and variety, as well as control of writing conventions.

Speaking and Listening

Targeted skills include:

- Listening comprehension

- Organization and delivery of oral communication

- Analysis and evaluation of oral and media communication

- Retellings, relating personal experiences, and providing descriptions

Informal assessments that allow you to document children's oral language development throughout the year are oral retellings, teacher-student conference records, ongoing teacher observation, and student portfolios. Student self-assessments are opportunities for children to monitor and evaluate their growth in speaking and listening and to set goals for improvement.

What instructional strategies will help to prepare children for formal assessments and high-stakes tests?

- Use the Scott Foresman *Reading Street* program to continually monitor children's progress and refine instruction to reflect your children's needs.

- Use the administration of the formal progress-monitoring and summative assessments as a way to teach test-taking skills.

- Literal, inferential, and critical-analysis questions on the Weekly, Unit, and End-of-Year Benchmark Tests are based on the question-answer framework used in instruction and are similar to question types on high-stakes assessments. Daily practice in answering literal, inferential, and critical-analysis questions will improve children's achievement on high-stakes standardized tests.

- Download and examine released items from standardized assessments, reviewing the various item constructions and test vocabulary. Model and discuss the thinking steps involved in responding to multiple-choice and constructed-response items, as well as writing prompts.

- Familiarize your children with the formal language of test directions. Instruct them to listen to, restate, follow, and write test directions.

- Pre-teach the "language of tests" encountered in directions and test items, including

  - Question words: *who, what, which, where, when, why,* and *how*

  - Emphasis words: *not, except, most likely, probably, major, both, neither, either, most,* and *least*

  - Action words: *explain, describe, discuss, persuade,* and *support with evidence*

- Encourage children to be careful readers and to check their own work.

- Provide repeated opportunities for practicing all of the techniques above.

References

Airasian, P. W. *Classroom Assessment: Concepts and Applications.* McGraw-Hill, 2000.

Blachowicz, C. L. Z. "Vocabulary Essentials: From Research to Practice for Improved Instruction." *Research-Based Vocabulary Instruction.* Scott Foresman, 2005.

Heritage, M. "Formative Assessment: What Do Teachers Need to Know and Do?" *Phi Delta Kappan*, vol. 89, no. 2 (October, 2007), 140–145.

McTighe, J., E. Seif, and G. Wiggins. "You Can Teach for Meaning." *Educational Leadership*, vol. 62, no. 1 (September 2004), pp. 26–30.

National Reading Panel. "Teaching Children to Read: An Evidence-Based Assessment of the Scientific Research Literature on Reading and Its Implications for Reading Instruction." *Reports of the Subgroups.* National Institute for Literacy, National Institute of Child Health and Human Development, 2000.

Popham, W. J. "Instructional Insensitivity of Tests: Accountability's Dire Drawback." *Phi Delta Kappan*, vol. 89, no. 2 (October 2007), pp. 146–150, 155.

Popham, W. J. "Tawdry Tests and AYP." *Educational Leadership*, vol. 62, no. 2 (October 2004), pp. 85–86.

Stiggins, R. J. "Assessment Crisis: The Absence of Assessment for Learning." *Kappan Professional Journal.* http://www.pdkintl.org/kappan/k020sti.htm (accessed May 8, 2005).

Stiggins, R. J. "New Assessment Beliefs for a New School Mission." *Phi Delta Kappan*, vol. 86, no. 1 (September 2004), 22–27.

Vaughn, S., and S. Thompson. *Research-Based Methods of Reading Instruction, Grades K–3.* Alexandria, VA: Association for Supervision and Curriculum Development, 2004.

| Chapter 2 | # Entry-Level Assessment: What to Do at the Beginning of the Year |

Overview

Entry-level assessments determine how well children have mastered specific standards or prerequisite skills and knowledge for a particular grade level. This is especially valuable in Kindergarten and First Grade because reading trajectories are established early. The later children are identified as needing support, the more likely they are to experience difficulties that may not be overcome in later grades. Entry-level assessments determine foci for initial instruction as well as interventions that might be needed for individual children or groups of children. There are many formal and informal assessment tools and practices that determine entry-level skills and provide the type of information needed to make decisions about where to begin instruction for individual children.

What is the purpose of using entry-level assessments?

Entry-level assessments are used for screening and diagnosis. The results of entry-level assessment tests are reported by specific knowledge and skill areas and can be used to:

- help you get to know your children and find a starting point for good instructional decisions;
- help you gather information about children's knowledge and skills in reading, writing, speaking, and listening at the beginning of the year; and
- gather specific information about children with special learning needs, such as English language learners, children with disabilities, struggling readers, and advanced learners.

What do I want to learn from entry-level assessments?

Learning where to begin instruction is the primary goal of entry-level assessments. The more you know about your children at the beginning of the year, the better equipped you are to maximize their learning experiences to ensure that they achieve continuous growth in writing, speaking, reading, and listening skills. Entry-level assessments identify children who are already proficient and need challenge, as well as those who need additional support and literacy intervention in areas such as:

- Letter recognition
- Phonemic awareness
- Phoneme segmentation
- Phonics and word reading
- Word reading fluency
- Reading comprehension
- Vocabulary
- Writing

What types of assessments should be used at the beginning of the year?

Use a variety of assessment practices early in the year to screen and diagnose children's achievement of writing, speaking, reading, and listening skills. Both formal and informal assessments will help you diagnose your children's prerequisite knowledge and skills, as well as gain a personal understanding of your children.

FORMAL ASSESSMENTS

- Formal entry-level assessments provide detailed analyses of children's performances in specific domains. They make available information about the degree to which children have acquired the knowledge and skills and identify areas in which additional instruction is needed for particular children.

- Formal entry-level assessments can be used to:
  - assess instructional needs of individual children;
  - focus instruction to meet targeted needs of all of the children in your classroom; and
  - determine what needs to be pretaught or retaught to individual children or groups of children.

INFORMAL ASSESSMENTS

- Informal entry-level assessments provide additional information about areas where instructional support is needed. They also provide useful background information, including knowledge about children's learning styles, confidence, and interests that will help you in designing effective instructional plans.

- Informal assessments, such as conferencing with children and administering developmentally appropriate inventories, surveys, and checklists at the beginning of the school year, will help you:
  - identify children's interests and attitudes about literacy;
  - assess instructional and motivational needs of individual children;
  - assess instructional needs of the class as a whole;
  - learn specifics about children with particular needs; and
  - make focused instructional decisions.

When do I gather the information?

The best time to administer entry-level assessments is during the first few weeks of the school year. However, it is important to avoid overwhelming children with too much assessment at one time. Plan carefully and spread a variety of assessment tasks throughout the first month of school. Prioritize the tools and tasks in relation to their importance to beginning instructional planning.

What techniques and tools are available?

FORMAL ENTRY-LEVEL ASSESSMENTS

- **Baseline Group Test** (See pages 38–39.)

  This Scott Foresman *Reading Street* test, one at each grade level, has both a written multiple-choice format and one-on-one teacher–student oral subtests for concepts of print (kindergarten) and phonemic awareness and fluency (grade 1). It enables you to establish baseline data for determining the level of instructional support children need and placing them into instructional groups.

- **Group Reading Assessment and Diagnostic Evaluation** (See pages 35–36.)

  GRADE is a norm-referenced, diagnostic reading assessment for grades PreK–Adult that provides information about the skills children have mastered and the skill areas in which they need mastery or intervention.

- **Developmental Reading Assessment® Second Edition (DRA2)** (See page 37.)

  This is a set of individually-administered criterion-referenced reading assessments for students in kindergarten through grade 8. The DRA2 is used to identify children's independent reading level in terms of accuracy, fluency, and comprehension.

INFORMAL ENTRY-LEVEL ASSESSMENTS

- **Getting to Know You Conference** (See page 40.)

  An individual conversation with a child that explores his or her learning interests, strengths, challenges, and goals

- **Knowledge about Books and Print** (See page 41.)

  A checklist that allows you to record observations about the knowledge your children have about print and books

- **Myself as a Learner** (See page 42.)

  An informal questionnaire that gives your children an opportunity to tell you about their reading and writing

- **Reading Behaviors Checklist** (See page 43.)

  A checklist that allows you to record observations about your children's reading skills and behaviors

- **Writing Behaviors Checklist** (See page 44.)

  A checklist that allows you to record observations about your children's writing skills and behaviors

- **Oral Language Behaviors Checklist** (See page 45.)

  A checklist that allows you to record observations about your children's oral language

- **Profile of English Language Learners** (See page 46.)

    A checklist that identifies the strengths and needs of children who are English language learners

- **My Child as a Learner** (See page 47.)

    A survey that provides information about your children's literacy behaviors at home

Want to learn more about entry-level assessment?

If you are interested in learning more about research that discusses the use of entry-level assessment tools and practices, you will find the following resources interesting.

References

Allinder, R. M.; M. Rose; L. S. Fuchs; and D. Fuchs. "Issues in Curriculum-Based Assessment." In *Critical Issues in Special Education: Access, Diversity, and Accountabiity*. Eds. A. M. Sorrells, H. J. Rieth, and P. T. Sindelar. Boston: Allyn and Bacon, 2004.

Buly, M. R., and S. W. Valencia. "Below the Bar: Profiles of Students Who Fail State Reading Tests." *Educational Evaluation and Policy Analysis*, vol. 24 (2002), pp. 219–239.

Chard, D.; S. McDonagh; S. Lee; and V. Reece. "Assessing Word Recognition." In *Classroom Literacy Assessment: Making Sense of What Students Know and Do*. Eds. J. R. Paratore and R. L. McCormack. New York: Guilford Press. pp. 85–100.

Cunningham, P. M. "The Multisyllabic Word Dilemma: Helping Students Build Meaning, Spell, and Read 'Big' Words." *Reading and Writing Quarterly*, vol.14 (1998), pp. 189–218.

Ehri, L. C. "Development of the Ability to Read Words: Update." In *Theoretical Models and Processes of Reading*, 3rd ed. Eds. R. B. Ruddell, M. R. Ruddell, and H. Singer. Newark, DE: International Reading Association.

Helman, L. A. "Using Literacy Assessment Results to Improve Teaching for English-Language Learners." *The Reading Teacher*, vol. 58, no. 7 (April 2005), pp. 668–677.

Johnston, P. H., and R. Roger. "Early Literacy Development: The Case for Informed Assessment." In *Handbook of Early Reading Research*. Eds. S. B. Neuman and D. K. Dickinson. New York: Guilford Press, 2001, pp. 377–389.

Kame'enui, E. J., R. H. Good, and B. A. Harn. "Beginning Reading Failure and the Quantification of Risk: Reading Behavior as the Supreme Index." In *Focus on Behavior Analysis in Education: Achievements, Challenges, and Opportunities*. Eds. W. L. Heward, et al. Upper River, N.J.: Pearson/Merrill/Prentice Hall, 2005.

McMillan, James H. "Essential Assessment Concepts for Teachers and Administrators." In *Experts in Assessment* series. Eds. T. R. Guskey and R. J. Marzano. Thousand Oaks, CA: Corwin Press, Inc., 2001.

Group Reading Assessment and Diagnostic Evaluation (GRADE)

What is it?

GRADE is an accurate, in-depth, and easy-to-use entry-level assessment for pre-kindergarten children through young adult, postsecondary students. It is a normative diagnostic reading assessment that determines developmentally which skills children have mastered and where they need instruction or intervention. GRADE is a research-based assessment that can be group-administered. It was standardized and normed using the most up-to-date methodology.

Why would I use it?

You will want to use GRADE for many reasons.

- It helps you screen your children and determine the strengths and weaknesses of individuals or groups of children in relation to specific skills.

- It helps you determine your children's prerequisite skills and knowledge.

- It allows you to save time through whole-group administration as opposed to individual administration.

- You can score the assessment and analyze assessment results using information in the teacher manual or with scoring and reporting software.

- Children who appear to have significantly above- or below-grade-level reading performance can be given an out-of-level test form.

- Parallel forms offer the opportunity to test up to four times a year.

- Results are linked to specific follow-up instruction and interventions.

- Using GRADE assessment to focus instruction will improve achievement and help deliver Adequate Yearly Progress gains.

What does it test?

In kindergarten and first grade, GRADE assesses essential elements of reading, including:

- Phonemic awareness
- Phonics
- Oral Language
- Vocabulary
- Comprehension

When do I use it?

When GRADE is used as an entry-level assessment, it should be administered by the end of the first month of school. GRADE can be used up to four times a year, with the recommendation that three months be allowed between testing sessions.

How do I use it?

- Give the appropriate grade-level assessment or an out-of-level assessment if you determine the child will perform below or above grade level.
- Analyze children's results using normative tables for converting raw scores to standard scores, stanines, percentiles, normal curve equivalents, grade equivalents, and growth-scale values.
- Use results to plan focused instruction for individuals or groups of children.
- Use activities and exercises that are correlated with the assessment results from the *GRADE Resource Library* and *Head for Success* to plan interventions for children with special learning needs.

Developmental Reading Assessment® ✓
Second Edition (DRA2)

What is it?

- The DRA2 is a set of individually-administered criterion-referenced reading assessments for students in kindergarten through grade 8. Modeled after an informal reading inventory, the DRA2 is designed to be administered, scored, and interpreted by a classroom teacher. The DRA2 for grades K–1 identifies a child's independent reading level based on the child's accuracy, fluency, and comprehension.

Why would I use it?

You will want to use the DRA2 for many reasons, including:

- To identify your children's strengths and weaknesses in relation to specific knowledge and skills for language arts and reading

- To evaluate the phonological awareness and phonics skills of children in kindergarten and early first grade and the word-analysis skills of below-grade-level readers in grade 1

What does it test?

The DRA2 assesses essential elements of reading and language arts, including:

- Phonological awareness and phonics skills
- Independent reading level
- Reading engagement
- Oral reading fluency (rate and accuracy)
- Reading comprehension

When do I use it?

The DRA2 can be given twice a year (fall and spring) to provide you with information to guide instruction. It can also be administered at mid-year to identify the needs or skills of children who are challenged readers, to monitor progress, and to provide more instructional guidance.

How do I use it?

- You have an individual reading conference with each child involving the child's reading a text orally.

- As the child reads aloud, you use a text-specific observation guide to record reading behaviors and errors.

- You convert the total number of oral reading errors to an accuracy score and calculate the child's reading fluency as words correct per minute (WCPM).

Baseline Group Test

What is it?	• A placement test given at the beginning of the school year to establish a baseline for each child
Why would I choose it?	• To identify children who are on grade level, those who need intervention, and those who could benefit from more challenge • To recognize how best to shape the curriculum to fit the needs of all children
What does it test?	• In kindergarten, readiness skills (such as understanding left/right directions and location prepositions), letter recognition, phonological awareness (such as initial and final consonant sounds), listening-comprehension skills, and concepts of print are tested. Also included is a graded oral vocabulary test (optional). • In grade 1, phonemic awareness, phonics, letter and word recognition, and listening-comprehension skills are tested. Also included are a graded oral vocabulary test and a passage for testing fluency and/or doing a running record (both optional).
When do I use it?	• At the beginning of the school year, to establish baselines for children and to place them in groups according to their level of ability • Throughout the year as needed to assess progress and determine instructional requirements of new children
How do I use it?	• Some sections of the test may be group administered. Other sections require an individual administration.
How do I use the results?	• Each test includes a table specifying how many correct responses indicate the various levels of mastery (Strategic Intervention, On-Level, or Advanced Level). • The teacher's manual includes charts with percentage scores, an evaluation chart, and an interpretation key that will allow you to place each child in an appropriate instructional group.

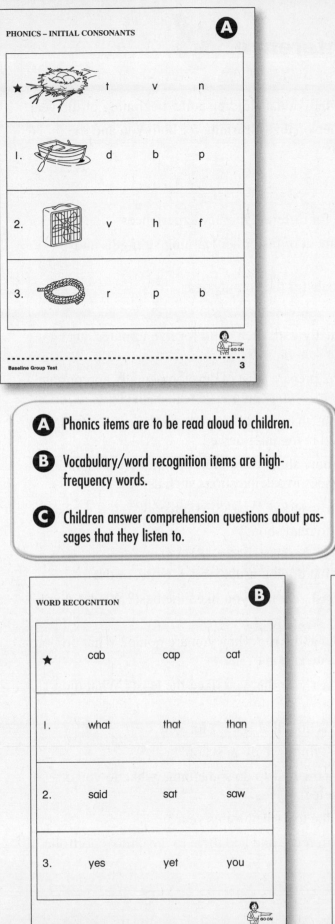

PHONICS – INITIAL CONSONANTS **A**

★ t v n

1. d b p

2. v h f

3. r p b

VOWEL SOUNDS **A**

★ pin mat fed

8. dud did dad

9. bun bin ban

10. bad bed bid

A Phonics items are to be read aloud to children.

B Vocabulary/word recognition items are high-frequency words.

C Children answer comprehension questions about passages that they listen to.

Samples are from Grade 1 Baseline Group Test.

WORD RECOGNITION **B**

★ cab cap cat

1. what that than

2. said sat saw

3. yes yet you

LISTENING COMPREHENSION **C**

Getting to Know You Conference

What is it?

- A conversation with individual children at the beginning of the year
- An experience that personalizes learning for both you and the children in your class

What does it show?

- A child's interests
- A child's preference for different literacy experiences
- A child's self-assessment of his or her learning strengths and challenges
- A child's learning goals for the coming year

How do I use it?

- Plan to meet individually with each child for five minutes during the first two weeks of school.
- Before the conference, prepare a list of developmentally appropriate questions to select from as you conference with each child.
- Highlight the questions that you think might be the most relevant for the particular child being interviewed.
- Consider what you know about the child's pre-kindergarten or kindergarten experiences to ask questions such as:
  - What is your favorite story? Why do you like it?
  - What do you like to read about?
  - During choice time at school, what would you rather do: read, write, or draw? What do you usually read, write, or draw?
  - What did you do last year that you liked the best? What did you like about it?
  - Do you like to read and write when you are home? What do you like to read and write at home?
  - What did you do last year that you liked the least? What didn't you like about it?
  - What do we do in school that is easy for you?
  - What is the hardest thing we do in school?
  - When you don't know how to do something, what do you do? How do you get help?
  - What would you like to do better this year?
- Keep notes of the conference and add them to the child's portfolio or cumulative folder.

Teacher Form
Knowledge About Books and Print

What is it?
- A brief survey of a child's familiarity with books and print

What does it show?
- A child's understanding of what a book is and how to handle it
- A child's awareness of print

How do I use it?
- Start using this form at the beginning of the year, as you begin shared reading with kindergartners and first graders.
- Begin with those children who are not joining in or who seem confused. Work with them individually.
- Share a book in an encouraging way and let the child handle the book as naturally as he or she can.
- Repeat this assessment periodically (every month or so) to monitor the child's progress. Record your observations.
- Place the completed form in the child's portfolio as additional information about him or her.
- Consider using the form during parent conferences.

A Checklist format is easy to interpret.

B Space is provided to include other behaviors you may want to track.

Form for reproduction is on page 128.

Teacher Form
Knowledge About Books and Print

Child Lee Thompson   Date 9/19

Behavior	Yes	Not Yet	Comments
Knows how to hold book right side up	✓		
Knows how to turn pages sequentially, front to back	✓		
Knows that books have titles, authors, and illustrators		✓	
Makes predictions from title, cover, and illustrations		✓	
Can differentiate between pictures and text	✓		starts at left, but at bottom of page
Knows that text and pictures relate to each other	✓		
Tracks print from left to right and top to bottom		✓	
Knows that print represents spoken words	✓		
Knows that there are spaces between words	✓		
Joins in reading text with a familiar, repetitive, or predictable pattern		✓	
After multiple class readings, revisits the book, "reading" the story independently	✓		went back to look at a favorite class book
Other:			

41

Survey
Myself as a Learner ✓

What is it?
- A survey that gives children an opportunity to tell you more about themselves
- A tool for getting children to reflect on their reading and writing

What does it show?
- Children's familiarity with books and print
- Children's exposure to print in the home

How do I use it?
- Read the questions to each child or have children read and complete the form on their own. You may need to act as a scribe for some children.
- Place the completed forms in the children's portfolios as information about each child.
- Consider using the form during parent conferences.

Ⓐ Checklist format is easy to complete and interpret

Ⓑ Comments space allows you to write down spontaneous remarks from the child or have child elaborate.

Form for reproduction is on page 133.

Child Form
Myself as a Learner ✓

Name Kristen C.   Date Sept. 6

	Yes	No	Comments
1. I like to listen to stories.	X		
2. I like to read books by myself.	X Ⓐ		Ⓑ
3. I know how to hold a book and turn the pages.	X		
4. I like to read out loud to others.	X		
5. I can figure out new words when I read.	X		
6. I like to write.	X		
7. I like to draw.	X		
8. I like to go to school.	X		
9. I read signs wherever I go.	X		

Teacher Form
Reading Behaviors Checklist

What is it?	• A form to record your observations of children's reading behaviors at the beginning of and throughout the year
What does it show?	• Children's awareness of print and word concepts • Children's knowledge of phonological awareness and phonics
How do I use it?	• Complete this form as you observe children interacting with print materials. • Use your observations to assess children's needs and to make instructional decisions. • Place the completed forms in the children's portfolios as additional information about each child.

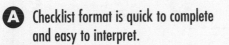

A Checklist format is quick to complete and easy to interpret.

B Checklist includes all important aspects of a child's early reading behaviors.

C "Not Applicable" column makes checklist adaptable to different grade levels.

Form for reproduction is on page 129.

Teacher Form
Reading Behaviors Checklist

Child Kristen Cleaver   Date 4/18

Behavior	Yes	No	Not Applicable
Recognizes letters of the alphabet	✓		
Recognizes name in print	✓		
Recognizes some environmental print, such as signs and logos	✓		
Knows the difference between letters and words	✓		
Knows the difference between capital and lowercase letters	✓		
Understands function of capitalization and punctuation	✓		
Recognizes that book parts such as cover, title page, and table of contents offer information		✓	
Recognizes that words are represented in writing by specific sequences of letters	✓		
Recognizes words that rhyme	✓		
Distinguishes rhyming and nonrhyming words	✓		
Knows sound-letter correspondences	✓		
Identifies and isolates initial sounds in words	✓		
Identifies and isolates final sounds in words	✓		
Blends sounds to make spoken words	✓		
Segments one-syllable/two-syllable spoken words into individual phonemes	✓		
Reads consonant blends and digraphs			✓
Reads and understands endings such as -es, -ed, -ing			✓
Reads vowels and vowel diphthongs			✓
Reads and understands possessives			✓
Reads and understands compound words			✓
Reads simple sentences	✓		
Reads simple stories		✓	
Understands simple story structure	✓		
Other:			

Teacher Form
Writing Behaviors Checklist ✓

What is it?	• A form to record your observations of children's writing behaviors at the beginning of and throughout the year
What does it show?	• Children's awareness of basic writing concepts • Children's ability to communicate through writing
How do I use it?	• Complete this form as you observe children drawing and/or writing. • Use your observations to assess children's needs and to make instructional decisions. • Place the completed forms in the children's portfolios as additional information about each child.

A Checklist format is quick to complete and easy to interpret.

B Checklist includes all important aspects of a child's early writing behaviors.

C "Not Applicable" column makes checklist adaptable to different grade levels.

Form for reproduction is on page 130.

Teacher Form
Writing Behaviors Checklist ✓

Child _Kristen Cleaver_   **A**   Date _9/28_

Behavior	Yes	No	Not Applicable
Produces detailed and relevant drawings	✓		
Dictates messages for others to write	✓		
Writes using scribble, drawing, or letterlike forms	✓		
Distinguishes between writing and drawing	✓		
Writes own name and other important words	✓		
Writes all letters of the alphabet, capital and lowercase		✓	
Writes labels or captions for illustrations and possessions	✓		
Writes messages that move from left to right and top to bottom		✓	
Uses phonological knowledge to map sounds to letters when writing		✓	
Holds pencil and positions paper correctly	✓		
Uses basic capitalization and punctuation		✓	
Writes messages that can be understood by others		✓	
Shows understanding of sequence in writing		✓	
Stays on topic when writing			✓
Expresses original ideas	✓		
Elaborates with details			✓
Has an identifiable voice			✓
Chooses precise and vivid words		✓	
Takes risks with vocabulary			✓
Uses descriptive words	✓		
Writes in different forms			✓
Writes for different audiences and purposes			✓
Writes to record ideas and reflections	✓		
Other: _Writes using rhyming words_			

Teacher Form
Oral Language Behaviors Checklist

What is it?
- A form to record your observations of children's speaking and listening behaviors at the beginning of and throughout the year

What does it show?
- Children's facility with oral language
- Children's ease at speaking and listening in various situations and for various purposes

How do I use it?
- Complete this form as you observe children speaking and listening, both individually and in groups.
- Use your observations to assess children's needs and to make instructional decisions.
- Place the completed forms in the children's portfolios as additional information about each child.

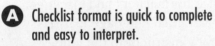

A Checklist format is quick to complete and easy to interpret.

B Checklist includes all important aspects of a child's early oral language behaviors.

Form for reproduction is on page 131.

Teacher Form
Oral Language Behaviors Checklist

Child **Kristen Cleaver**   Date **9/26**

Behavior	Yes	No	Example
Follows simple oral directions	✔		
Follows directions of several steps		✔	got confused making a book page
Listens to stories read aloud	✔		
Participates actively when predictable rhymes and songs are read aloud	✔		
Understands and retells spoken messages	✔		
Gives precise directions		✔	couldn't explain how to get to office
Expresses ideas clearly	✔		
Responds appropriately to questions	✔		
Knows and uses many words	✔		
Participates in conversations and discussions	✔		
Listens in small-group situations	✔		
Listens in whole-group situations	✔		
Stays on topic in discussions		✔	led TV discussion away from topic
Uses language conventions appropriately	✔		
Listens to others courteously without interrupting	✔		
Can retell simple stories in sequence			forgot order in "Three Bears"
Recalls details from stories	✔		
Listens and speaks for various purposes	✔		
Adapts speaking to audience		✔	
Listens critically to oral readings, discussions, and messages	✔		
Connects cultural experiences and prior knowledge through speaking and listening	✔		
Other:			

Survey
Profile of English Language Learners

What is it?
- A form to help identify the strengths and needs of children whose first language is not English

What does it show?
- An English language learner's proficiency with speaking, reading, and writing English

How do I use it?
- Identify children whose English proficiency you are uncertain about.
- Use the criteria on the form to assess children's abilities in the various language areas, noting specific examples.
- Use the form as a rough guideline of where children are in their English language development and where they may need help.

What do I do next?

Scott Foresman *Reading Street* offers your English language learners

- standards-based instruction at all levels of language acquisition—Beginning, Early Intermediate, Intermediate, Early Advanced, and Advanced.
- the English Language Learners Handbook with instructional material and comprehensive guidance for teachers and effective, efficient, and explicit instruction for English language learners. Building on the *Reading Street* literacy instruction, the guide uses components such as ELL Posters, ELL Readers, and English Language Support (blackline masters).

A Checklist format is easy to interpret.

B Space is provided for you to note your own responses.

Form for reproduction is on page 132.

Teacher Form
Profile of English Language Learners

Child: Tomás Alvarez

Trait	Mostly	Unevenly	Rarely	Date/Comment
Speaks and/or understands a few basic words	✓			
Speaks fluently but makes frequent errors			✓	10/16 seems to know more words than he is comfortable using
Uses names of many objects		✓		
Uses and understands basic everyday vocabulary		✓		
Asks and answers simple questions			✓	10/16 reluctant to ask for help
Follows simple directions		✓		
Takes part in discussions			✓	10/16 good at communicating through art
Conveys ideas or stories through drawings	✓			
Needs pictures to comprehend simple text		✓		
Recognizes basic sound/letter relationships in words		✓		
Follows text being read aloud		✓		
Joins in choral reading	✓			10/16 likes to join in with the class
Retells predictable text		✓		

Survey
My Child as a Learner ✔

What is it?
- A survey to help you get to know your children better from their families' perspectives
- An opportunity to establish a positive relationship with your children's families from the start

What does it show?
- Children's behaviors that families observe at home
- A family's view of a child as a learner

How do I use it?
- Send the survey home at the beginning of the school year with a cover letter explaining the value of family input.
- Place the completed forms in the children's portfolios as additional information about each child.
- Discuss it during parent conferences.

Parent Form
My Child as a Learner ✔

Child **Kristen Cleaver**   Parent/Guardian/Caregiver **Jeff Cleaver**   Date **10/21**

	Always	Sometimes	Never	Comments
1. My child asks to be read to.	**Ⓐ**	✓		
2. My child can retell a book we have read or a television program we have watched.	✓			**Ⓑ**
3. My child can predict what will happen next when reading a book or watching a television program.		✓		
4. My child picks up a book to read or look at alone.		✓		
5. My child reads or pretends to read at home.		✓		
6. My child knows how to hold a book, how to turn pages, and that print goes from left to right	✓			
7. My child likes to write or pretend to write.		✓		writes some letters backwards—should we be concerned?
8. My child likes to talk about what he or she has written.		✓		
9. My child can follow an oral direction when given.		✓		
10. My child can follow a series of oral directions when given one time.		✓		
11. My child likes working with others.	✓			
12. My child tries to read words in the environment—signs, labels, logos.		✓		
13. My child likes to go to school.	✓			

Ⓐ Checklist format is quick to complete and easy to interpret.

Ⓑ Comments provide information specific to each child in your class.

Form for reproduction is on page 134.

Chapter 3

Progress-Monitoring Assessments: What to Do During the Year

Overview

Assessments designed to monitor child progress take many forms, including weekly tests, unit tests, checklists and rubrics used in self-assessment, and teacher-managed activities, such as collecting and analyzing work samples and observing children while engaged in literacy tasks. Progress-monitoring involves using a variety of formal and classroom-based assessment formats that are characterized by timely feedback aligned with instructional goals. After using entry-level assessments to determine where to begin instruction for individuals and groups of children, it becomes equally important to monitor the progress that your children make throughout the year and the effectiveness of your instruction. The assessments labeled progress-monitoring tools in this handbook provide ongoing feedback on the progress your children make toward achievement of the skills and knowledge described in the strands and domains of the national and state reading and language arts standards.

What are the benefits of progress-monitoring?

- It helps you determine if all children are progressing as expected and helps you focus instruction for individuals and groups of children, as opposed to teaching to the middle performance level in your classes.

- It allows you to determine children's progress in meeting or exceeding national and state reading and language arts standards based on a regular process of observing, monitoring, and judging the quality of their work.

- You can guide children's learning better if you have an up-to-date understanding of the children's current performance levels—wasting no time on skills children have already mastered and focusing instead on the areas that need additional attention.

- Frequent use of progress-monitoring assessments gives *all* your children a more equitable opportunity to demonstrate their skills because high standards are most reliably achieved in small, consistent increases that occur over time.

- Because many progress-monitoring assessments are curriculum-embedded and aligned to instruction, they provide feedback on the effectiveness of your instruction.

What are the purposes of progress-monitoring?

- To identify mastery of national and state reading and language arts standards both at the individual level and at the class level

- To determine when differentiation of instruction is required for individuals or groups of children

- To provide a basis for focused instructional decision-making

- To help you modify or emphasize parts of your curriculum and instruction to reflect the results of progress-monitoring assessments

- To determine report card grades and/or communicate progress to parents

- To encourage child self-assessment and evaluation by helping children learn how to make judgments about the quality of their own work

- To evaluate instructional approaches

- To promote continuous improvement

What are some typical classroom-based activities that might be used to monitor progress?

- Participation during read-alouds and shared-book discussions

- Oral readings, dramatizations, and retellings

- Drawings, sculpture, and other artwork

- Graphic organizers

- Collaborative activities and projects

- Journals and reports in the form of pictures and beginning writing

> "…quality is the result of regular inspections (assessments) along the way, followed by needed adjustments based on the information gleaned from the inspections."
> (McTighe, 1997)

When do I use progress-monitoring assessment activities?

Use these activities throughout the school year to measure children's growth and development. Make assessment part of your classroom culture, an established classroom routine, and a natural step in learning.

Who should engage in progress-monitoring?

Although you are the primary initiator of progress-monitoring assessments, your children should be given opportunities to engage in ongoing self-monitoring. There are many benefits to involving children in their own progress-monitoring. When your children participate in self-assessment practices, they are more likely to develop metacognitive awareness and exhibit self-regulating skills. This means they will become consciously aware of their learning and actively set goals designed to increase their performances. Engaging in self-assessment leads to the development of positive attitudes toward learning. Furthermore, self-assessment emphasizes application of the knowledge and skills identified in the statewide and district-wide reading and language arts standards and promotes higher-order thinking and the development of reasoning skills.

- **How can I help children become better self-assessors?**

  – Model self-monitoring by sharing your thoughts with children as you evaluate and reflect on a project you are doing, such as putting up a bulletin board, writing a note to another teacher, or drafting directions for an assignment you are going to give them.

  – Allow students to participate in generating criteria for assessing a task or activity.

  – Make the criteria on which children are assessed public so that they can use this information to self-assess.

  – Schedule regular times for self-assessment.

  – Provide opportunities for children to engage in activities that encourage thinking, writing, and talking about their performances.

- **What kinds of activities support self-assessment?**

  – Writing and Reading Conferences with you

  – Writing and Reading Conferences with classmates

  – Portfolio reviews

  – Use of self-assessment checklists and rubrics

What techniques and tools are available?

FORMAL ASSESSMENTS FOR MONITORING PROGRESS

- **Weekly Tests (Grade 1 only)** (See pages 56–57.)
  These multiple-choice tests measure children's understanding of each week's high-frequency words, word-reading/phonics skills, and comprehension skills as applied to a new passage.

- **Fresh Reads for Fluency and Comprehension (Grade 1 only)** (See pages 58–59.)
  These multiple-choice and constructed-response tests allow children to practice comprehension skills with a new selection matched to their instructional reading level. They also provide a check of reading fluency.

- **Unit Benchmark Assessments (Grade K)** and **Unit Benchmark Tests (Grade 1)** (See pages 60–61.)
  These tests are designed to measure children's abilities to apply target comprehension skills and other literacy skills taught in each unit.

INFORMAL ASSESSMENTS FOR MONITORING PROGRESS

- **Questioning Strategies** (See pages 62–63.)

  Skillful questioning is an important assessment technique. Your ability to frame and ask powerful questions is an effective way to monitor the children's learning progress.

- **Ongoing Teacher Observation** (See page 64.)

  Observation of individual children allows you to monitor their performances in the context of classroom activities and provide helpful feedback while children are in the process of learning, rather than after-the-fact.

- **Fluency Check for Grade 1** (See pages 65–66.)

  This assessment technique is an individually-administered procedure for recording and analyzing your children's reading rates and reading behaviors.

- **Retelling and Summarizing** (See pages 67–68.)

  These oral or written recountings of narrative or expository text in your children's own words serve as indicators of what they can remember after reading or listening to a text.

- **Work Habits Conference Record** (See page 69.)

  This record sheet can be used when conferencing with children and provides a way to monitor children's understanding of task completion and time management behaviors.

- **Skills Conference Record** (See page 70.)

  This checklist allows you to capture information about your children's reading, writing, speaking, and listening behaviors and strategies.

- **Observing English Language Learners** (See page 71.)

  This form allows you to record ongoing observations about English language learners' progress in developing reading skills.

- **Observing My Child's Reading** (See page 72.)

  This form allows parents to comment on behaviors they notice as their children read aloud to them.

- **Peer Assessment** (See page 73.)

  This form allows children to assess their peers' portfolio work.

- **Student Portfolios** (See pages 74–75.)

  Maintaining a portfolio is a process that allows children to use work samples to document and reflect on their growth in reading, writing, speaking, and listening. See Chapter 7 for descriptions of the Portfolio Guide and the Portfolio Selection Slips.

> "Any decision of consequence deserves more than one piece of evidence."
>
> (Pearson, 1998)

- **Reading Log** (See page 76.)
  This form allows children to keep track of the literature they have read, as well as rate the quality of the selections.

- **Writing Log** (See page 77.)
  This form helps children keep track of and reflect on the pieces they have written.

- **Early Literacy Behaviors Checklist** (See page 146.)
  This checklist enables teachers to compile their dated observations of a child's literacy progress over time.

"Research on accomplished readers demonstrates that they are planful and aware and capable of online monitoring of their reading."
(Afflerbach, 2001)

3 • Progress Monitoring

Want to learn more about progress-monitoring assessment?

If you would like to learn more about how to use progress-monitoring assessment practices in your classroom, you will find the following resources interesting.

References

Afflerbach, P. *Understanding and Using Reading Assessment, K–12* (2nd ed.). Newark, DE: International Reading Association, 2012.

Afflerbach, P. "Teaching Reading Self-Assessment Strategies." In *Comprehension Instruction: Research-Based Best Practices*. Eds. C. Block and M. Pressley. New York: The Guilford Press, 2001, pp. 96–111.

Bailey, J. M., and T. R. Guskey. "Implementing Student-Led Conferences." In *Experts in Assessment Series*. Eds. T. R. Guskey and R. J. Marzano. Thousand Oaks, CA: Corwin Press, Inc., 2001.

Danielson, C., and L. Abrutyn. *An Introduction to Using Portfolios in the Classroom*. Alexandria, VA: ASCD, 1997.

Gambrell, L. B., P. S. Koskinen, and B. A. Kapinus. "Retelling and the Reading Comprehension of Proficient and Less-Proficient Readers." *Journal of Educational Research*, vol. 84 (1991), pp. 356–363.

Gambrell, L. B., W. Pfeiffer, and R. Wilson. "The Effects of Retelling Upon Reading Comprehension and Recall of Text Information." *Journal of Educational Research*, vol. 78 (1985), pp. 216–220.

Good, R. H., D. C. Simmons, and S. Smith. "Effective Academic Interventions in the United States: Evaluating and Enhancing the Acquisition of Early Reading Skills." *School Psychology Review*, vol. 27, no. 1 (1998), pp. 45–56.

Hasbrouck, J. E., and G. Tindal. "Curriculum-Based Oral Reading Fluency Norms for Students in Grades 2 through 5." *Teaching Exceptional Children*, vol. 24 (1992), pp. 41–44.

Keene, E. O., and S. Zimmermann. *Mosaic of Thought*. Portsmouth, NH: Heinemann, 1997.

Marzano, R. J., D. Pickering, and J. E. Pollock. *Classroom Instruction That Works: Research-Based Strategies for Increasing Student Achievement*. Alexandria, VA: ASCD, 2001.

Marzano, R. J., et al. *Handbook for Classroom Instruction That Works*. Alexandria, VA: ASCD, 2001.

McMillan, J. H. "Essential Assessment Concepts for Teachers and Administrators." In *Experts in Assessment* series. Eds. T. R. Guskey and R. J. Marzano. Thousand Oaks, CA: Corwin Press, Inc., 2001.

McTighe, J. "What Happens Between Assessments?" *Educational Leadership*, Vol. 54, no. 4 (1997), pp. 6–12.

Morrow, L. M. "Effects of Structural Guidance in Story Retelling on Children's Dictation of Original Stories." *Journal of Reading Behavior*, vol. 18, no. 2 (1986), pp. 135–152.

Moss, B. "Teaching Expository Text Structures Through Information Trade Book Retellings." *The Reading Teacher*, vol. 57, no. 8 (May 2004), pp. 710–718.

Pappas, C. C. "Fostering Full Access to Literacy by Including Information Books." *Language Arts*, vol. 68, no. 6 (October 1991), pp. 449–462.

Raphael, T. E. "Teaching Question Answer Relationships, Revisited." *The Reading Teacher*, vol. 39, no. 6 (February 1986), pp. 516–522.

Wixson, K. K., and M. N. Yochum. "Research on Literacy Policy and Professional Development: National, State, District, and Teacher Contexts." *Elementary School Journal*, vol. 105, no. 2 (November 2004), pp. 219–242.

Wood, K. D.; D. B. Taylor; B. Drye; and M. J. Brigman. "Assessing Students' Understanding of Informational Text in Intermediate- and Middle-Level Classrooms." In *Classroom Literacy Assessment: Making Sense of What Students Know and Do*. Eds. J.R. Paratore and R.L. McCormack. New York: The Guilford Press, 2007, pp. 195–209.

Weekly Tests (Grade 1 only) ✓

What are they?
- Tests designed to measure first-grade children's understanding of the skills and high-frequency words of the week
- Tests consisting of multiple-choice questions

Why would I choose them?
- To assess children's understanding of the high-frequency words, phonics skill, and comprehension skill of the week
- To monitor mastery of skills

What do they test?
- Phonemic awareness (Unit R)
- Understanding of high-frequency words (all units)
- Word reading (Unit R) and phonics skills (Units 1–5)
- Comprehension—target skills (all units)
- Ability to respond in writing to the "Look Back and Write" assignments in the Student Edition

When do I use them?
- At the end of Day 5 in each week

How do I use them?
- The tests are designed to be group-administered.

How do I use the results?
- To identify children who can successfully construct meaning from a reading selection and to identify which children need intervention
- To identify the specific high-frequency words, phonics skills, and comprehension skills a child has and has not mastered

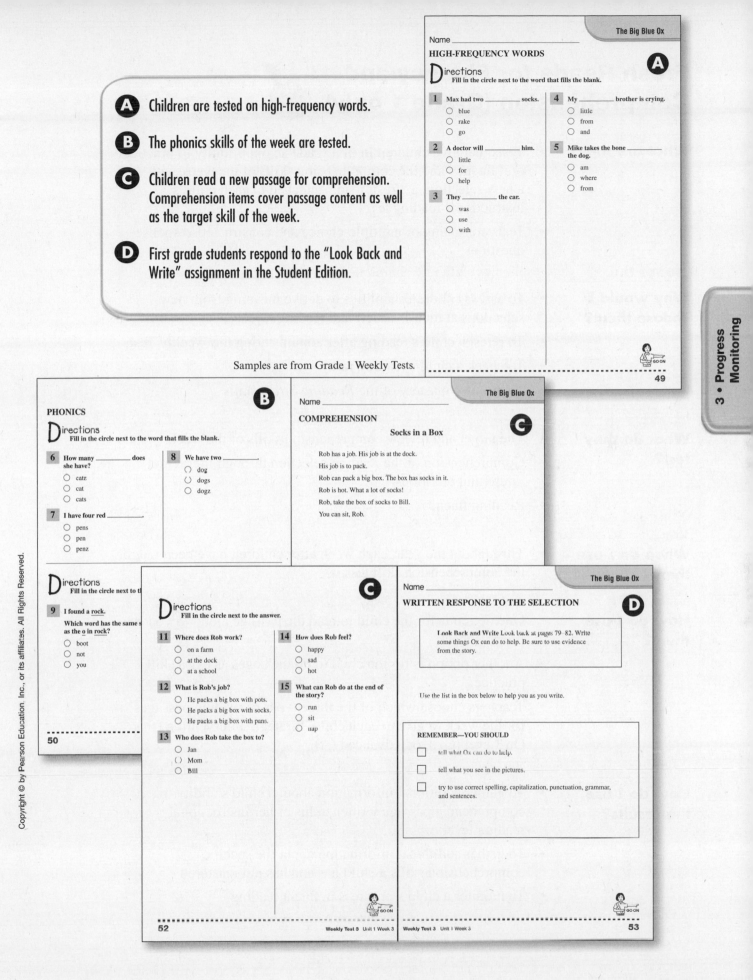

A Children are tested on high-frequency words.

B The phonics skills of the week are tested.

C Children read a new passage for comprehension. Comprehension items cover passage content as well as the target skill of the week.

D First grade students respond to the "Look Back and Write" assignment in the Student Edition.

Samples are from Grade 1 Weekly Tests.

Name _____

The Big Blue Ox

A

HIGH-FREQUENCY WORDS

Directions
Fill in the circle next to the word that fills the blank.

1. Max had two _____ socks.
   - ○ blue
   - ○ rake
   - ○ go

2. A doctor will _____ him.
   - ○ little
   - ○ for
   - ○ help

3. They _____ the car.
   - ○ was
   - ○ use
   - ○ with

4. My _____ brother is crying.
   - ○ little
   - ○ from
   - ○ and

5. Mike takes the bone _____ the dog.
   - ○ am
   - ○ where
   - ○ from

49

PHONICS

B

Directions
Fill in the circle next to the word that fills the blank.

6. How many _____ does she have?
   - ○ catz
   - ○ cat
   - ○ cats

7. I have four red _____.
   - ○ pens
   - ○ pen
   - ○ penz

8. We have two _____.
   - ○ dog
   - ○ dogs
   - ○ dogz

Directions
Fill in the circle next to t

9. I found a <u>rock</u>.
   Which word has the same s as the o in <u>rock</u>?
   - ○ boot
   - ○ not
   - ○ you

50

Name _____

The Big Blue Ox

C

COMPREHENSION

Socks in a Box

Rob has a job. His job is at the dock.

His job is to pack.

Rob can pack a big box. The box has socks in it.

Rob is hot. What a lot of socks!

Rob, take the box of socks to Bill.

You can sit, Rob.

C

Directions
Fill in the circle next to the answer.

11. Where does Rob work?
    - ○ on a farm
    - ○ at the dock
    - ○ at a school

12. What is Rob's job?
    - ○ He packs a big box with pots.
    - ○ He packs a big box with socks.
    - ○ He packs a big box with pans.

13. Who does Rob take the box to?
    - ○ Jan
    - ○ Mom
    - ○ Bill

14. How does Rob feel?
    - ○ happy
    - ○ sad
    - ○ hot

15. What can Rob do at the end of the story?
    - ○ run
    - ○ sit
    - ○ nap

52

Weekly Test 3 Unit 1 Week 3

Name _____

The Big Blue Ox

D

WRITTEN RESPONSE TO THE SELECTION

Look Back and Write Look back at pages 79–82. Write some things Ox can do to help. Be sure to use evidence from the story.

Use the list in the box below to help you as you write.

REMEMBER—YOU SHOULD

☐ tell what Ox can do to help.

☐ tell what you see in the pictures.

☐ try to use correct spelling, capitalization, punctuation, grammar, and sentences.

Weekly Test 3 Unit 1 Week 3

53

3 • Progress Monitoring

Fresh Reads for Fluency and Comprehension (Grade 1 only) ✔

What are they?
- Tests that give children in first grade an opportunity to practice oral fluency and the comprehension skills of the week with a new selection, a "fresh read," matched to each child's instructional reading level
- Tests consisting of multiple-choice and constructed-response questions

Why would I choose them?
- To assess children's abilities to derive meaning from new selections at their instructional reading levels
- To retest a child's reading after administering the Weekly Tests
- To check a child's reading rate
- To monitor mastery of the *Reading Street* skills

What do they test?
- The target and review comprehension skills of the week
- Comprehension of the reading selection through literal and inferential questions
- Reading fluency

When do I use them?
- Throughout the year, each week after children have been taught the comprehension skill lesson

How do I use them?
- One option is for the child to read the passage aloud to you as a fluency check.
- Another option is for the child to do the pages as extra skill practice.
- Teachers choose which of the three types of reading passages for the week to give to each child: Strategic Intervention (SI), On-Level (OL), or Advanced (A).

How do I use the results?
- To gather additional information about a child's ability to comprehend a passage written at his or her instructional reading level
- To gather additional information about the specific comprehension skills a child has and has not mastered
- To monitor a child's progress in fluent reading

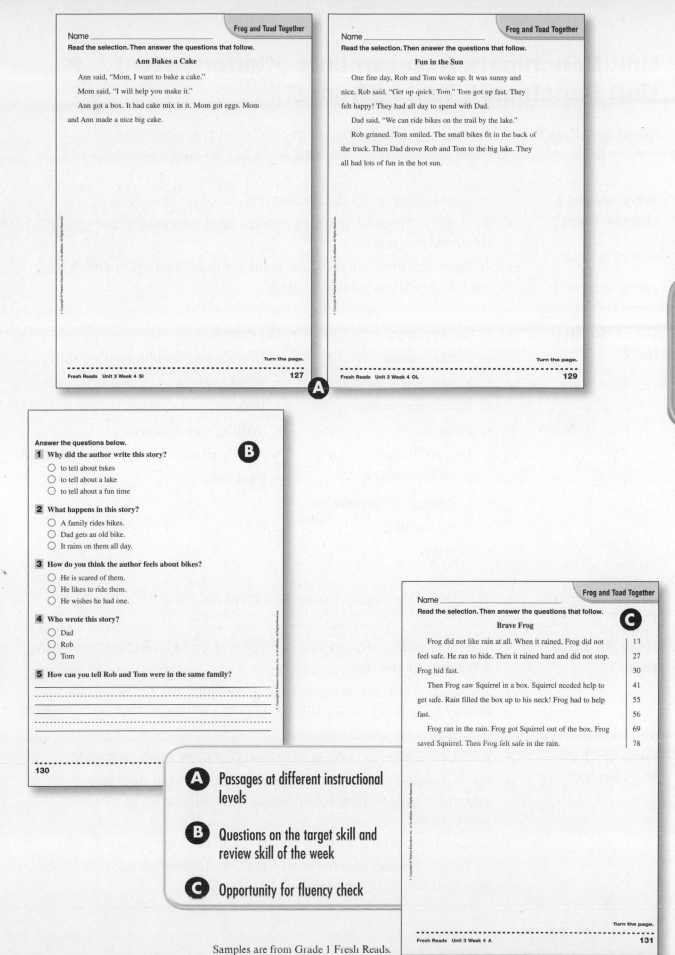

Frog and Toad Together

Name _____

Read the selection. Then answer the questions that follow.

Ann Bakes a Cake

Ann said, "Mom, I want to bake a cake."

Mom said, "I will help you make it."

Ann got a box. It had cake mix in it. Mom got eggs. Mom and Ann made a nice big cake.

Turn the page.

Fresh Reads Unit 3 Week 4 SI   127

Frog and Toad Together

Name _____

Read the selection. Then answer the questions that follow.

Fun in the Sun

One fine day, Rob and Tom woke up. It was sunny and nice. Rob said, "Get up quick, Tom." Tom got up fast. They felt happy! They had all day to spend with Dad.

Dad said, "We can ride bikes on the trail by the lake."

Rob grinned. Tom smiled. The small bikes fit in the back of the truck. Then Dad drove Rob and Tom to the big lake. They all had lots of fun in the hot sun.

Turn the page.

Fresh Reads Unit 3 Week 4 OL   129

Answer the questions below.

1 Why did the author write this story?
- ○ to tell about bikes
- ○ to tell about a lake
- ○ to tell about a fun time

2 What happens in this story?
- ○ A family rides bikes.
- ○ Dad gets an old bike.
- ○ It rains on them all day.

3 How do you think the author feels about bikes?
- ○ He is scared of them.
- ○ He likes to ride them.
- ○ He wishes he had one.

4 Who wrote this story?
- ○ Dad
- ○ Rob
- ○ Tom

5 How can you tell Rob and Tom were in the same family?

_____

130

Frog and Toad Together

Name _____

Read the selection. Then answer the questions that follow.

Brave Frog

Frog did not like rain at all. When it rained, Frog did not	13
feel safe. He ran to hide. Then it rained hard and did not stop.	27
Frog hid fast.	30
Then Frog saw Squirrel in a box. Squirrel needed help to	41
get safe. Rain filled the box up to his neck! Frog had to help	55
fast.	56
Frog ran in the rain. Frog got Squirrel out of the box. Frog	69
saved Squirrel. Then Frog felt safe in the rain.	78

Turn the page.

Fresh Reads Unit 3 Week 4 A   131

A Passages at different instructional levels

B Questions on the target skill and review skill of the week

C Opportunity for fluency check

Samples are from Grade 1 Fresh Reads.

Unit Benchmark Assessments (Kindergarten)
Unit Benchmark Tests (Grade 1)

What are they?

- Tests designed to measure each child's ability to apply target comprehension skills and other literacy skills taught during the unit

Why would I choose them?

- To assess children's understanding and use of specific skills
- To identify skill areas in which children need intervention and continued practice
- To know that there are sufficient items per individual skill to track a child's proficiency with that skill

What do they test?

- In Kindergarten:
  - Letter naming
  - Phonological awareness
  - Phonemic awareness
  - Phonics
  - High-frequency word knowledge
  - Listening comprehension
  - Word reading
  - Writing

- In Grade 1:
  - Unit reading comprehension skills
  - Word reading
  - Phonics
  - Writing conventions
  - Ability to respond to a writing prompt
  - Oral fluency

When do I use them?

- Throughout the year, at the end of each of the six-week units

How do I use them?

- The kindergarten tests are designed to be given to individuals or to groups depending on the task.
- The grade 1 tests are designed to be group-administered except for the fluency passages. Fluency checks in grade 1 are individually administered.

How do I use the results?

- For kindergarten, to make instructional decisions about each child
- For first grade, to identify children who can successfully construct meaning from a reading selection and to identify children who need intervention
- To identify specific skills children have and have not mastered
- As feedback about the effectiveness of your instruction and to help you plan instruction for the next unit

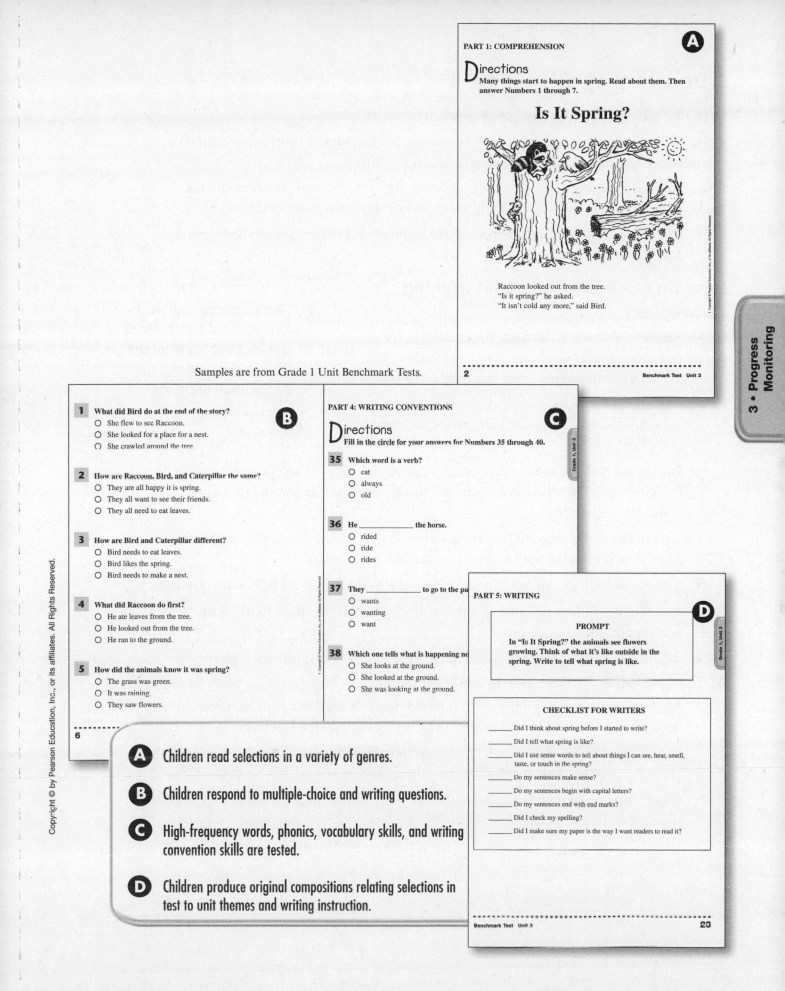

PART 1: COMPREHENSION

Directions
Many things start to happen in spring. Read about them. Then answer Numbers 1 through 7.

Is It Spring?

Raccoon looked out from the tree.
"Is it spring?" he asked.
"It isn't cold any more," said Bird.

Samples are from Grade 1 Unit Benchmark Tests.

1 What did Bird do at the end of the story?
- ○ She flew to see Raccoon.
- ○ She looked for a place for a nest.
- ○ She crawled around the tree.

2 How are Raccoon, Bird, and Caterpillar the same?
- ○ They are all happy it is spring.
- ○ They all want to see their friends.
- ○ They all need to eat leaves.

3 How are Bird and Caterpillar different?
- ○ Bird needs to eat leaves.
- ○ Bird likes the spring.
- ○ Bird needs to make a nest.

4 What did Raccoon do first?
- ○ He ate leaves from the tree.
- ○ He looked out from the tree.
- ○ He ran to the ground.

5 How did the animals know it was spring?
- ○ The grass was green.
- ○ It was raining.
- ○ They saw flowers.

6

PART 4: WRITING CONVENTIONS

Directions
Fill in the circle for your answers for Numbers 35 through 40.

35 Which word is a verb?
- ○ cat
- ○ always
- ○ old

36 He _____ the horse.
- ○ rided
- ○ ride
- ○ rides

37 They _____ to go to the pa
- ○ wants
- ○ wanting
- ○ want

38 Which one tells what is happening no
- ○ She looks at the ground.
- ○ She looked at the ground.
- ○ She was looking at the ground.

Grade 1, Unit 3

PART 5: WRITING

PROMPT

In "Is It Spring?" the animals see flowers growing. Think of what it's like outside in the spring. Write to tell what spring is like.

CHECKLIST FOR WRITERS

_____ Did I think about spring before I started to write?

_____ Did I tell what spring is like?

_____ Did I use sense words to tell about things I can see, hear, smell, taste, or touch in the spring?

_____ Do my sentences make sense?

_____ Do my sentences begin with capital letters?

_____ Do my sentences end with end marks?

_____ Did I check my spelling?

_____ Did I make sure my paper is the way I want readers to read it?

A Children read selections in a variety of genres.

B Children respond to multiple-choice and writing questions.

C High-frequency words, phonics, vocabulary skills, and writing convention skills are tested.

D Children produce original compositions relating selections in test to unit themes and writing instruction.

3 • Progress Monitoring

Questioning Strategies

Why is questioning important?

- While asking questions is a routine practice for teachers, it is often overlooked as our most powerful tool for instruction and assessment.

- Artfully crafted questions engage children, focus their attention, stimulate their thinking, facilitate their understanding, and deepen their comprehension.

- Child self-generated questions improve learning and strengthen problem-solving and critical-thinking skills.

How do I use effective questioning strategies?

- Selectively choose questions for specific purposes (e.g., recall-level questions about sequence of ideas and analytic questions about the theme of a story).

- Ask questions that represent diverse thinking activities—recall, analysis, comparison, inference, and evaluation.

> "Our questions help us formulate our beliefs about teaching and learning, and those beliefs underlie our instructional decisions."
> (Keene & Zimmermann, 1997)

- Design developmentally appropriate questions that emphasize both content and the thinking needed to process the content, using verbs such as *list, define, compare, conclude,* and *defend*.

- Remember that when children are asked to analyze information, they will learn more than if asked simply to recall or identify information.

- Listen carefully to children's answers in order to shape skillful follow-up questions.

- Ask probing follow-up questions that help children extend their thinking and clarify and support their points of view.

- Allow wait time because it gives children time to think and provides answering opportunities for those who process more slowly.

- Model question-asking and question-answering behavior, and provide repeated opportunities for children to practice generating their own questions.

- Model questioning with a variety of texts and, through reading conferences with the children, monitor their developing use of questioning.

- Guide children in understanding that through their own questions, they can actively regulate their reading and learning.

How does Scott Foresman *Reading Street* support effective questioning practices?

- Questioning strategies are based on a question-answer framework suggesting an interaction among the question, the text to which it refers, and the prior knowledge of the reader (Raphael, 1986).

- Children are taught that answering comprehension questions in class and on tests demands thinking: they have to analyze the questions in order to provide the right answers.

- Children learn that answers to questions can be found **In the Book** and **In My Head.**

- **In the Book** questions can be:

  - **Right There** questions, which are *literal* and focus on ideas explicitly stated in the text. The words in the question may match the words in the passage.

  - **Think and Search** questions, which are also *literal* and require children to locate and integrate information from within different sections of the text.

- **In My Head** questions can be:

  - **Author and Me** questions, which are *inferential* in nature, requiring children to interpret information and connect themes and major ideas with their own background knowledge. The most demanding **Author and Me** questions necessitate use of critical analysis as readers evaluate and justify the purpose, content, and quality of text.

  - **On My Own** questions are not based on the text and can be answered from children's general background knowledge and experience. These questions are often posed by teachers in order to activate prior knowledge before reading and/or to extend the learning beyond the lesson.

- The Scott Foresman *Reading Street* formal assessments offer children a variety of engaging narrative and expository texts, and children respond to test items designed to assess how they use their comprehension skills in constructing meaning.

- Literal, inferential, and critical-analysis questions on the formal assessments are based on the question-answer framework used in instruction and are similar to question types on high-stakes assessments.

- Daily practice in answering, analyzing, and asking **Right There, Think and Search,** and **Author and Me** questions will improve children's achievement on high-stakes standardized tests.

Ongoing Teacher Observation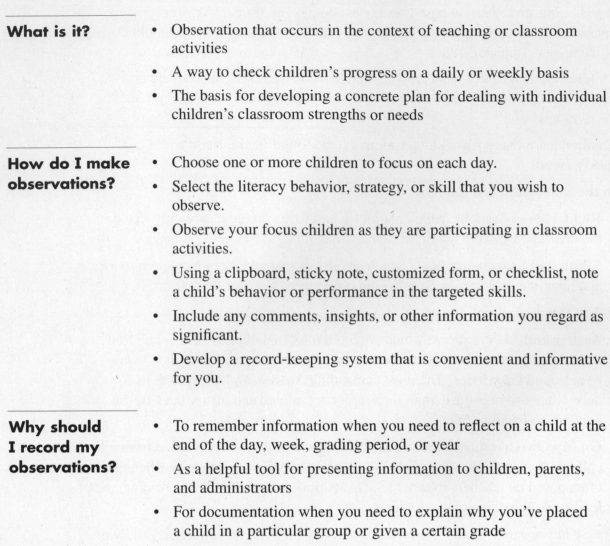

What is it?

- Observation that occurs in the context of teaching or classroom activities
- A way to check children's progress on a daily or weekly basis
- The basis for developing a concrete plan for dealing with individual children's classroom strengths or needs

How do I make observations?

- Choose one or more children to focus on each day.
- Select the literacy behavior, strategy, or skill that you wish to observe.
- Observe your focus children as they are participating in classroom activities.
- Using a clipboard, sticky note, customized form, or checklist, note a child's behavior or performance in the targeted skills.
- Include any comments, insights, or other information you regard as significant.
- Develop a record-keeping system that is convenient and informative for you.

Why should I record my observations?

- To remember information when you need to reflect on a child at the end of the day, week, grading period, or year
- As a helpful tool for presenting information to children, parents, and administrators
- For documentation when you need to explain why you've placed a child in a particular group or given a certain grade
- To plan intervention strategies for children needing special attention

Fluency Check (Grade 1 only) ✓

What is it?

- An individually-administered procedure of recording and analyzing a child's specific reading behaviors
- A method of deciding whether a text is at the appropriate instructional level for a child
- A means of determining the level of support a child will need while reading the material

What does it show?

- Teachers who administer regular fluency checks gather evidence about the following:
  - oral reading skills and fluency calculated as words correct per minute
  - decoding and word recognition strategies
  - reading strategies a child uses and how he or she uses them to derive meaning

When do I use it?

- As often as necessary to get a clear and ongoing picture of a child's precise reading behaviors (for example, at the beginning or end of a unit or grading period or when you need to report progress to interested parties)

How do I use it?

- Use an excerpt from Scott Foresman *Reading Street*, from a trade book, or any other text that is at an appropriate reading level for the child.
- Make one photocopy of the passage for yourself and one for the child.
- Use a watch with a second hand to time the child's reading for exactly one minute.
- Observe the child closely as he or she reads aloud, and note the miscues or errors that are made.

3 • Progress Monitoring

How do I use it? (continued)

- Use the following notations and symbols for errors:

  - **Last Word Read** ( ]) – Put a bracket after the last word the child reads in one minute.

  - **Mispronunciation/misreading** (/) – Write the child's pronunciation of the word.

  - **Substitutions** – Write the substituted word above the text word. Cross out the text word. If it is a nonsense word, write it phonetically.

  - **Self-correction** (sc) – Write *sc* in a circle next to the corrected word/text; this is not considered an error.

  - **Insertions** (∧) – Write the text word/phrase and the inserted word/phrase. Mark each insertion with a caret. Include any repetitions of words.

  - **Omissions** – Circle the word(s) or word part(s) omitted.

The formula is:

Total number of words read in one minute – Number of errors = Words correct per minute

Teacher Form
Retelling

What is retelling?

- A post-reading recall of what children can remember from reading or listening to a particular text

- An oral or written recounting of narrative or expository text in a child's own words

- A reminder for children that the purpose of reading is to make sense of text

What does it show?

- Children's abilities to understand narrative text elements and author's purpose and to connect stories to personal experiences and other texts

- Children's abilities to understand expository text—the relationship of main ideas and details, organizational structure, author's purpose, and inferences—and to connect texts to personal experiences and prior knowledge (Moss, 2004)

- Oral and written language development

What does the research say?

- Several researchers (Gambrell, Koskinen, and Kapinus, 1991; Gambrell, Pfeiffer, and Wilson, 1985; Morrow, 1986) have found that using retellings improves children's understanding of text.

- Pappas (1991) found that kindergarten children were just as capable of summarizing informational text as they were of retelling narrative text.

How do I do it?

- In preparation:

  - Have children attempt to retell narrative or summarize expository texts only after you have taught and modeled the procedure and the children understand the task.

  - Have children practice in groups before retelling or summarizing for assessment purposes.

  - Teach text structures (narrative and expository) separately to avoid confusing children.

- Oral retellings should be administered individually. Written retellings can be administered individually or in a group.

- For oral retellings, read the passage aloud to the child or have the child read the selected text. Remind the child to remember everything he or she has heard or read. Then ask the child to tell you everything about what was read. Use prompts, such as "Can you tell me more about that?"; "What happened next?"; and "What else do you remember?" At the end of the retelling, use follow-up questions (e.g., main idea, author's purpose, personal response, etc.) to gain a deeper understanding of the child's comprehension.

How do I do it? (continued)

- For written retellings, read the text aloud to children or ask them to read it silently. Remind the children to remember everything they can. Immediately after reading, have children write out what they remember about the text.

How do I use the Retelling and Summarizing Forms?

- Record your scores and observations on either the narrative or the expository checklist. Try to record at least one narrative retelling and one expository retelling from each child per unit.

Teacher Form
Narrative Retelling Chart ✓

Unit __4__ Selection Title _The Three Billy Goats Gruff_ Name _David Romero_ Date _2/4/09_

Retelling Criteria/Teacher Prompt	Teacher-Aided Response	Student-Generated Response	Rubric Score (Circle one.)
Connections Did you like this book? Why or why not? How does this story remind you of other stories? **Ⓐ**		I liked this book because the goats tricked the troll. It reminds me of the Three Little Pigs because the pigs tricked the wolf too.	④ 3 2 1
Author's Purpose What was the author trying to teach us?		Being mean will get you in trouble.	4 ③ 2 1
Characters Describe _____ (character's name).		The littlest goat was brave and smart.	4 ③ 2 1
Setting Where and when did the story happen?		It happened on the troll's bridge.	4 3 ② 1
Plot Tell me what happened in the story.		The troll tried to scare the goats so they wouldn't cross the bridge. The goats tricked the troll and the biggest goat scared him away	4 ③ 2 1

Summative Retelling Score 4 ③ 2 1
Comments _____

Ⓐ **Criteria reflect comprehension skills.**

Ⓑ **Criteria help children pinpoint key information.**

Teacher Form
Expository Retelling Chart ✓

Unit __4__ Selection Title _Snakes_ Name _David Romero_ Date _10/28/08_

Retelling Criteria/Teacher Prompt	Teacher-Aided Response	Student-Generated Response	Rubric Score (Circle one.)
Connections Did this selection make you think about something else you have read? What did you learn about as you read this selection?		This book made me think of the green snake in Armadillo's Orange	④ 3 2 1
Author's Purpose Why do you think the author wrote this selection?		I think he wants us to know about snakes so we can be careful but not scared of them.	④ 3 2 1
Topic What was the selection mostly about?		snakes	4 ③ 2 1
Important Ideas What is important for me to know about _____ (topic)?		Some are poisonous and some are not. Sankes live in many different places.	4 ③ 2 1
Conclusions What did you learn from reading this selection? **Ⓑ**		I learned where different kinds of snakes live and what they eat.	4 ③ 2 1

Summative Retelling Score 4 ③ 2 1
Comments _David is motivated to read books about animals._

Forms for reproduction are on pages 135–136.

Teacher Form
Work Habits Conference Record ✓

What is it?
- A means of assessing a child's work habits and task-completion behaviors

What does it show?
- A child's ability to set priorities and manage time
- A child's behavior toward problem-solving tasks
- A child's progress toward working independently

How do I use it?
- Plan to confer with each child at least once per grading period.
- Use the form for frequent, ongoing, informal conversations about the child's ability to manage time, set priorities, seek help, follow directions, and explain task completion processes.
- Tailor each conference to the child's needs, interests, and abilities; encourage him or her to take an active role.

Teacher Form
Work Habits Conference Record ✓

Child Kristen Cleaver

Use the key at the bottom of the page to assess student's performance.

Date	Understands tasks (A)	Sets priorities (B)	Uses time appropriately (C)	Solves problems effectively	Seeks help when needed (D)	Completes tasks on time	Can explain process/ project effectively	Comments
10\21	4	3	2	3	3	2	3	distracted by other activities in room
12\4	4	3	2	4	4	2	4	works well in small groups

4 Independent   3 With Some Assistance   2 With Frequent Assistance   1 Not Observed

A Did the child understand the assignment's purpose and procedures? Did he or she follow directions?

B Was the child able to decide which parts of the assignment had to be done first?

C Did the child allot time appropriately and use the time productively?

D Did the child know when it was time to seek help? Did he or she seek out the right resources (books, peers, teacher, and so on)?

Form for reproduction is on page 137.

Teacher Form
Skills Conference Record

What is it?

- A means of focusing and recording results of conversations with a child about his or her reading, writing, speaking, and listening

What does it show?

- A child's behaviors, strategies, and proficiencies in the areas of reading, writing, speaking, and listening

How do I use it?

- Plan to confer with each child at least once per grading period.

- Use the form for frequent, ongoing, informal conversations about the child's progress, strengths, and areas for improvement.

- Tailor each conference to the child's needs, interests, and abilities; encourage him or her to take an active role.

A Specific criteria in each area show particular strengths and needs.

B Comments can be made to record child's behavior or a specific concern.

C Checklist covers the continuum of child's skill growth.

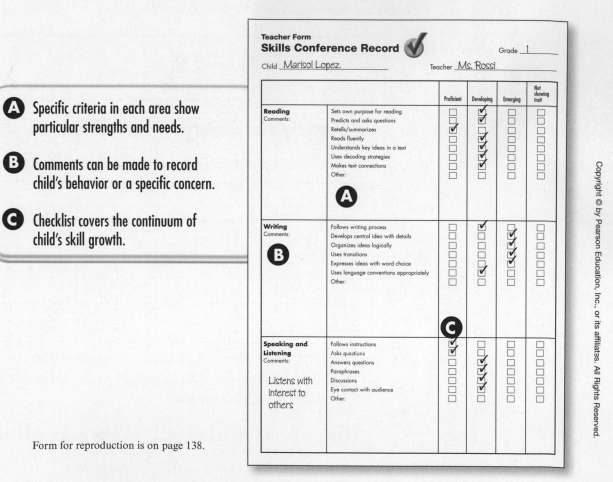

Form for reproduction is on page 138.

Teacher Form
Observing English Language Learners

What is it?
- A form to record your ongoing observations about how English language learners process what they read

What does it show?
- How English language learners use strategies to make sense of materials they read
- Children's growth and development in processing what they read

How do I use it?
- Use this form with first graders beginning in the second half of the year as children become capable of reading passages.
- Work with children individually as they read a new selection.
- Record your observations about how children deal with new words and concepts.
- Continue to review and record children's behaviors periodically.
- Consider using the information on the form in parent conferences.

A Behaviors identify common strategies for success in reading a new language.

B Space is provided to record children's development over time.

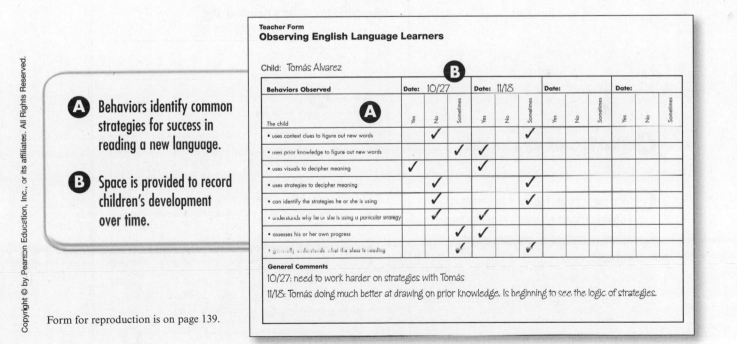

Teacher Form
Observing English Language Learners

Child: Tomás Alvarez

Behaviors Observed	Date: 10/27			Date: 11/18			Date:			Date:		
The child	Yes	No	Sometimes	Yes	No	Sometimes	Yes	No	Sometimes	Yes	No	Sometimes
• uses context clues to figure out new words		✓				✓						
• uses prior knowledge to figure out new words			✓	✓								
• uses visuals to decipher meaning	✓					✓						
• uses strategies to decipher meaning		✓				✓						
• can identify the strategies he or she is using		✓				✓						
• understands why he or she is using a particular strategy	✓				✓							
• assesses his or her own progress		✓		✓								
• generally understands what the class is reading		✓				✓						

General Comments

10/27: need to work harder on strategies with Tomás

11/18: Tomás doing much better at drawing on prior knowledge. Is beginning to see the logic of strategies.

Form for reproduction is on page 139.

Parent Form
Observing My Child's Reading

What is it?

- A form to allow parents to monitor, evaluate, and comment on their child's reading

- A way to keep parents knowledgeable about and involved in their child's reading progress

What does it show?

- Reading behaviors that parents notice as their child reads aloud to them

How do parents use it?

- Give multiple copies of the form to parents during a conference or other meeting early in the school year.

- Ask parents to use the forms every few weeks to note their responses as their child reads aloud to them.

- Encourage parents to include comments on any other noteworthy aspects of their child's reading progress.

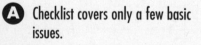

A Checklist covers only a few basic issues.

B Parents are encouraged to comment on any aspect of child's reading that they've noticed or are concerned about.

Form for reproduction is on page 140.

Parent Form
Observing My Child's Reading

Child David Hill

Parent/Guardian/Caregiver Becky Townsend

Date 10/10

1. Story or article my child read to me:

I Like My Bike

2. Here are some things I noticed about my child's

Vocabulary A

	yes	no	not sure
• understands most words that he or she reads	☑ yes	☐ no	☐ not sure
• can figure out word meanings from other words in passage	☐ yes	☐ no	☑ not sure
• is not afraid to attempt reading new words	☐ yes	☑ no	☐ not sure

Comprehension

	yes	no	not sure
• understands what he or she is reading	☐ yes	☐ no	☑ not sure
• remembers the important ideas from a reading	☑ yes	☐ no	☐ not sure
• can tell back what he or she has read	☑ yes	☐ no	☐ not sure
• remembers the order things happened in	☐ yes	☐ no	☑ not sure

Read-Aloud Ability

	yes	no	not sure
• reads most sentences without pausing	☐ yes	☑ no	☐ not sure
• reads in a manner that shows he or she makes sense of what is being read	☐ yes	☑ no	☐ not sure
• reads with expression	☐ yes	☑ no	☐ not sure
• pronounces most words correctly	☐ yes	☐ no	☐ not sure

3. Here are some general comments about what I noticed as my child read: **B**

David does all right until he encounters a word he doesn't know. Then he ignores it and loses the sense of what he's reading. He reads with such little expression that I wonder how much he understands.

Child Form
Peer Assessment

What is it?	• A form that allows children to evaluate and comment on each other's work
	• A way to help children become aware of and value different points of view

What does it show?	• Constructive feedback that children provide to their peers
	• Different perspectives children have on their peers' work and/or performance

How do children use it?	• Children should assess a piece of a peer's work at least once per grading period.
	• Children might keep this form in their portfolios and use it during peer conferences.

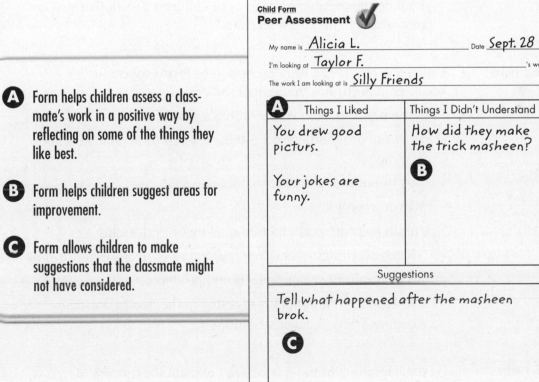

A Form helps children assess a class-mate's work in a positive way by reflecting on some of the things they like best.

B Form helps children suggest areas for improvement.

C Form allows children to make suggestions that the classmate might not have considered.

Form for reproduction is on page 143.

Child Form
Peer Assessment

My name is _Alicia L._   Date _Sept. 28_

I'm looking at _Taylor F._ 's work.

The work I am looking at is _Silly Friends_

A Things I Liked	Things I Didn't Understand
You drew good picturs.	How did they make the trick masheen? **B**
Your jokes are funny.	

Suggestions
Tell what happened after the masheen brok. **C**

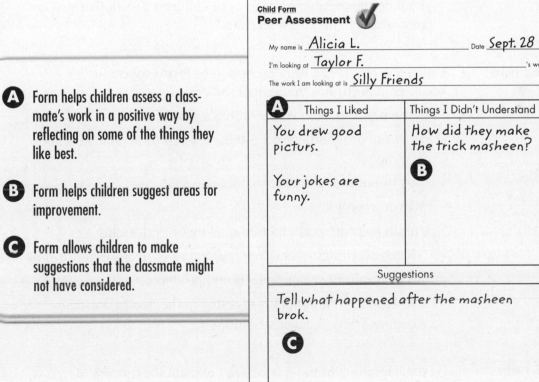

Student Portfolios

What is a portfolio?

- A teacher-guided process in which children collect representative samples of their own reading, writing, speaking, and listening as a means of demonstrating growth over time

- A method of documenting growth by using the actual products children create during normal day-to-day learning

- A way to encourage children to feel ownership of their learning

What is the purpose of a portfolio?

- Portfolios may accomplish any or all of the following:
  - Demonstrate children's growth and progress
  - Show children's strengths and needs
  - Help you make instructional decisions about children
  - Encourage children to assess their own growth and progress and to set new goals
  - Make it possible to share evidence of children's growth during parent conferences
  - Include representative samples of children's work that you can pass along to their next teachers

What goes into a portfolio?

- Chapter 7 provides a full description of forms to use for organizing portfolios throughout the year.
- Possible items to include in children's portfolios are:
  - Drawing or writing projects that children have done at school or at home
  - List of books children have read
  - Works in progress
  - Audio recordings of children reading or performing
  - Video recordings of children presenting projects or performing
  - Photographs of group projects and products
  - Children's work samples suggested in the Scott Foresman *Reading Street* Teacher's Editions

How do I help children choose samples for their portfolios?

- At the beginning of the school year, explain the process of developing a portfolio.
- Show models of portfolios and sample entries. Explain that portfolios should include:
  - a wide variety of materials
  - samples that demonstrate learning experiences

How do I help children choose samples for their portfolios? (continued)

- – pieces that show growth or improvement over time
- – materials that indicate that children have challenged themselves to try something different

- Periodically set aside time for children to examine their work and think about which pieces they would like to include in their portfolios.
  - – Ask children to complete or help them complete a Portfolio Selection Slip that can be attached to each piece of work selected for inclusion in the portfolio.
  - – Ask children to briefly describe the work sample, the rationale for including it, and a reflection on the quality of the work (for example, *What I Chose*, *Why I Chose It*, and *What I Like About It*).

- Encourage children to include other documentation of literacy growth and progress, such as journal entries, inventories, writing samples, and reading and writing logs.

How do I involve the family in the portfolio process?

- At the beginning of the year, send home a letter to parents informing them about portfolios.

- Share children's portfolios during parent conferences as children explain the contents, how projects were developed, and how portfolio pieces were selected.

- While viewing portfolios with parents, point out children's strengths and progress over time.

What can I do at the end of each grading period?

- Hold portfolio conferences toward the end of each grading period to help children reflect on the contents of their portfolios.

- Have children decide which pieces to take home, which pieces to keep in the portfolio, and which pieces to lend to you to update their Portfolio Guides.

What can I do at the end of the school year?

- Hold final conferences with children to help them reflect on their portfolios and decide what to save and what to eliminate.

- Have children decide what to take home and what to pass along to their next teachers (for example, the pieces they are most proud of or the ones that show the most growth).

Child Form
Reading Log

What is it?
- A form to help children keep track of the literature they have read

What does it show?
- Literature children have read and how they evaluate what they read
- Children's reading growth over time

How do children use it?
- Children may list either materials from the reading program or pieces of literature they have selected on their own.
- Children may put this form in their portfolios as a way of documenting what they have read.

Child Form
Reading Log   Ⓐ

Name _Derrick Johnson_

Dates Read	Title and Author	What is it about?	How would you rate it?	Explain your rating.
From 1/20 to 1/28	Frog and Toad Are Friends by Arnold Lobel	The adventures of two friends	Great **Ⓑ** Awful (5) 4 3 2 1	I like how they help each other.
From 2/4 to 2/10	Trains by Lee Sullivan Hill	train cars on freight and passenger trains and workers	Great Awful 5 4 (3) 2 1	I wanted to learn about more kinds of trains.
From ___ to ___			Great Awful 5 4 3 2 1	
From ___ to ___			Great Awful 5 4 3 2 1	
From ___ to ___			Great Awful 5 4 3 2 1	

Ⓐ Children should list the titles and authors of selections they have read.

Ⓑ Have children circle the rating they would give each selection. Children should give a reason or two to explain or support their ratings.

Form for reproduction is on page 141.

Child Form
Writing Log

What is it?

- A form to help children keep track of and reflect on the pieces they have written

What does it show?

- Titles and types of compositions children have written
- Children's feelings toward their writing and what they liked/disliked about each piece

How do children use it?

- Children can make notes in their Writing Logs during any stage of the writing process for any pieces they choose.
- Children may put this form in their portfolios as a way of keeping track of what they have written.

Child Form
Writing Log

Child **Taylor F.** Date **10/30**
Teacher **Ms Rossi** Grade **2**

Date	Title (A)	Type of writing	How I felt about this piece	What I liked or disliked (B)	Put in portfolio
Oct 15	Silly Friends		④ 3 2 1	the funny parts	✓
Oct 27	My Halloween Costume		4 ③ 2 1	the surprise at the end	
			4 3 2 1		
			4 3 2 1		
			4 3 2 1		
			4 3 2 1		

Key
4 = Excellent
3 = Good
2 = Fair
1 = Poor

A If children haven't titled a piece yet, they can use a working title such as "My Puppy" or "Mystery Story."

B Encourage children to assess their own writing and to point out the strengths of each piece.

Form for reproduction is on page 142.

Chapter 4

Summative Assessment: What to Do After Instruction Has Taken Place

Overview

Summative assessments are formal assessments used to determine how well children have met or exceeded state reading and language arts curriculum standards. They are designed to document long-term growth in the development of literacy skills and include state-required assessments as well as Scott Foresman *Reading Street* assessments and tests developed by school districts. They focus on end-of-year standards and outcomes.

What are the benefits of summative assessments?

Summative assessments help you determine if all children are making expected academic growth and provide you with information to:

- determine your children's progress in meeting or exceeding state reading and language arts curriculum standards;

- gather information in a systematic way to validate judgments and decisions about learning;

- standardize opportunities for each child taking the test;
  - Each child receives the same directions.
  - Each test is scored by the same criteria.

- give feedback to your children that enables them to learn about their own literacy development; and

- continually refine and modify instruction in your classroom to meet the needs of your children.

What is the purpose of using summative assessments?

Summative assessments are used for measuring long-term growth. The results of summative assessment tests can be used to:

- determine the degree to which your children have achieved the goals defined by a given standard or group of standards; and

- gather specific information about children with particular needs, such as English language learners and children with disabilities.

What do I want to learn from summative assessments?

Summative assessments provide you with information about how well your children have mastered the content of previously taught lessons. They include feedback on child achievement of standards in the following grade-level strands of national and state reading and language arts standards.

- Phonics, word analysis, and fluency development
- Reading comprehension
- Literary response and analysis
- Writing prompt
- Written language conventions (e.g., sentence structure, grammar, punctuation, capitalization, spelling)

What type of assessments should be used as summative assessment?

- Use formal assessments that provide a detailed analysis of how well your children have mastered the knowledge and skills described in the national and state reading and language arts standards.

When do I gather the information?

- Summative assessments should be given at the end of the year.

What techniques and tools are available?

FORMAL ASSESSMENT TOOL AND TECHNIQUES FOR SUMMATIVE ASSESSMENT

- **End-of-Year Benchmark Assessment (Kindergarten)** and **End-of-Year Benchmark Test (Grade 1)** (See pages 82–83.)

    A group-administered, summative assessment is used to determine your children's growth in mastering the content in the national and state reading and language arts standards and to document achievement of skills taught throughout the school year.

INFORMAL ASSESSMENT TOOLS AND TECHNIQUES FOR SUMMATIVE ASSESSMENT

- Additional classroom-based assessment forms can be found in Chapter 7. These include:

    – Reading Strategic Assessment

    – Writing Strategic Assessment

    – Cumulative Folder Form

Want to learn more about summative assessment?

If you are interested in learning more about research that supports the use of summative assessment tools and practices, you will find the following resources interesting.

References

Afflerbach, P. "Teaching Reading Self-Assessment Strategies." In *Comprehension Instruction: Research-Based Best Practices*. Eds. C. Block and M. Pressley. New York: Guilford Press, 2001, pp. 96–111.

Guthrie, J. T. "Preparing Students for High-Stakes Test Taking in Reading." In *What Research Has To Say About Reading Instruction*. Eds. A. E. Farstrup and S. J. Samuels. Newark, DE: International Reading Association, 2002, pp. 370–391.

Howell, K. W., and V. Nolet. *Curriculum-Based Evaluation: Teaching and Decision Making*, 3rd Ed. Belmont, CA: Wadsworth and Thompson Learning Company, 2000.

Johnston, P., and P. Costello. "Principles for Literacy Assessment." *Reading Research Quarterly*. vol. 40, no. 2 (2005), pp. 256–267.

Marzano, R,. et al. *Classroom Instruction That Works: Research-Based Strategies for Increasing Student Achievement*. Alexandria, VA: ASCD, 2001.

Pearson, P. D.; S. Vyas; L. M. Sensale; and Y. Kim. "Making Our Way Through the Assessment and Accountability Maze: Where Do We Go Now?" *The Clearing House*, vol. 74, no. 4 (2001), pp. 175–182.

Shepard, L. "The Role of Classroom Assessment in Teaching and Learning." In *Handbook of Research on Teaching*. 4th Ed. Ed. V. K. Richardson. Washington, DC: American Educational Research Association, 2001, pp. 1066–1101.

Valencia, S. W. "Inquiry-Oriented Assessment." In *Classroom Literacy Assessment: Making Sense of What Students Know and Do*. Eds. J. R. Paratore and R. L. McCormack. New York: The Guilford Press, 2007, pp. 3–20.

Wixson, K. K.; S. W. Valencia; and M. Y. Lipson. "Issues in Literacy Assessment: Facing the Realities of Internal and External Assessment." *Journal of Reading Behavior*, vol. 26, no. 3 (1994), pp. 315–337.

4 • Summative

End-of-Year Benchmark Assessment (Kindergarten)
End-of-Year Benchmark Test (Grade 1)

What is it?

- A multiple-choice and constructed-response test designed to measure your children's proficiency at specific skills taught throughout the school year
- A means to document your children's long-term growth

Why would I choose it?

- To evaluate your children's end-of-year mastery in specific reading and language arts skills
- To identify skill areas in which children need intervention and continued practice
- To document academic growth

What does it test?

The kindergarten End-of-Year Benchmark Assessment and grade 1 End-of-Year Benchmark Test include subtests for the following grade-level strands:

- Listening comprehension (kindergarten)
- Reading comprehension (grade 1)
- Phonics
- High-frequency words
- Writing conventions—usage, mechanics, grammar, and spelling
- Writing application—response to a prompt
- Oral reading fluency (grade 1)

When do I use it?

- At the end of the year

How do I use it?

- The test is designed to be group-administered.
- The fluency check is administered individually.

How do I use the results?

- To document and record individual children's growth in cumulative skills taught during the school year
- To diagnose and record individual children's needs for the next year
- To inform and improve the delivery of curriculum and instruction
- To provide guidance for teacher teams in the next school year who plan interventions for children who need additional support
- To provide helpful feedback to children and parents
- To help determine children's overall grades
- To guide parents in working with their children during vacation, so learning continues throughout the summer months

Samples are from Grade 1 End-of-Year Benchmark Test.

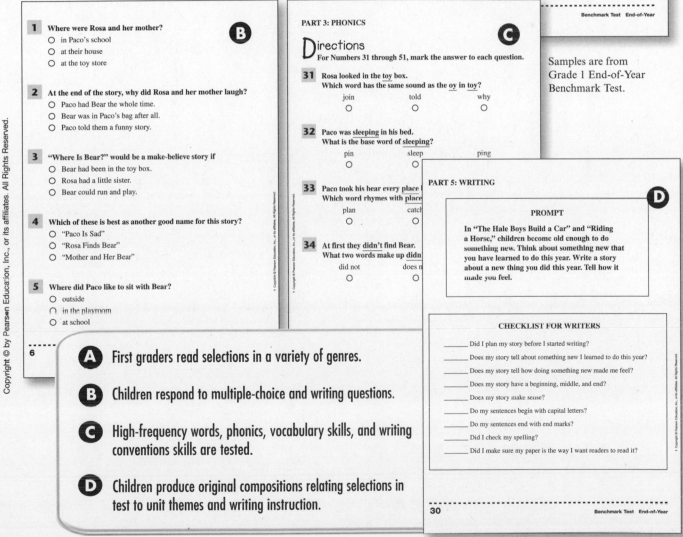

PART 1: COMPREHENSION

Directions
Paco's favorite toy is missing! Read about how Paco's sister and mother look for the toy. Then answer Numbers 1 through 7.

A

Where Is Bear?

Rosa's little brother, Paco, had a favorite toy bear. He took it every place he went.

One day Rosa's mother said, "I can't find Bear. I thought Bear was in Paco's bag. Now Bear isn't there. Paco will be very sad."

Rosa's mother said, "Rosa, I need your help to look for Bear. Let's think like detectives. Where are the places that Paco goes with Bear?"

Benchmark Test End-of-Year

B

1 Where were Rosa and her mother?
- ○ in Paco's school
- ○ at their house
- ○ at the toy store

2 At the end of the story, why did Rosa and her mother laugh?
- ○ Paco had Bear the whole time.
- ○ Bear was in Paco's bag after all.
- ○ Paco told them a funny story.

3 "Where Is Bear?" would be a make-believe story if
- ○ Bear had been in the toy box.
- ○ Rosa had a little sister.
- ○ Bear could run and play.

4 Which of these is best as another good name for this story?
- ○ "Paco Is Sad"
- ○ "Rosa Finds Bear"
- ○ "Mother and Her Bear"

5 Where did Paco like to sit with Bear?
- ○ outside
- ○ in the playroom
- ○ at school

6

PART 3: PHONICS

Directions
For Numbers 31 through 51, mark the answer to each question.

C

31 Rosa looked in the toy box.
Which word has the same sound as the oy in toy?

join   told   why
○   ○   ○

32 Paco was sleeping in his bed.
What is the base word of sleeping?

pin   sleep   ping
○   ○   ○

33 Paco took his bear every place
Which word rhymes with place

plan   catch
○   ○

34 At first they didn't find Bear.
What two words make up didn

did not   does n
○   ○

PART 5: WRITING

D

PROMPT

In "The Hale Boys Build a Car" and "Riding a Horse," children become old enough to do something new. Think about something new that you have learned to do this year. Write a story about a new thing you did this year. Tell how it made you feel.

CHECKLIST FOR WRITERS

_____ Did I plan my story before I started writing?

_____ Does my story tell about something new I learned to do this year?

_____ Does my story tell how doing something new made me feel?

_____ Does my story have a beginning, middle, and end?

_____ Does my story make sense?

_____ Do my sentences begin with capital letters?

_____ Do my sentences end with end marks?

_____ Did I check my spelling?

_____ Did I make sure my paper is the way I want readers to read it?

30   Benchmark Test End-of-Year

A First graders read selections in a variety of genres.

B Children respond to multiple-choice and writing questions.

C High-frequency words, phonics, vocabulary skills, and writing conventions skills are tested.

D Children produce original compositions relating selections in test to unit themes and writing instruction.

4 • Summative

83

Copyright © by Pearson Education, Inc., or its affiliates. All Rights Reserved.

Chapter 5 | Writing as Learning and Assessment

Overview

Writing is an important component of the state reading and language arts curriculum standards. Writing facilitates learning by providing a means through which children can develop complex thinking and express depth of understanding. As you design writing instruction, you will not only want to consider how to assess the development of writing, but also how your children use writing as a tool for demonstrating the knowledge and skills.

Writing as Learning

The process and products of emergent writing are in themselves educative. The act of writing helps your children organize and clarify their thoughts. It helps them discover meaning and express what they understand about a topic or concept. Writing gives your children an opportunity to explore thoughts and deepen their understanding. When your children write down their ideas using scribble writing, letter strings, or conventional writing, and then have an opportunity to rethink and revise them, they also have an opportunity to expand their thinking. During this process, their ideas are extended and refined, especially if you are able to give children opportunities to participate in writing conferences in which they share their drafts with you and their peers. Some activities that give your children opportunities to learn as they write are:

- Making class lists of ideas as they brainstorm information on a specific topic
- Talking about their ideas before they sit down to write
- Taking class notes on a topic they are studying
- Writing responses to stories
- Writing reports (shared writing and/or individual writing)
- Reflecting on what they have learned (shared writing and/or individual writing)
- Writing observations as they watch class science experiments (shared writing and/or individual writing)

Writing as a Demonstration of Knowledge and Skill

Because writing illustrates thinking, it provides you with an opportunity to assess what your children have learned during or following instruction. Constructed-response items are very effective forms of assessment. The checklists and rubrics used to evaluate constructed-response items allow you to provide clear feedback to your children so that they can improve their performance.

5 • Writing

Assessment and Evaluation of Writing

Writing assessment is an essential part of a comprehensive writing program. In order to ensure growth in writing, a balanced approach to assessment is needed—one that includes entry-level, progress-monitoring, and summative assessments. Through the combination of these assessments, you will gain an in-depth view of your children's knowledge and skill in using the writing process. The assessments labeled progress-monitoring tools in this handbook provide ongoing feedback on the progress your children make toward achievement of the skills and knowledge.

What are the benefits of a balanced approach to writing assessment?

- Using a balanced approach to writing assessment allows you to collect data throughout the year and respond specifically to the learning trajectory of your children.

    - Entry-level writing assessments, given at the beginning of the year, help you diagnose where to begin writing instruction for individual children and help you plan specific instructional activities designed to meet the learning needs of each of the writers in your class.

    - Progress-monitoring assessments, given throughout the year, help you determine if all children are making expected progress toward the goal of writing brief narratives and brief descriptions of objects, persons, places, or events.

    - Summative assessments, and at the end of the year, determine how well your children have learned the writing skills you have taught and how well how your children have met or exceeded statewide and district-wide curriculum standards.

- You can guide your children's writing development better if you have an up-to-date understanding of their current performance levels—wasting no time on skills they have already mastered and focusing instead on the areas that represent the next step in their growing writing proficiency or areas that need additional attention.

- Because high standards in writing achievement are most reliably achieved in small, consistent increases that occur over time, a balanced approach to writing assessment affords you the opportunity to monitor and adjust curriculum and instruction as needed to maximize the writing improvement for all children.

- Providing feedback to children about their performance on writing assessments will help them develop skills required to successfully complete writing tasks (e.g., writing letters, words, sentences, friendly letters) included in high-stakes assessments such as the STAR California Standards Tests.

What are the purposes of writing assessment?

- To promote continuous improvement in your children's successful use of the writing process and language conventions

- To identify mastery of state curriculum standards, both at the individual child level and at the class level, which address:

  - Organization and focus

  - Penmanship

  - Research

  - Evaluation and revision

  - Written language conventions (sentence structure, grammar, punctuation, capitalization, spelling)

- To determine when differentiation of instruction is required for individuals or groups of children who have not demonstrated mastery in writing

- To provide a basis for focused instructional decision-making, mini-lessons on the writing process and skills, and feedback to be shared during writing conferences with your children

- To encourage child self-assessment and evaluation by helping children learn how to make judgments about the quality of their writing

- To determine report card grades and/or communicate progress to parents

- To evaluate instructional approaches and modify curriculum to reflect results from writing assessments

When do I use writing assessments?

- Use entry-level writing assessments at the beginning of the year to gather baseline data regarding children's writing proficiency levels.

- Use progress-monitoring writing assessments throughout the school year to measure children's growth in developing writing proficiency.

- Use summative writing assessments at the end of the year to determine students' proficiency levels in the area of writing at the close of each grading period.

5 • Writing

How do I help children assess their own writing?

Self-assessment is very important to your children's writing development. Although you are the primary evaluator of your children's writing, you should give your children opportunities to engage in ongoing self-assessment and peer assessment. The benefits are many—such assessments will help them analyze their writing and the writing of their peers, set goals for improvement, and evaluate their performance in achieving the goals.

- **How can I help children become better self-assessors?**

  - Model self-monitoring by sharing your thoughts with children as you evaluate and reflect on a writing project you are doing.

  - Make the criteria on which children are assessed (e.g., checklists, rubrics) public so that they can use this information to self-assess.

  - Schedule regular times for self-assessment.

  - Give children opportunities to draft criteria for assessing their own work.

  - Provide opportunities for children to engage in activities that encourage thinking, writing, and talking about their writing.

- **What kinds of activities support self-assessment?**

  - Writing conferences with you

  - Writing conferences with classmates

  - Reflections about writing goals and progress in achieving the goals

  - Reviews of student portfolios

  - Use of self-assessment checklists and rubrics

The Role of Rubrics in Assessing Writing

Rubrics play an important role in assessing writing. They identify criteria upon which writing is evaluated, and they identify levels of performance. Using rubrics helps you and your children in many ways.

- Rubrics help you focus your children's attention on elements of quality writing, especially if you share the rubrics with them before they begin writing.

- Rubrics help you achieve consistency when evaluating your children's work.

- Rubrics allow you to provide focused feedback to children so that they can improve their writing.

- Rubrics help you identify objectives for individuals and groups of children.

- Your children will become better writers by using rubrics to guide their self-assessment.

- Peer assessment will be more effective when children have rubrics to guide their analysis of writing samples.

There are several types of rubrics:

- Some rubrics are general and describe the features of good writing that can be applied to a variety of genres.

- Some rubrics describe the features of a specific type or genre of writing.

- Some rubrics are holistic, assessing writing on how well the parts (e.g., ideas, organization, voice, conventions) interact to create a quality piece of writing.

- Some rubrics are analytic, assessing the individual characteristics of writing that serve as criteria for assessing the quality of a piece of writing.

A general four-point writing rubric is included in this chapter.

For guidance in creating your own rubric see page 120.

What techniques and tools are available?

These assessments are simply defined here and are explained and/or pictured on the pages listed.

ENTRY-LEVEL ASSESSMENT TOOL AND TECHNIQUES

- **First Writing Sample** (See page 93.)

    A baseline piece of writing used to assess emergent and beginning writing behaviors.

PROGRESS-MONITORING ASSESSMENT TOOLS AND TECHNIQUES

- **Unit Benchmark Assessments (Kindergarten)** and **Unit Benchmark Tests (Grade 1)** (See pages 60–61.)

    These tests are designed to measure your children's ability to apply target comprehension skills and other literacy skills. Included in each assessment is a writing prompt.

- **Ongoing Teacher Observation** (See page 64.)

    Observation of your children allows you to monitor their performance in the context of classroom writing activities and provide helpful feedback while children are in the process of learning, rather than after the fact.

- **Writing Behaviors Checklist** (See page 44.)

    This form may be used to record your observations of children's writing behaviors at the beginning of the year.

- **Skills Conference Record** (See page 70.)

    This checklist allows you to capture information about your children's writing.

- **Peer Assessment** (See page 73.)

    This form allows you to model peer assessment by collaboratively reviewing a child's writing and helping children apply what they are learning about the quality of effective writing.

- **Student Portfolios** (See pages 74–75.)

    Maintaining a portfolio is a process that allows your children to use work samples to document and reflect on their growth in writing.

- **Writing Log** (See page 77.)

    This form helps children keep track of the pieces they have written, as well as rate the quality of their own writing.

SUMMATIVE ASSESSMENT TOOLS

- **End-of-Year Benchmark Assessment (Kindergarten)** and **End-of-Year Benchmark Test (Grade 1)**
  (See pages 82–83.)

  A group-administered, summative assessment is used to determine your children's growth in mastering the *Reading Street* content. Additionally, this test documents achievement of skills taught throughout the school year. The writing section requires children to write to a prompt.

5 • Writing

Want to learn more about writing assessment?

If you would like to learn more about how to use writing assessment practices in your classroom, you will find the following resources interesting.

References

Bromley K. "Assessing Student Writing." In *Classroom Literacy Assessment: Making Sense of What Students Know and Do*. Eds. J. R. Paratore and R. L. McCormack. New York: The Guilford Press, 2007, pp. 227–245.

Calfee, R. C. "Writing Portfolios: Activity, Assessment, Authenticity." In *Perspectives on Writing: Research, Theory, and Practice*. Eds. R. Indrisano and J. R. Squire. Newark, DE: International Reading Association, 2000, pp. 278–304.

Fisher, D., and N. Frey. *Checking for Understanding: Formative Assessment Techniques for Your Classroom*. Alexandria, VA: Association for Supervision and Curriculum Development, 2007.

Glazer, S. M. "A Classroom Portfolio System: Assessment Instruction." In *Classroom Literacy Assessment: Making Sense of What Students Know and Do*. Eds. J. R. Paratore and R. L. McCormack. New York: The Guilford Press, 2007, pp. 227–245.

Spandel, V. *Seeing with New Eyes: A Guidebook on Teaching and Assessing Beginning Writers*. Portland, OR: Northwest Regional Educational Laboratory, 1998.

Spandel, V. *Creating Writers through 6-Trait Writing Assessment and Instruction*. Boston: Allyn and Bacon, 2000.

Vacca, R. T., and J. L. Vacca. "Writing Across the Curriculum." In *Perspectives on Writing: Research, Theory, and Practice*. Eds. R. Indrisano and J. R. Squire. Newark, DE: International Reading Association, 2000, pp. 214–232.

Zamel, V. "Writing: The Process of Discovering Meaning." *TESOL Quarterly*, vol. 16, no. 2 (1982), pp. 195–209.

First Writing Sample

What is it?

- A baseline piece of writing used as an informal assessment that gives you evidence about a child's initial writing ability

What does it show?

- Child's awareness of letters, words, and the concept of sentences

How do I use it?

- For kindergartners:
  - Give children a piece of paper and a developmentally appropriate writing instrument.
  - Ask them to write all the letters they know.
  - Ask them to write their name.
  - Ask them to write all the words they know.
  - Ask them to draw a picture and write about what they have drawn.

- For grade 1:
  - Give children a piece of paper and developmentally appropriate writing instrument.
  - Ask them to write their name.
  - Ask them to write all the words they know.
  - Ask them to draw a picture and write about what they have drawn.

- Encourage children to do as much as they can without putting pressure on them.

How do I use the results?

- Assess what the children have written
  - Count the number of letters formed correctly and make note of letters that need to be taught.
  - Count the number of words written correctly and take note of the words that appear to be in the child's sight vocabulary so that you can build on them.
  - Observe whether or not the child can write his or her name correctly.
  - Notice if the child produces one or more sentences connected to his or her drawing.

- Use the information observed in this informal writing sample to plan instructional goals for individual children.

Four-Point Scoring Rubric

4 **The writing/drawing—**

- Addresses the task.
- May or may not explicitly state the purpose, but it can be *easily inferred* by the reader.
- Is related to the topic and organized in a logical structure with an effective beginning, middle, and end.
- Develops the topic with appropriate details and/or examples based on the student's prior knowledge and experience.
- Exhibits interesting word usage.
- Contains *some errors* in the conventions of the English language (grammar, punctuation, capitalization, spelling). These errors do **not** interfere with the reader's understanding of the text.

3 **The writing/drawing—**

- Addresses *most* of the task.
- Does *not* explicitly state the purpose, but the reader *may* be able to infer it.
- Is *generally* organized in a logical structure with a beginning, middle, and end.
- Demonstrates *some* development of the topic with appropriate details and/or examples.
- Includes *some* interesting word usage.
- Contains *some* errors in the conventions of the English language (grammar, punctuation, capitalization, spelling). These errors do **not** interfere with the reader's understanding of the text.

2 **The writing/drawing—**

- Addresses *some* of the task.

- Does not explicitly state the purpose, and the reader will have *difficulty* inferring it.

- *Lacks* a clear organizational structure.

- Demonstrates *limited* development of the topic with details and/or examples.

- Includes *little* variety in word usage.

- Contains *many errors* in the conventions of the English language (grammar, punctuation, capitalization, spelling). These errors **may** interfere with the reader's understanding of the text.

1 **The writing/drawing—**

- Addresses *only one part, or none*, of the task.

- Demonstrates *no* understanding of purpose.

- Lacks organization.

- Demonstrates *little* development of the topic with *marginally related* details and/or examples.

- Includes *no* variety in word usage.

- Contains *serious errors* in the conventions of the English language (grammar, punctuation, capitalization, spelling). These errors interfere with the reader's understanding of the text.

5 • Writing

Student Portfolios

What is a portfolio as it relates to writing?

- A teacher-guided process in which children collect representative samples of their own writing as a means of demonstrating growth over time

- A way to encourage children to feel ownership of their writing

What is the purpose of a portfolio as it relates to writing?

- Portfolios may accomplish any or all of the following:

  - Demonstrate children's writing progress

  - Show children's writing strengths and needs

  - Help you make instructional decisions for each child's writing

  - Encourage children to assess their own growth and progress in writing and to set new writing goals

  - Make it possible to share evidence of children's writing growth during parent conferences

  - Compile representative samples of children's writing that you can pass along to their next teachers

Which writing pieces go into a portfolio?

- Chapters 3 and 7 provide full descriptions of techniques and forms to use for compiling and organizing portfolios.

- Possible writing pieces to include in Student Portfolios are:

  - Drawing/writing projects that children have done at school or at home

  - Examples of pre-writing activities

  - Examples of first drafts

  - Examples of revisions

  - Documentation of peer assessment

  - Documentation of self-assessment

  - Examples of a variety of genres, including:

    - Expository descriptions of objects, people, places or events

    - Brief narratives (fictional or autobiographical)

How do I help children choose writing samples for their portfolios?

- At the beginning of the school year, explain the process of developing a portfolio.
- Show models of portfolios and sample writing entries. Explain that portfolios should include:
  - different types of compositions—drawings as well as written works
  - samples that demonstrate learning experiences in writing
  - pieces that show growth or improvement in writing over time
  - materials that indicate that children have challenged themselves to try something different with their writing
- Periodically set aside time for children to examine their writing samples and think about which pieces they would like to include in their portfolios.

What can I do at the end of each grading period?

- Hold writing conferences toward the end of each grading period to help children reflect on the written pieces they have placed in their portfolios.
- Have children decide which pieces to take home, which ones to keep in the portfolio, and which ones to lend to you to update their Portfolio Guides.

What can I do at the end of the school year?

- Hold final conferences with children to help them reflect on their writing and decide which pieces to save and which to eliminate.
- Have children decide which writing samples to take home and which to pass along to their next teachers (for example, the pieces they are most proud of or the ones that show the most growth).

| Chapter 6 | # Assessing the Progress of English Language Learners |

Overview

Classrooms through out the United States are populated with children representing diverse cultures, ethnicities, and languages. This diversity offers rich benefits to learners, but also places enormous demands upon teachers, who are expected to guide *all* students with vastly different literacy and learning abilities toward achievement of state reading and language arts standards.

English language learners pose unique challenges to educators. Teachers must monitor the language acquisition of these children in an ongoing, systematic way, in addition to assessing their understanding of concepts, skills, and strategies. This chapter is designed to assist teachers of English language learners in recognizing the assessment challenges, utilizing appropriate assessment accommodations, preparing children for high-stakes tests, and implementing classroom-based strategies for assessing the strengths and needs of English language learners.

What are the unique challenges in assessing achievement of English language learners?

- Many English language learners may quickly master *social* English, the conversational language skills and conventions used in everyday interactions with classmates. These same learners frequently encounter difficulty with the *academic* English found on formal assessments.

- The structure of academic English is complex, e.g., fiction and nonfiction text structures, paragraph organization, and syntax, including prepositional phrases, introductory clauses, and pronoun references. There are structural analysis constraints at the word, sentence, paragraph, and text levels.

- The vocabulary of academic English consists of specialized meanings of common words, abstract concepts and multiple-meaning words, and words based on Latin and Greek roots. (Bielenberg, 2004/2005)

- The topics and concepts of comprehension passages are frequently unfamiliar, and the purposes of assessment tasks divorced from real-life contexts can be difficult to perceive.

- Formal assessments often fail to reflect the diverse cultural and linguistic experiences of English learners and then have limited value for helping teachers select appropriate instructional strategies. (Garcia, 1994)

How are Scott Foresman *Reading Street* assessments sensitive to the needs of English language learners?

- Both formal and informal classroom-based *Reading Street* assessments help teachers monitor growth in the basic reading and expression skills of alphabetic understanding, decoding, sight vocabulary, and grammar, along with measurement of the more complex skills of fluency, comprehension, and vocabulary.

- Reading comprehension test passages reflect diverse ethnic content and cultural experiences.

- Texts are matched to the age, interest, and background knowledge of children.

- Most assessment tasks are embedded in contexts with which children are familiar. The comprehension assessments are generally based on themes and topics explored in instruction; vocabulary is assessed within the context of the passage; and writing tasks relate to central ideas of the texts.

- Visual cues, pictures, and other non-print features accompany assessment passages.

- The language of the test directions and assessment items is straightforward and unambiguous.

What instructional strategies will help prepare my English language learners for formal assessments?

- Preteach the "language of tests" encountered in directions and test items, including:

  - Question words, such as *who, what, which, where, when, why,* and *how*

  - Emphasis words, such as n*ot, except, most likely, probably, major, both, neither, either, most,* and *least*

  - Action words, such as *explain, describe,* and *discuss*

- Teach use of context clues to interpret meaning of unfamiliar terms.

- Highlight and discuss routinely the *academic* language, vocabulary, syntax, and narrative and expository text structures encountered in textbooks and trade books.

- Coach children in oral and written retelling and summarization, so they develop a "sense" of text types, features, conventions, and organization. English language learners relate to the concrete nature of informational text, and expository summarization helps to familiarize them with common text structures, such as sequence, description, classification, compare/contrast, cause/effect, and problem/ solution.

- Review academic vocabulary particular to tests. Model and discuss the thinking steps involved in responding to various types of test items.

- Provide regular opportunities for meaningful oral language experiences in which English language learners participate in discussion of important topics and perform the activities required on tests, such as explaining, describing, and stating and supporting opinions. Encourage them to use vocabulary that will support academic language development.

- Read aloud, think aloud, and model purposeful and strategic behaviors of effective readers, speakers, and writers of English.

- Provide repeated opportunities for practicing all the techniques above.

What accommodations are appropriate to use with the Scott Foresman *Reading Street* assessments?

- Accommodating the needs of English language learners ensures fairness and full participation in formal assessments. A general rule of thumb is to use the same accommodations in testing situations as used in instruction. For instance, if children receive part of their instruction in their first languages, then it is appropriate to translate test directions and comprehension questions into the children's first languages.

> "Accommodation in assessment allows students to best demonstrate their reading development and achievement."
> (Afflerbach, 2007)

- Other acceptable accommodations might include the following:

  - providing additional testing time and allowing frequent or extended breaks

  - administering the tests at times most beneficial to children

  - administering the tests in small groups or in one-on-one settings

  - reading test directions to children in English (or in the children's first languages, if this is possible), and repeating as often as needed

  - simplifying the language and sentence structure of test directions

  - requesting that children restate and clarify test directions in their own words

  - discussing the pictures and any graphics, such as maps, to ensure that children can interpret them

  - reading test passages to children in English, and repeating as often as necessary, when listening comprehension is being assessed

  - reading comprehension questions orally in English or in the children's first languages

  - allowing children to respond orally to questions or dictate answers for transcription

  - encouraging children to draw pictures to demonstrate their thinking and learning

- In providing accommodations to children, it is important not to compromise the intent of the assessment. For example, with the exception of selected units in Grade 1, the reading comprehension assessments are designed to measure both word recognition and understanding, so reading aloud the selections to the children actually alters the construct of the test.

- While the language-specific modifications above may be most appropriate for English language learners, many of the listed accommodations are also beneficial for children with learning and reading disabilities and other special needs. The use of appropriate accommodations in assessment ensures that all children have fair and equal opportunities to demonstrate evidence of learning and achievement.

- Following the administration of formal assessments, note which accommodations were used, and interpret scores with that information in mind.

What are the *best* ways to assess the strengths and needs of English language learners?

- Through ongoing classroom-based assessment, teachers can observe, monitor, and judge the quality of student work.

- Using multiple assessments mirrors the learning process, while single assessments capture one moment at a time, much like the difference between an album of photographs and a single snapshot.

- Ask children frequently to communicate orally or in writing their understanding of concepts and processes. In this way, teachers are provided with instant insight about children's thinking and depth of learning.

- Observing small, consistent increases in learning over time is most reliable. The goal is continuous improvement.

- Frequent monitoring addresses learning in progress, allows for correction of misconceptions as they occur, and provides helpful feedback to English language learners.

- Teaching children to self-assess their reading progress helps to build independence in language and learning. For example, encourage them to monitor their progress by comparing work samples and voice recordings over time.

- Authentic assessment activities enhance, rather than diminish, instructional time, because they are inseparable from instruction. Activities include classroom observation, language-experience stories, storytelling or writing, voice recordings of oral reading, reading-response logs, and journals. (Garcia, 1994)

- Scott Foresman *Reading Street* provides many resources to help you tailor instruction and assessment for all your children; administer and score entry-level, progress-monitoring, and summative assessments; interpret scores; and make decisions based on test results.

What are examples of classroom-based assessment techniques and tools?

- **Profile of English Language Learners** (See page 105.)
  A checklist that identifies the strengths and needs of children who are English language learners

- **Observing English Language Learners** (See page 106.)
  A form that allows you to record ongoing observations about your English language learners' progress in developing reading skills

6 • English Learners

References

Afflerbach, P. *Understanding and Using Reading Assessment, K–12* (2nd ed.). Newark, DE: International Reading Association, 2012.

Bielenberg, B., and L. W. Fillmore. "The English They Need for the Test." *Educational Leadership*, 2004, pp. 45–49.

Garcia, G. E. "Assessing the Literacy Development of Second-Language Students: A Focus on Authentic Assessment." In *Kids Come in All Languages: Reading Instruction for ESL Students*. Eds. K. Spangenberg-Urbshat and R. Pritchard. Newark, DE: International Reading Association, 1994, pp. 180–205.

Lenters, K. "No Half Measures: Reading Instruction for Young Second-Language Learners." *The Reading Teacher*, vol. 58 (2004), pp. 328–336.

Moss, B. "Teaching Expository Text Structures through Information Trade Book Retellings." *The Reading Teacher*, vol. 57 (2004), pp. 710–718.

Zwiers, J. "The Third Language of Academic English." *Educational Leadership*, vol. 62, no. 4 (2004), pp. 60–63.

Profile of English Language Learners

What is it?	• This checklist helps to identify the strengths and needs of children whose first language is not English.
What does it show?	• An English language learner's proficiency with speaking, reading, and writing English
How do I use it?	• Identify children whose English proficiency you are uncertain about. • Use the criteria on the form to assess children's abilities in the various language areas, noting specific examples. • Use the form as a rough guideline of where children are in their English language development and where they may need help.
What do I do next?	Scott Foresman *Reading Street* offers your English language learners • standards-based instruction at all levels of language acquisition—Beginning, Early Intermediate, Intermediate, Early Advanced, and Advanced • the English Language Learners Handbook with instructional material and comprehensive guidance for teachers and effective, efficient, and explicit instruction for English language learners. Building on the *Reading Street* literacy instruction, the guide uses components such as ELL Posters, ELL Readers, and English Language Support (blackline masters).

A Checklist format is easy to interpret.

B Space is provided for you to note your own responses.

Form for reproduction is on page 132.

Teacher Form
Profile of English Language Learners

Child: Tomás Alvarez

Trait	Mostly	Unevenly	Rarely	Date/Comment
Speaks and/or understands a few basic words	✓			
Speaks fluently but makes frequent errors			✓	10/16 seems to know more words than he is comfortable using
Uses names of many objects		✓		
Uses and understands basic everyday vocabulary		✓		
Asks and answers simple questions			✓	10/16 reluctant to ask for help
Follows simple directions		✓		
Takes part in discussions			✓	10/16 good at communicating through art
Conveys ideas or stories through drawings	✓			
Needs pictures to comprehend simple text		✓		
Recognizes basic sound/letter relationships in words		✓		
Follows text being read aloud		✓		
Joins in choral reading	✓			10/16 likes to join in with the class
Retells predictable text		✓		

6 • English Learners

Observing English Language Learners

What is it?

- A form to record your ongoing observations about how English language learners process what they read

What does it show?

- How English language learners use strategies to make sense of materials they read
- Children's growth and development in processing what they read

How do I use it?

- Work with children individually as they read a new selection.
- Record your observations about how children deal with new words and concepts.
- Continue to review and record children's behaviors periodically as needed.
- Consider using the information on the form in parent conferences.

A Behaviors identify common strategies for success in reading a new language.

B Space is provided to record children's development over time.

Teacher Form
Observing English Language Learners

Child: Tomás Alvarez

Behaviors Observed	Date: 10/27			Date: 11/18			Date:			Date:		
The child	Yes	No	Sometimes	Yes	No	Sometimes	Yes	No	Sometimes	Yes	No	Sometimes
• uses context clues to figure out new words		✓				✓						
• uses prior knowledge to figure out new words			✓	✓								
• uses visuals to decipher meaning	✓			✓								
• uses strategies to decipher meaning		✓				✓						
• can identify the strategies he or she is using		✓				✓						
• understands why he or she is using a particular strategy		✓		✓								
• assesses his or her own progress			✓	✓								
• generally understands what the class is reading		✓				✓						

General Comments

10/27: need to work harder on strategies with Tomás

11/18: Tomás doing much better at drawing on prior knowledge. Is beginning to see the logic of strategies.

Form for reproduction is on page 139.

| Chapter 7 | # Collecting, Evaluating, and Reporting Evidence of Learning |

Overview

Information about the three levels of assessment, entry-level (diagnostic and screening), progress-monitoring, and summative assessment, explained in Chapters 2–4, suggests that teachers will be compiling large amounts of information about children. Access to this data informs sound decision-making related to the focus of curriculum instruction, effectiveness of instruction, meaningful feedback to children and parents, and improved achievement.

Teacher Record Keeping

Learning goals are met by shaping effective instruction and assessment to meet the needs of each child. Checking for understanding contributes to improved instruction and learning. The evidence of this learning can be collected on a variety of record forms.

Why collect evidence of learning?

- A roadmap of each child's learning is created by keeping records of learning from classroom assessment, including:

  - the Scott Foresman *Reading Street* Baseline Group Test, entry-level (diagnostic) inventories, and surveys (Chapter 2)

  - progress-monitoring discussions, logs, journal entries, portfolios, projects, and Scott Foresman *Reading Street* tests (Chapter 3)

  - summative measurements, such as state-required tests, the Scott Foresman *Reading Street* End-of-Year Benchmark Test, and district tests (Chapter 4)

- Pace, content, and type of instruction may be adjusted after evaluating the child's collected evidence of learning to see that learning goals are met.

How do I collect evidence of learning?

- Collect records of children's learning throughout the year—at the beginning of the school year, daily, weekly, after clusters of instructional time such as units, and at the end of the year.

- Collect a variety of records of children's learning (e.g., notes from observations, responses to questions, checklists, portfolios, self-assessment, rubric and test scores, and grading).

- Collect key indicators about the skills and concepts (e.g., words correct per minute, recognition of multiple meanings, summaries of readings).

Tools and Techniques for Teacher Record Keeping

- **Teacher Summary Reports** (See page 115.)
  Compilations of assessment data that help describe children's growth in reading, writing, speaking, and listening over time

- **Early Literacy Behaviors Checklist** (See page 116.)
  This checklist enables teachers to compile their dated observations of a child's literacy progress over time

- **Cumulative Folder Form** (See page 117.)
  A cumulative record of children's reading progress that can be placed in their permanent files and follow them from year to year

How do I share assessment information?

- Assessment information is shared in two ways, communication and grading. Communication of assessment information may occur as written remarks or as conversation in which the quality or level of learning is discussed.

- Conferences provide excellent opportunities to convey assessment information and to maintain ongoing communication between teacher and child, teacher and parent, and child and child.

  - Teacher-child conferences can be part of your classroom routine and allow you time to learn about the unique learning needs and successes of individual children in your class.

  - Teacher-parent conferences are held formally during regularly scheduled school conference days but can also be held informally when you want to share concerns and accomplishments with your children's parents.

  - Child-led conferences with a teacher and parent allow children to talk about personal strengths and weaknesses and set goals for their next steps in learning, as well as help children become more aware of what to say and do about their learning.

- Conferencing about reading, writing, speaking, or listening or collections of work may include:
  - examining and discussing a reading response with comments about why its attributes meet a learning standard
  - analyzing and discussing how the traits on a written work match the descriptions on a rubric
  - providing feedback about an inference skill or questioning strategy
  - explaining the reasons for a score on a vocabulary progress test
  - discussing a child's self-assessment reflection
  - evaluating a collection of work in a portfolio together with the child
- Evaluative communication provides feedback with a judgment about the quality of the work. This type of formal communication is typically shared by mark or symbol—check, score, or grade to designate the quality or level of learning. Symbols are often used on
  - checklists
  - continuums
  - assessment reports
  - report cards
- Narrative statements are often found on children's work, in portfolios, or as an addition to a report marked with symbols.

Student Portfolios

A portfolio is a collection of representative work done by the child in reading, writing, speaking, and listening, serving as documentation of change and growth over a period of time. It centers discussion about learning on actual samples of work among teachers, children, and parents. The collection may be evaluated in process or as a completed product with narrative comments or symbols, such as rubric scores, and is a credible form of progress monitoring. A rubric is a valuable way to score entries in a portfolio because criteria in a rubric serve as a clear vision for children during the writing process, in drafting as well as the final product. The final rubric scores awarded in the portfolio contribute to an overall evaluation of learning along with other requirements for a grade.

What is the teacher's role?

- To make decisions with your children about the purpose, process, content, and time line of the portfolio

- To consider options for the format of the portfolio (e.g., folder, binder, or electronic versions)

- To decide the method for evaluating the process and contents of the portfolio (e.g., conferencing with the child and parents, narrative feedback, scoring, grading, or perhaps review by other teachers or children)

- To share examples of portfolios, showing children how portfolios might be organized and what might be kept in a portfolio

- To model metacognition (the awareness of the internal thinking that influences the choices for selection and revision of portfolio contents) by keeping a personal portfolio and sharing how you select and reflect on the pieces you include in it

What is the child's role?

- To add, change, or remove portfolio items demonstrating evidence of reading, writing, speaking, and listening to their portfolios with assistance from the teacher

- To explain and reflect about their collections of work

- To set and monitor goals for learning, as well as discuss strengths and weaknesses with teachers and family

- To participate in self-assessment activities to improve their skills in collecting and learning from evidence in their portfolios.

Tools and Techniques for Maintaining Portfolios

- **Student Portfolios** (See pages 96–97.)
  Maintaining a portfolio is a process that allows children to use work samples to document and reflect on their growth in reading, writing, speaking, and listening.

- **Portfolio Guide** (See page 118.)
  This form helps you manage the contents of students' portfolios.

- **Portfolio Selection Slips** (See page 119.)
  These forms help your children select items to include in their portfolios and reflect on how the items demonstrate their growing skills in reading, writing, speaking, and listening.

- **Reading Log** (See page 76.)
  This form allows children to keep track of the literature they have read, as well as rate the quality of the selections.

- **Writing Log** (See page 77.)
  This form helps children keep track of and reflect on the pieces they have written.

Grading

As mentioned earlier in this chapter, grading is a formal, summative form of communication about learning. Grading provides information for children, parents, teacher record keeping, and sometimes district reporting, and often leads to decisions about future learning goals for each child. Guidelines about grading attempt to ensure fairness to the child and sound grading practices.

What is a grade?

A grade is the evaluative symbol reported at the end of an instructional unit of time. It is a summary of performance or achievement, showing whether the child met learning goals or standards. The symbol is usually a number or letter and answers, "How well is the child achieving at this point in time?" The primary purposes of grading are

- to inform children, parents, teachers, and others about the child's current level of achievement

- to support learning goals and inform progress of learning

- to improve children's achievement by providing feedback that explains the criteria upon which the grade is based

- to answer the question, "Has the child met the intended learning goals for this period?"

What are some general guidelines for grading?

- Base grades on academic achievement. Feedback on effort, behavior, ability, and attendance should be documented and reported separately.

- Communicate achievement of clear learning goals and standards with grades.

- Discuss expectations for grading with children and parents at the beginning of the instruction. Explain the criteria for grades in the classroom and school. Display models of graded work to children and parents at the beginning of the year to clarify and demonstrate expectations for children.

- Develop criteria for grades which may include test scores, rubric scores, completed work, and narrative records.

- Use rubrics as a lead-in to fair grading with clear descriptive criteria for scoring and alignment to learning standards.

- Add narrative and descriptive feedback with grades whenever possible.

- Do not grade all work—some work is in draft form or for practice only.

- Use *recent* summative classroom assessments to measure achievement of learning goals.

- Determine marking period grades from multiple types of scores. Summarize overall achievement for a marking period into one score or grade.

- Check with the district's grading policy to ensure that your procedures are fair and consistent with the guidelines established by your school and district.

What are some opportunities for grading in Scott Foresman *Reading Street*?

The program offers many opportunities to grade children's work, including:

- activities and projects
- writing assignments
- pages from the Reader's and Writer's Notebook
- pages from Fresh Reads for Fluency and Comprehension
- oral presentations
- Weekly Tests
- Unit Benchmark Tests
- End-of-Year Benchmark Test

Tools and Techniques for Grading

- **Rubrics in the Teacher's Editions**
  Your Scott Foresman *Reading Street* Teacher's Editions contain a variety of rubrics to help you assess your children's performance.

- **Creating a Rubric** (See page 120.)
  This form is used to identify criteria for assessing reading, writing, speaking, and listening and to evaluate how well children meet those criteria on various assignments.

- **Grading Writing** (See page 121.)
  Teachers can use the Creating a Rubric form to develop grading criteria for children's responses to writing prompts.

- **Grading Products and Activities** (See pages 122–125.)
  Teachers can use the Creating a Rubric form to develop grading criteria for a wide variety of children's products and activities.

Want to learn more about record keeping and grading?

If you are interested in learning more about record keeping and sharing assessment information, you will find the following resources interesting.

7 • Evidence of Learning

References

Afflerbach, P. *Understanding and Using Reading Assessment, K–12* (2nd ed.). Newark, DE: International Reading Association, 2012.

Fisher, D. and N. Frey. *Checking for Understanding: Formative Assessment Techniques for Your Classroom.* Alexandria, VA: Association for Supervision and Curriculum Development, 2007.

Guskey, T. R. *How's My Kid Doing? A Parent's Guide to Grades, Marks, and Report Cards.* San Francisco, CA: Jossey-Bass, 2002.

Marzano, R. J. *Transforming Classroom Grading.* Alexandria, VA: Association for Supervision and Curriculum Development, 2000.

O'Connor, K. *How to Grade for Learning.* Arlington Heights, IL: Skylight Professional Development, 2002.

Stiggins, R., J. Arter, J. Chappuis, and S. Chappuis. *Classroom Assessment for Student Learning: Doing It Right—Using It Well.* Portland, OR: Assessment Training Institute, 2004.

Teacher Forms
Teacher Summary Reports ✓

What are they?	• Various forms that teachers can compile as a way of summarizing and assessing a child's literacy growth over time
What do they show?	• A child's reading, writing, speaking, and listening behaviors and strategies
How do I use them?	• In order to document a child's progress, compile and synthesize information from any or all of these sources:

- Ongoing teacher observations
- Behavior checklists
- Profiles and inventories
- Self and peer assessments
- Conference records
- Reading and writing logs
- Rubrics
- Student portfolios
- Cumulative folder form
- Test scores

• Use what you have gathered when you prepare grades and as you get ready for conferences with children, parents, administrators, or resource teachers.

7 • Evidence of Learning

Teacher Form
Early Literacy Behaviors Checklist

What is it?

- A cumulative list of major skills, behaviors, and concepts covered in kindergarten and first grade
- A place to compile information collected from various teacher observations and child performances

What does it show?

- Where a child is in his or her growth as a reader and language user
- Specific information about the following:
  - The child's familiarity with books and print
  - The child's language development
  - The child as a reader
  - The child as a writer
  - The child as a speaker and listener

How do I use them?

- Whenever a summary of a child's progress is required, compile the information from your various assessment tools onto this form.
- You can use this checklist at parent-teacher conferences, at the end of each grading period, or at any other time a detailed yet concise report is needed.
- Some teachers also choose to use this checklist as an inventory at the beginning of the school year.

A Specific information gives a clear picture of the child's growth

B Multiple observations allow you to track a child's literacy development

Forms for reproduction are on pages 146–147.

Teacher Form
Cumulative Folder Form

What is it?	• A cumulative record of a child's reading progress, to be placed in the child's permanent record that follows him or her from year to year.
What does it show?	• The most basic and permanent information on how the child performed during each school year—namely, his or her score on the Baseline Group Test, scores for each Unit Benchmark Test, group placement, and any additional comments from the teacher.
How do I use it?	• Record scores and comments from unit to unit.
	• Place the form into the child's cumulative folder at the end of the school year.

A Categories reflect early literacy skills.

B Scores serve as a guide for flexible group placement.

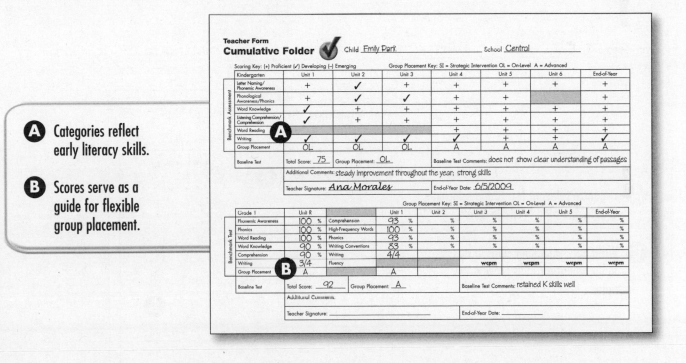

Form for reproduction is on page 150.

Teacher Form
Portfolio Guide

What is it?
- A form for managing the contents of a student's portfolio, whether teacher or child selected
- A cover sheet showing the portfolio contents at-a-glance

What does it show?
- An overall composite of a child's strengths, needs, interests, and attitudes throughout the year
- A child's selected work throughout the year

How do I use it?
- Track forms and work samples submitted at various times during the year.
- Fill in dates as a reminder of when items were submitted and when to collect additional submissions.

A Organize relevant forms and selected work behind the Portfolio Guide.

B Write dates of submissions in boxes to document a child's growth over time.

Form for reproduction is on page 144.

Teacher Form
Portfolio Guide

Grade __1__

Child: James Russell

Date: 9/16

Form		Date Submitted		
Knowledge About Books and Print	**A**	☐		
Reading Behaviors Checklist		☐	☐	☐
Writing Behaviors Checklist		☐	☐	☐
Oral Language Behaviors Checklist		☐	☐	☐
Myself as a Learner		9/16		
My Child as a Learner		☐		
Other: _____		☐		

Record of Child's Work **B**

Selected Writing Piece	9/23	10/17	☐	☐	☐
Selected Drawing Piece	9/16	10/13	☐	☐	☐
Unit R (Grade1) Benchmark Test Evaluation Chart	☐				
Unit 1 Benchmark Test Evaluation Chart	☐				
Unit 2 Benchmark Test Evaluation Chart	☐				
Unit 3 Benchmark Test Evaluation Chart	☐				
Unit 4 Benchmark Test Evaluation Chart	☐				
Unit 5 Benchmark Test Evaluation Chart	☐				
Unit 6 (Kindergarten) Benchmark Assessment Evaluation Chart	☐				
Other: _____	☐				
Other: _____	☐				
Other: _____	☐				

Child Form
Portfolio Selection Slips

What are they?

- Forms to help children select work samples to include in their portfolios
- Opportunities for children to think about what they have included in their portfolios and why they have chosen those items

What do they show?

- A child's rationale for including each piece in the portfolio
- What children think of their own work

How do children use them?

- Give children time to look over their work, decide which items to submit to their portfolios, and complete the forms.
- Attach one slip to each work sample and place it in the portfolio for future review of contents.

A Form gives children a chance to assess their work.

B Form gives children a chance to assess their own growth as learners.

Child Form
Portfolio Selection Slips

Name _Taylor F._

Date _Oct. 3_

I chose this piece of work because **A**

It is funny.

The pictures are my

best work.

Name _Taylor F._

Date _Oct. 3_ **B**

I chose this piece of work because

I like the colors.

Form for reproduction is on page 145.

Teacher Form
Creating a Rubric

What is it?

- A form that may be used for evaluation of reading, writing, speaking, or listening assignments
- A tool that allows you to focus assessment on the key concepts emphasized during instruction

What does it show?

- How well a child exhibits his or her understanding of the key features of the assignment
- Areas in which a child may require additional instruction

How do I use it?

- Decide which assessment criteria are most relevant to a particular assignment. List them in the Features column.
- Rate and comment on those features as you assess the assignment.
- If desired, teachers may choose to convert the ratings into letter grades.

A The open-endedness of this form allows you to customize assessment features to meet the needs of every assignment.

B Your comments help you remember why you arrived at a rating and give you a starting point for discussing the assignment with the child or family.

C When desired, the rating may be turned into a letter grade.

Form for reproduction is on page 151.

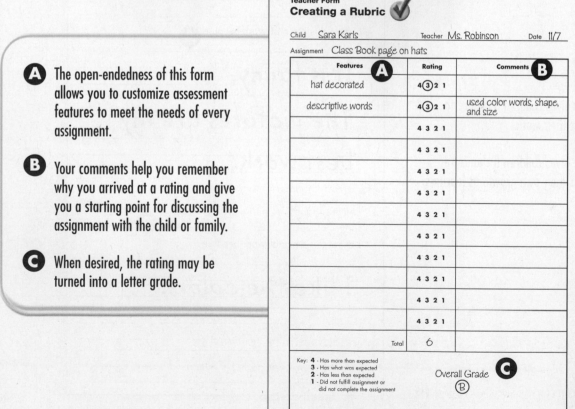

Teacher Form
Creating a Rubric

Child Sara Karls   Teacher Ms. Robinson   Date 11/7

Assignment   Class Book page on hats

Features **A**	Rating	Comments **B**
hat decorated	4 ③ 2 1	
descriptive words	4 ③ 2 1	used color words, shape, and size
	4 3 2 1	
	4 3 2 1	
	4 3 2 1	
	4 3 2 1	
	4 3 2 1	
	4 3 2 1	
	4 3 2 1	
	4 3 2 1	
	4 3 2 1	
	4 3 2 1	
Total	6	

Key: **4** - Has more than expected
3 - Has what was expected
2 - Has less than expected
1 - Did not fulfill assignment or did not complete the assignment

Overall Grade **C**
Ⓑ

Teacher Form
Grading Writing

Grading Responses to Writing Prompts

- Writing prompts occur in several places in Scott Foresman *Reading Street*:
  - Following each selection and in the end-of-unit writing-process activity in the teacher's guide
  - In the Unit Benchmark Assessments (kindergarten) or Tests (grade 1) and the End-of-Year Benchmark Assessment (kindergarten) or Test (grade 1)
- To grade children's writing, you can use the Creating a Rubric form. For your convenience, an example scale for a how-to response has been completed for you below. Actual determinations about what score equals which grade will, however, vary with different teachers and districts.

A Decide which features of a story are important and list your own criteria.

B Comments help you remember why you arrived at a rating and give you a starting point for discussing the writing with the child.

C To determine the possible score, multiply the number of features by 4 (4 features x 4 = 16). Then add the ratings you've given the features to find the child's actual score. In this example 14 out of 16 = B.

Score	Grade
15–16	A
13–14	B
11–12	C
10	D
9 and below	F

Form for reproduction is on page 151.

Teacher Form
Creating a Rubric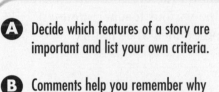

Child __Jaime Novarro__   Teacher __Mr. Brownlee__   Date __2/19__

Assignment __Narrative Writing__

Features	Rating	Comments
The story is entertaining.	4 ③ 2 1	needs a little more punch
The story has a beginning, middle, and end.	④ 3 2 1	good sequence of events
The story has well-defined characters.	4 ③ 2 1	could use more description
The end ties the story together.	④ 3 2 1	surprise ending!
A	4 3 2 1	**B**
	4 3 2 1	
	4 3 2 1	
	4 3 2 1	
	4 3 2 1	
	4 3 2 1	
	4 3 2 1	
	4 3 2 1	
Total	14	

Key: **4** - Has more than expected
    3 - Has what was expected
    2 - Has less than expected
    1 - Did not fulfill assignment or did not complete the assignment

C

Overall Grade
    Ⓑ

7 • Evidence of Learning

Grading Products and Activities

Grading Products and Activities

- The Creating a Rubric form lends itself to grading a variety of children's products and activities, including:
    - Class discussions
    - Speeches
    - Retellings
    - Oral readings and dramatizations
    - Drawings, sculptures, and other artwork
    - Graphic organizers such as Venn diagrams, story maps, concept maps, and KWL charts

- Two examples and grading scales—for a class discussion and for a graphic organizer—are provided here. Actual determinations about what score equals which grade will, however, vary with different teachers and districts.

- In determining the criteria on which to evaluate children's work, you may find it helpful to refer to the various teacher summary reports described earlier or to the other checklists in this handbook.

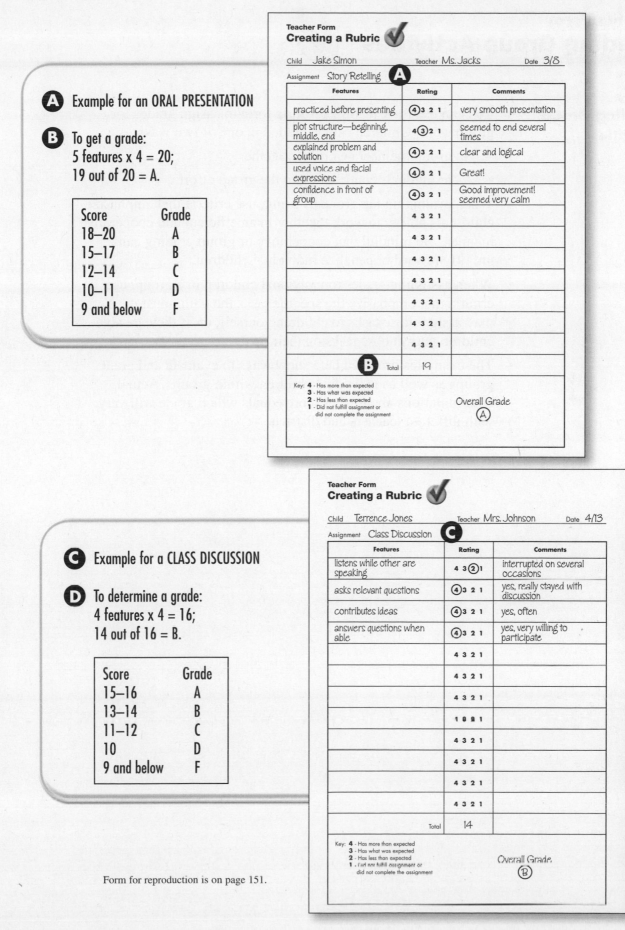

A Example for an ORAL PRESENTATION

B To get a grade:
5 features x 4 = 20;
19 out of 20 = A.

Score	Grade
18–20	A
15–17	B
12–14	C
10–11	D
9 and below	F

Teacher Form
Creating a Rubric ✓

Child _Jake Simon_   Teacher _Ms. Jacks_   Date _3/8_

Assignment _Story Retelling_   **A**

Features	Rating	Comments
practiced before presenting	④ 3 2 1	very smooth presentation
plot structure—beginning, middle, end	4 ③ 2 1	seemed to end several times
explained problem and solution	④ 3 2 1	clear and logical
used voice and facial expressions	④ 3 2 1	Great!
confidence in front of group	④ 3 2 1	Good improvement! seemed very calm
	4 3 2 1	
	4 3 2 1	
	4 3 2 1	
	4 3 2 1	
	4 3 2 1	
	4 3 2 1	
	4 3 2 1	

B Total **19**

Key: **4** - Has more than expected
3 - Has what was expected
2 - Has less than expected
1 - Did not fulfill assignment or did not complete the assignment

Overall Grade
Ⓐ

C Example for a CLASS DISCUSSION

D To determine a grade:
4 features x 4 = 16;
14 out of 16 = B.

Score	Grade
15–16	A
13–14	B
11–12	C
10	D
9 and below	F

Teacher Form
Creating a Rubric ✓

Child _Terrence Jones_   Teacher _Mrs. Johnson_   Date _4/13_

Assignment _Class Discussion_   **C**

Features	Rating	Comments
listens while other are speaking	4 3 ② 1	interrupted on several occasions
asks relevant questions	④ 3 2 1	yes, really stayed with discussion
contributes ideas	④ 3 2 1	yes, often
answers questions when able	④ 3 2 1	yes, very willing to participate
	4 3 2 1	
	4 3 2 1	
	4 3 2 1	
	4 3 2 1	
	4 3 2 1	
	4 3 2 1	
	4 3 2 1	
	4 3 2 1	

Total **14**

Key: **4** - Has more than expected
3 - Has what was expected
2 - Has less than expected
1 - Did not fulfill assignment or did not complete the assignment

Overall Grade
Ⓑ

Form for reproduction is on page 151.

Grading Group Activities

**Grading Group
Activities**

- You can use the Creating a Rubric form to assign grades for group work. Children can be graded in one of two ways:
  - As group members working together
  - As individuals contributing to the group effort

- When evaluating the group as a unit, use criteria that emphasize children's ability to work together in an efficient and cooperative manner. Be mindful that cooperative or group grading can unfairly reward or penalize individual children.

- When assigning grades to individual children in a group, use criteria that emphasize the specific tasks the child must do. You may assign those tasks to children yourself, or, if they are able, children may choose tasks on their own.

- The examples provided here show ways to evaluate and grade groups as well as individual children within groups. Actual determinations about what score equals which grade will vary with different teachers and districts.

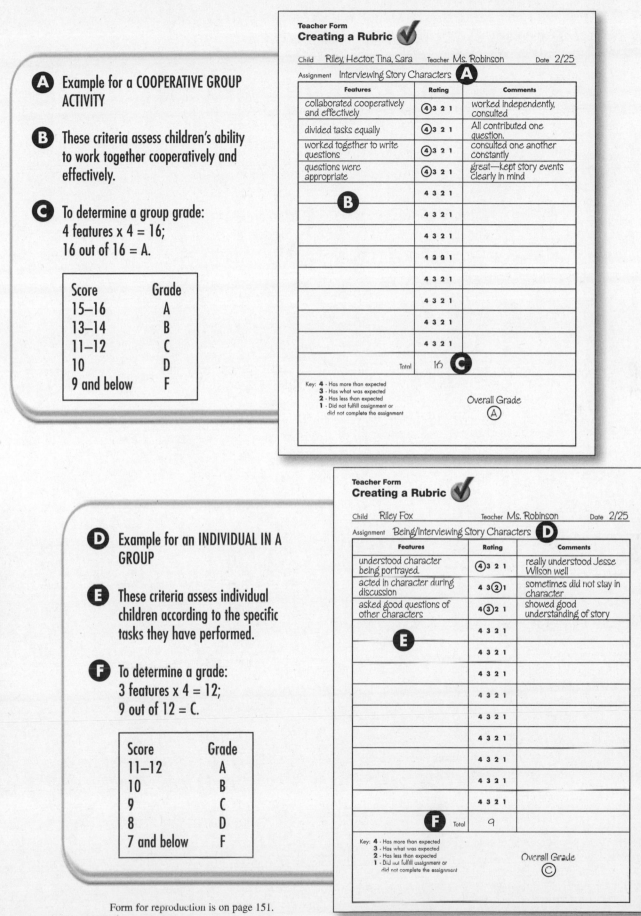

A Example for a COOPERATIVE GROUP ACTIVITY

B These criteria assess children's ability to work together cooperatively and effectively.

C To determine a group grade:
4 features x 4 = 16;
16 out of 16 = A.

Score	Grade
15–16	A
13–14	B
11–12	C
10	D
9 and below	F

Teacher Form
Creating a Rubric ✓

Child Riley, Hector, Tina, Sara   Teacher Ms. Robinson   Date 2/25 **A**

Assignment Interviewing Story Characters

Features	Rating	Comments
collaborated cooperatively and effectively	④ 3 2 1	worked independently, consulted
divided tasks equally	④ 3 2 1	All contributed one question.
worked together to write questions	④ 3 2 1	consulted one another constantly
questions were appropriate	④ 3 2 1	great—kept story events clearly in mind
B	4 3 2 1	
	4 3 2 1	
	4 3 2 1	
	4 3 2 1	
	4 3 2 1	
	4 3 2 1	
	4 3 2 1	
	4 3 2 1	
Total	16 **C**	

Key: **4** - Has more than expected
 3 - Has what was expected
 2 - Has less than expected
 1 - Did not fulfill assignment or did not complete the assignment

Overall Grade
Ⓐ

D Example for an INDIVIDUAL IN A GROUP

E These criteria assess individual children according to the specific tasks they have performed.

F To determine a grade:
3 features x 4 = 12;
9 out of 12 = C.

Score	Grade
11–12	A
10	B
9	C
8	D
7 and below	F

Teacher Form
Creating a Rubric ✓

Child Riley Fox   Teacher Ms. Robinson   Date 2/25

Assignment Being/Interviewing Story Characters **D**

Features	Rating	Comments
understood character being portrayed.	④ 3 2 1	really understood Jesse Wilson well
acted in character during discussion	4 3 ② 1	sometimes did not stay in character
asked good questions of other characters	4 ③ 2 1	showed good understanding of story
E	4 3 2 1	
	4 3 2 1	
	4 3 2 1	
	4 3 2 1	
	4 3 2 1	
	4 3 2 1	
	4 3 2 1	
	4 3 2 1	
	4 3 2 1	
F Total	9	

Key: **4** - Has more than expected
 3 - Has what was expected
 2 - Has less than expected
 1 - Did not fulfill assignment or did not complete the assignment

Overall Grade
Ⓒ

Form for reproduction is on page 151.

Classroom-based Assessment Tools

Knowledge About Books and Print

Child   Date

Behavior	Yes	Not Yet	Comments
Knows how to hold book right side up			
Knows how to turn pages sequentially, front to back			
Knows that books have titles, authors, and illustrators			
Makes predictions from title, cover, and illustrations			
Can differentiate between pictures and text			
Knows that text and pictures relate to each other			
Tracks print from left to right and top to bottom			
Knows that print represents spoken words			
Knows that there are spaces between words			
Joins in reading text with a familiar, repetitive, or predictable pattern			
After multiple class readings, revisits the book, "reading" the story independently			
Other:			

Reading Behaviors Checklist

Child   Date

Behavior	Yes	No	Not Applicable
Recognizes letters of the alphabet			
Recognizes name in print			
Recognizes some environmental print, such as signs and logos			
Knows the difference between letters and words			
Knows the difference between capital and lowercase letters			
Understands function of capitalization and punctuation			
Recognizes that book parts such as cover, title page, and table of contents offer information			
Recognizes that words are represented in writing by specific sequences of letters			
Recognizes words that rhyme			
Distinguishes rhyming and nonrhyming words			
Knows sound-letter correspondences			
Identifies and isolates initial sounds in words			
Identifies and isolates final sounds in words			
Blends sounds to make spoken words			
Segments one-syllable/two-syllable spoken words into individual phonemes			
Reads consonant blends and digraphs			
Reads and understands endings such as *-es, -ed, -ing*			
Reads vowels and vowel diphthongs			
Reads and understands possessives			
Reads and understands compound words			
Reads simple sentences			
Reads simple stories			
Understands simple story structure			
Other:			

Writing Behaviors Checklist ✓

Child   Date

Behavior	Yes	No	Not Applicable
Produces detailed and relevant drawings			
Dictates messages for others to write			
Writes using scribble, drawing, or letterlike forms			
Distinguishes between writing and drawing			
Writes own name and other important words			
Writes all letters of the alphabet, capital and lowercase			
Writes labels or captions for illustrations and possessions			
Writes messages that move from left to right and top to bottom			
Uses phonological knowledge to map sounds to letters when writing			
Holds pencil and positions paper correctly			
Uses basic capitalization and punctuation			
Writes messages that can be understood by others			
Shows understanding of sequence in writing			
Stays on topic when writing			
Expresses original ideas			
Elaborates with details			
Has an identifiable voice			
Chooses precise and vivid words			
Takes risks with vocabulary			
Uses descriptive words			
Writes in different forms			
Writes for different audiences and purposes			
Writes to record ideas and reflections			
Other:			

Teacher Form

Oral Language Behaviors Checklist

Child   Date

Behavior	Yes	No	Example
Follows simple oral directions			
Follows directions of several steps			
Listens to stories read aloud			
Participates actively when predictable rhymes and songs are read aloud			
Understands and retells spoken messages			
Gives precise directions			
Expresses ideas clearly			
Responds appropriately to questions			
Knows and uses many words			
Participates in conversations and discussions			
Listens in small-group situations			
Listens in whole-group situations			
Stays on topic in discussions			
Uses language conventions appropriately			
Listens to others courteously, without interrupting			
Can retell simple stories in sequence			
Recalls details from stories			
Listens and speaks for various purposes			
Adapts speaking to audience			
Listens critically to oral readings, discussions, and messages			
Connects cultural experiences and prior knowledge through speaking and listening			
Other:			

Teacher Form
Profile of English Language Learners

Child:

Trait	Mostly	Unevenly	Rarely	Date/Comment
Speaks and/or understands a few basic words				
Speaks fluently but makes frequent errors				
Uses names of many objects				
Uses and understands basic everyday vocabulary				
Asks and answers simple questions				
Follows simple directions				
Takes part in discussions				
Conveys ideas or stories through drawings				
Needs pictures to comprehend simple text				
Recognizes basic sound/letter relationships in words				
Follows text being read aloud				
Joins in choral reading				
Retells predictable text				

Child Form
Myself as a Learner

Name   Date

	Yes	No	Comments
1. I like to listen to stories.			
2. I like to read books by myself.			
3. I know how to hold a book and turn the pages.			
4. I like to read out loud to others.			
5. I can figure out new words when I read.			
6. I like to write.			
7. I like to draw.			
8. I like to go to school.			
9. I read signs wherever I go.			

Parent Form
My Child as a Learner

Child _____ Parent/Guardian/
Caregiver _____ Date _____

	Always	Sometimes	Never	Comments
1. My child asks to be read to.				
2. My child can retell a book we have read or a television program we have watched.				
3. My child can predict what will happen next when reading a book or watching a television program.				
4. My child picks up a book to read or look at alone.				
5. My child reads or pretends to read at home.				
6. My child knows how to hold a book, how to turn pages, and that print goes from left to right.				
7. My child likes to write or pretend to write.				
8. My child likes to talk about what he or she has written.				
9. My child can follow an oral direction when given.				
10. My child can follow a series of oral directions when given one time.				
11. My child likes working with others.				
12. My child tries to read words in the environment—signs, labels, logos.				
13. My child likes to go to school.				

Teacher Form

Expository Retelling Chart

Unit _____ Selection Title _____

Name _____ Date _____

Retelling Criteria/Teacher Prompt	Teacher-Aided Response	Student-Generated Response	Rubric Score (Circle one.)			
Connections Did this selection make you think about other selections?			4	3	2	1
Author's Purpose Why do you think the author wrote this selection?			4	3	2	1
Topic What was the selection about?			4	3	2	1
Important Ideas What is important for me to know about _____ (topic)?			4	3	2	1
Conclusions What did you learn from this selection?			4	3	2	1

Summative Score 4 3 2 1

Comments _____

Teacher Form

Narrative Retelling Chart

Unit _____ Selection Title _____   Name _____ Date _____

Retelling Criteria/Teacher Prompt	Teacher-Aided Response	Student-Generated Response	Rubric Score (Circle one)
Connections Did you like this book? Why or why not? How does this story remind you of other stories?			4 3 2 1
Author's Purpose What was the author trying teach us?			4 3 2 1
Characters Describe _____ (character's name)?			4 3 2 1
Setting Where and when did the story happen?			4 3 2 1
Plot Tell me what happened in the story?			4 3 2 1

Summative Retelling Score 4 3 2 1

Comments _____

Teacher Form

Work Habits Conference Record

Child

Use the key at the bottom of the page to assess child's performance.

Date	Understands tasks	Sets priorities	Uses time appropriately	Solves problems effectively	Seeks help when needed	Completes tasks on time	Can explain process/ project effectively	Comments

4 Independent   **3** With Some Assistance   **2** With Frequent Assistance   **1** Not Observed

Teacher Form

Skills Conference Record

Grade _____

Child _____   Teacher _____

		Proficient	Developing	Emerging	Not showing trait
Reading Comments:	Sets own purpose for reading	☐	☐	☐	☐
	Predicts and asks questions	☐	☐	☐	☐
	Retells/summarizes	☐	☐	☐	☐
	Reads fluently	☐	☐	☐	☐
	Understands key ideas in a text	☐	☐	☐	☐
	Uses decoding strategies	☐	☐	☐	☐
	Makes text connections	☐	☐	☐	☐
	Other:	☐	☐	☐	☐
Writing Comments:	Follows writing process	☐	☐	☐	☐
	Develops central idea and with details	☐	☐	☐	☐
	Organizes ideas logically	☐	☐	☐	☐
	Uses transitions	☐	☐	☐	☐
	Expresses ideas with word choice	☐	☐	☐	☐
	Uses language conventions appropriately	☐	☐	☐	☐
	Other:	☐	☐	☐	☐
Speaking and Listening Comments:	Follows instructions	☐	☐	☐	☐
	Asks questions	☐	☐	☐	☐
	Answers questions	☐	☐	☐	☐
	Paraphrases	☐	☐	☐	☐
	Discussions	☐	☐	☐	☐
	Eye contact with audience	☐	☐	☐	☐
	Other:	☐	☐	☐	☐

Teacher Form

Observing English Language Learners

Child:

Behaviors Observed	Date:			Date:			Date:			Date:		
	Yes	No	Sometimes	Yes	No	Sometimes	Yes	No	Sometimes	Yes	No	Sometimes
The child												
• uses context clues to figure out new words												
• uses prior knowledge to figure out new words												
• uses visuals to decipher meaning												
• uses strategies to decipher meaning												
• can identify the strategies he or she is using												
• understands why he or she is using a particular strategy												
• assesses his or her own progress												
• generally understands what the class is reading												

General Comments

139

Parent Form
Observing My Child's Reading

Child   Parent/Guardian/
Caregiver   Date

1. Story or article my child read to me:

2. Here are some things I noticed about my child's

Vocabulary

- understands most words that he or she reads   ☐ yes   ☐ no   ☐ not sure

- can figure out word meanings from other words in passage   ☐ yes   ☐ no   ☐ not sure

- is not afraid to attempt reading new words   ☐ yes   ☐ no   ☐ not sure

Comprehension

- understands what he or she is reading   ☐ yes   ☐ no   ☐ not sure

- remembers the important ideas from a reading   ☐ yes   ☐ no   ☐ not sure

- can tell back what he or she has read   ☐ yes   ☐ no   ☐ not sure

- remembers the order things happened in   ☐ yes   ☐ no   ☐ not sure

Read-Aloud Ability

- reads most sentences without pausing   ☐ yes   ☐ no   ☐ not sure

- reads in a manner that shows he or she makes sense of what is being read   ☐ yes   ☐ no   ☐ not sure

- reads with expression   ☐ yes   ☐ no   ☐ not sure

- pronounces most words correctly   ☐ yes   ☐ no   ☐ not sure

3. Here are some general comments about what I noticed as my child read:

Child Form

Reading Log

Name _____

Dates Read	Title and Author	What is it about?	How would you rate it?	Explain your rating.
From ___ to ___			**Great** 5 4 3 2 1 **Awful**	
From ___ to ___			**Great** 5 4 3 2 1 **Awful**	
From ___ to ___			**Great** 5 4 3 2 1 **Awful**	
From ___ to ___			**Great** 5 4 3 2 1 **Awful**	
From ___ to ___			**Great** 5 4 3 2 1 **Awful**	

Child Form
Writing Log

Child _____   Date _____

Teacher _____   Grade _____

Date	Title	Type of writing	How I felt about this piece	What I liked or disliked	Put in portfolio
			4 3 2 1		
			4 3 2 1		
			4 3 2 1		
			4 3 2 1		
			4 3 2 1		
			4 3 2 1		

Key
4 = Excellent
3 = Good
2 = Fair
1 = Poor

Peer Assessment ✓

My name is _____ Date _____

I'm looking at _____'s work.

The work I am looking at is _____.

Things I Liked	Things I Didn't Understand

Suggestions

Portfolio Guide

Grade _____

Child: _____

Date: _____

Form   Date Submitted

Form	Date Submitted
Knowledge About Books and Print	☐
Reading Behaviors Checklist	☐ ☐ ☐
Writing Behaviors Checklist	☐ ☐ ☐
Oral Language Behaviors Checklist	☐ ☐ ☐
Myself as a Learner	☐
My Child as a Learner	☐
Other: _____	☐

Record of Child's Work

Selected Writing Piece	☐ ☐ ☐ ☐ ☐ ☐
Selected Drawing Piece	☐ ☐ ☐ ☐ ☐ ☐
Unit R (Grade1) Benchmark Test Evaluation Chart	☐
Unit 1 Benchmark Test Evaluation Chart	☐
Unit 2 Benchmark Test Evaluation Chart	☐
Unit 3 Benchmark Test Evaluation Chart	☐
Unit 4 Benchmark Test Evaluation Chart	☐
Unit 5 Benchmark Test Evaluation Chart	☐
Unit 6 (Kindergarten) Benchmark Assessment Evaluation Chart	☐
Other: _____	☐
Other: _____	☐
Other: _____	☐

Portfolio Selection Slips

Name _____

Date _____

I chose this piece of work because

_____

_____

_____

_____

_____

_____

Name _____

Date _____

I chose this piece of work because

_____

_____

_____

_____

_____

_____

Early Literacy Behaviors Checklist

Name _____

Date _____ Grade _____

| A = Always |
| S = Sometimes |
| N = Never |

Dates of Observations

Concepts of Print							
recognizes environmental print							
knows how to hold a book							
knows the parts of a book (front cover, back cover)							
distinguishes between title, author, and illustrator							
turns pages in sequence from front to back							
understands that print represents spoken language and conveys meaning							
knows the difference between letters and words							
tracks print from left to right and top to bottom							
knows that letters make up words							
matches spoken to written words							
Phonological/Phonemic Awareness							
identifes rhyming words							
produces rhyming words							
knows that words are made up of syllables							
isolates phonemes							
identifies initial phonemes in words							
identifies final phonemes in words							
segments and blends phonemes in words							
Phonics and Decoding							
identifies letters of the alphabet, both uppercase and lowercase							
recognizes own name in print							
connects sound to letter—consonants							
connects sound to letter—vowels							
uses sound-letter knowledge to read words							
uses context and picture clues to help identify words							

Early Literacy Behaviors Checklist (continued)

Name _____

Date _____ Grade _____

	A = Always
	S = Sometimes
	N = Never

Dates of Observations

Comprehension						
retells stories with story structure, including setting, characters, and plot						
uses illustrations to understand stories						
predicts what will happen next						
connects concepts from literature to own life						
can identify genres of children's literature						
asks appropriate questions and makes appropriate comments about text and pictures						
infers and evaluates ideas and feelings						
demonstrates an understanding of thematic concepts						
Writing						
writes own name—first and last						
is moving from scribble writing to random letters and letter strings						
uses letter-sound knowledge to write words						
understands the correspondence between spoken and written words in dictation when recording thoughts						
writes for a variety of purposes						
writes in a variety of genres: narrative, exposition, and poetry						
Speaking and Listening						
speaks in complete sentences						
engages freely in conversation in varied situations						
attends to others while they are speaking						
discriminates sounds appropriately						
pronounces sounds appropriately for age and language background						
uses increasingly complex oral language that is appropriate for age and language background						
follows oral directions						

Teacher Form

Reading Strategy Assessment

Child _____ Date _____

Teacher _____ Grade _____

		Proficient	Developing	Emerging	Not showing trait
Building Background Comments:	Previews	☐	☐	☐	☐
	Asks questions	☐	☐	☐	☐
	Predicts	☐	☐	☐	☐
	Activates prior knowledge	☐	☐	☐	☐
	Sets own purposes for reading	☐	☐	☐	☐
	Other:	☐	☐	☐	☐
Comprehension Comments:	Retells/summarizes	☐	☐	☐	☐
	Questions, evaluates ideas	☐	☐	☐	☐
	Paraphrases	☐	☐	☐	☐
	Rereads/reads ahead for meaning	☐	☐	☐	☐
	Visualizes	☐	☐	☐	☐
	Uses text structure to locate information	☐	☐	☐	☐
	Uses decoding strategies	☐	☐	☐	☐
	Uses vocabulary strategies	☐	☐	☐	☐
	Understands key ideas of a text	☐	☐	☐	☐
	Relates text to other texts, experiences, or understanding	☐	☐	☐	
	Other:	☐	☐	☐	☐
Fluency Comments:	Reads fluently and accurately	☐	☐	☐	☐
	Paces appropriately	☐	☐	☐	☐
	Uses appropriate intonation and expression	☐	☐	☐	☐
	Other:	☐	☐	☐	☐
Self-Assessment Comments:	Is aware of: Strengths	☐	☐	☐	☐
	Needs	☐	☐	☐	☐
	Improvement/Achievement	☐	☐	☐	☐
	Sets and implements learning goals	☐	☐	☐	☐
	Maintains logs, records, portfolio	☐	☐	☐	☐
	Works with others	☐	☐	☐	☐
	Shares ideas and materials	☐	☐	☐	☐
	Other:	☐	☐	☐	☐

Teacher Form
Writing Strategy Assessment ✓

Child _____ Date _____

Teacher _____ Grade _____

		Proficient	Developing	Emerging	Not showing trait
Focus/Ideas Comments:	Addresses the writing task	☐	☐	☐	☐
	Demonstrates understanding of purpose	☐	☐	☐	☐
	States central idea	☐	☐	☐	☐
	Details support central idea	☐	☐	☐	☐
	Conclusion reinforces central idea	☐	☐	☐	☐
	Other:	☐	☐	☐	☐
Organization Comments:	Product of writing process	☐	☐	☐	☐
	Clearly presents central idea with details	☐	☐	☐	☐
	Begins with a topic sentence	☐	☐	☐	☐
	Uses transitions between sentences and paragraphs				
	Uses order words *(first, then, after, finally)*	☐	☐	☐	☐
	Other:	☐	☐	☐	☐
Voice Comments:	Speaks directly to audience	☐	☐	☐	☐
	Voice matches writer's purpose	☐	☐	☐	☐
	Shows rather than tells	☐	☐	☐	☐
	Shows writer's feelings and personality	☐	☐	☐	☐
	Keeps reader's attention	☐	☐	☐	☐
	Other:	☐	☐	☐	☐
Word Choice Comments:	Uses vivid words to elaborate ideas	☐	☐	☐	☐
	Avoids slang and jargon	☐	☐	☐	☐
	Uses strong images or figurative language	☐	☐	☐	☐
	Uses action verbs versus linking verbs	☐	☐	☐	☐
	Uses new words to express ideas	☐	☐	☐	☐
	Other:	☐	☐	☐	☐
Sentences Comments:	Expresses thoughts in lively, varied sentences	☐	☐	☐	☐
	Mixes short and long sentences	☐	☐	☐	☐
	Includes questions, commands, and exclamations	☐	☐	☐	
	Sentences flow logically from one to another	☐	☐	☐	☐
	Avoids choppy and wordy sentences	☐	☐	☐	☐
	Other:	☐	☐	☐	☐
Conventions Comments:	Uses subjects and verbs in agreement	☐	☐	☐	☐
	Uses correct punctuation for grade level	☐	☐	☐	☐
	Capitalizes proper nouns and sentence beginnings	☐	☐		☐
	Forms noun plurals correctly	☐	☐	☐	☐
	Spells words correctly	☐	☐	☐	☐
	Other:	☐	☐	☐	☐

Teacher Form
Cumulative Folder ✓

Child _____   School _____

Scoring Key: (+) Proficient (✓) Developing (−) Emerging   Group Placement Key: SI = Strategic Intervention OL = On-level A = Advanced

Benchmark Assessment

Kindergarten	Unit 1	Unit 2	Unit 3	Unit 4	Unit 5	Unit 6	End-of-Year
Letter Naming/Phonemic Awareness							
Phonological Awareness/Phonics							
Word Knowledge							
Listening Comprehension/Comprehension							
Word Reading							
Writing							
Group Placement							
Baseline Test							

Total Score: _____   Group Placement: _____

Teacher Signature: _____   End-of-Year Date: _____

Additional Comments:

Baseline Test Comments:

Benchmark Test

Grade 1	Unit R	Unit 1	Unit 2	Unit 3	Unit 4	Unit 5	End-of-Year
Phonemic Awareness	%	%	%	%	%	%	%
Phonics	%	%	%	%	%	%	%
Word Reading	%	%	%	%	%	%	%
Word Knowledge	%	%	%	%	%	%	%
Comprehension	%	%	%	%	%	%	%
Writing							
Group Placement							
Baseline Test							

Unit R	Unit 1	Unit 2	Unit 3	Unit 4	Unit 5	End-of-Year
Comprehension	%	%	%	%	%	%
High-Frequency Words	%	%	%	%	%	%
Phonics	%	%	%	%	%	%
Writing Conventions	%	%	%	%	%	%
Writing	%	%	%	%	%	%
Fluency		wcpm	wcpm	wcpm	wcpm	wcpm

Total Score: _____   Group Placement: _____

Teacher Signature: _____   End-of-Year Date: _____

Additional Comments:

Baseline Test Comments:

Group Placement Key: SI = Strategic Intervention OL = On-level A = Advanced

Teacher Form
Creating a Rubric

Child _____ Teacher _____ Date _____

Assignment _____

Features	Rating	Comments
	4 3 2 1	
	4 3 2 1	
	4 3 2 1	
	4 3 2 1	
	4 3 2 1	
	4 3 2 1	
	4 3 2 1	
	4 3 2 1	
	4 3 2 1	
	4 3 2 1	
	4 3 2 1	
	4 3 2 1	
Total		

Key: **4** - Has more than expected
3 - Has what was expected
2 - Has less than expected
1 - Did not fulfill assignment or
did not complete the assignment

Kindergarten Formal Assessment Tools

Kindergarten
Forms from
Baseline Group Test
Teacher's Manual

Name _____ Date _____

Concepts of Print Checklist

Directions: Place a check mark in the appropriate column beside each concept. Record notes and observations in the box at the bottom. Count the number correct and record the results of this assessment on the Evaluation Chart for Kindergarten.

Concepts	Yes	No
The child ...		
1. holds the book right-side up.		
2. points to the title of the book on the front cover.		
3. correctly indicates where to start reading.		
4. tracks print left to right on a line.		
5. tracks print from top to bottom on a page.		
6. understands how to turn the pages for reading.		
7. identifies a capital letter.		
8. identifies a word.		
9. identifies a sentence.		
10. tells what a period means.		
Notes/Observations:		

Kindergarten Baseline Test Evaluation Chart

Child's Name _____ Date _____

Teacher's Name _____ Class _____

SUBTEST Skills/ Item Numbers			Subtest Percentages		Total Number Correct	Total Percentage
Readiness _____/8 Correct					1	2%
1.	0	1	1=13%		2	4%
2.	0	1	2=25%		3	6%
3.	0	1	3=38%		4	8%
4.	0	1	4=50%		5	10%
5.	0	1	5=63%		6	12%
6.	0	1	6=75%		7	14%
7.	0	1	7=88%		8	16%
8.	0	1	8=100%		9	18%
Letter Recognition _____/12 Correct					10	20%
					11	22%
1.	0	1	1=8%		12	24%
2.	0	1	2=16%		13	26%
3.	0	1	3=25%		14	28%
4.	0	1	4=34%		15	30%
5.	0	1	5=42%		16	32%
6.	0	1	6=50%		17	34%
7.	0	1	7=58%		18	36%
8.	0	1	8=66%		19	38%
9.	0	1	9=75%		20	40%
10.	0	1	10=83%		21	42%
11.	0	1	11=91%		22	44%
12.	0	1	12=100%		23	46%
Phonological Awareness _____/12 Correct					24	48%
1.	0	1	1=8%		25	50%
2.	0	1	2=16%		26	52%
3.	0	1	3=25%		27	54%
4.	0	1	4=34%		28	56%
5.	0	1	5=42%		29	58%
6.	0	1	6=50%		30	60%
7.	0	1	7=58%		31	62%
8.	0	1	8=66%		32	64%
9.	0	1	9=75%		33	66%
10.	0	1	10=83%		34	68%
11.	0	1	11=91%		35	70%
12.	0	1	12=100%		36	72%
Listening Comprehension _____/8 Correct					37	74%
1.	0	1	1–13%		38	76%
2.	0	1	2=25%		39	78%
3.	0	1	3=38%		40	80%
4.	0	1	4=50%		41	82%
5.	0	1	5=63%		42	84%
6.	0	1	6=75%		43	86%
7.	0	1	7=88%		44	88%
8.	0	1	8=100%		45	90%
Concepts of Print _____/10 Correct					46	92%
					47	94%
Total Test _____/50 Correct					48	96%
					49	98%
Alternate Baseline Test _____/10 Correct					50	100%

Forms from Kindergarten Unit and End-of-Year Benchmark Assessments Teacher's Manual

CLASS RECORD CHART
Skills Assessment   Unit _____

Teacher's Name _____ **Date** _____

Directions: Use this chart to record the results for all children on any of the Unit Benchmark Assessments or the End-of-Year Assessment. Fill in the number of the unit at the top. Beside each child's name, record the results by marking Proficient (+), Developing (✓), or Emerging (−) under each assessed skill.

Child's Name	Phonemic Awareness	Phonological Awareness	Letter Naming	Phonics	Word Knowledge	Word Reading	Comprehension	Writing
1.								
2.								
3.								
4.								
5.								
6.								
7.								
8.								
9.								
10.								
11.								
12.								
13.								
14								
15								
16.								
17.								
18.								
19.								
20.								
21.								
22.								
23.								
24.								

INDIVIDUAL RECORD

End-of-Year Benchmark Assessment

Child's Name _____ **Date** _____

Directions: Record the results of the End-of-Year Benchmark Assessment by marking Proficient (+), Developing (✓), or Emerging (–) beside each assessed skill.

End-of-Year Assessed Skills	Proficient (+)	Developing (✓)	Emerging (–)	Common Core State Standard
Phonemic Awareness: Recognizing Initial and Final Sounds; Blending Individual Phonemes				Foundational Skills 2.c., 2.d.
Phonics: Letter-Sound Correspondence				Foundational Skills 3.a., 3.b.
Word Reading: CVC, CVCC, CCVC Words				Foundational Skills 3.
Word Knowledge: High-Frequency Words				Foundational Skills 3.c.
Listening Comprehension: Plot, Main Idea, Character, Setting				Literature 3.
Writing: Nouns and Pronouns				Writing 2.

Monitor Progress Pages
from
Kindergarten Teacher's Editions

Name _____

Name the Letters

A   b   C   d   B

e   D   a   E   c

Read the Words

I   ☐

am   ☐

Note to Teacher: Children name each letter. Children read words.

Scoring for Name the Letters/Read the Words: Score 1 point for each correct letter/word.

Letter Recognition (*Aa, Bb, Cc, Dd, Ee*) _____ /__10__

High-Frequency Words (*I, am*) _____ /__2__

| MONITOR PROGRESS | • Letters *Aa, Bb, Cc, Dd, Ee*
 • High-frequency words |

The Little School Bus • 99

Name _____

Character

Note to Teacher: Have children color the pictures that show characters from "Mary Had a Little Lamb."

Name _____

Name the Letters

F	g	G	M	H	i
L	f	j	h	K	l
k	N	l	m	J	n

Read the Words

am ☐

I ☐

Note to Teacher: Children name each letter. Children read the words.

Scoring for Name the Letters/Read the Words: Score 1 point for each correct letter/word.

Letter Recognition (*Ff, Gg, Hh, Ii, Jj, Kk, Ll, Mm, Nn*) ———— / __18__
High-Frequency Words (*am, I*) ———— / __2__

MONITOR PROGRESS
• Letters *Ff, Gg, Hh, Ii, Jj, Kk, Ll, Mm, Nn*
• High-frequency words

Name _____

Setting

Note to Teacher: Have children color the picture that shows where "Mr. Spuffington Fixes It Himself" takes place.

MONITOR PROGRESS • Setting

Name _____

Name the Letters

O   r   s   P   q

p   o   Q   S   R

Read the Words

the   ☐

little   ☐

Note to Teacher: Children name each letter. Children read the words.

Scoring for Name the Letters/Read the Words: Score 1 point for each correct letter/word.

Letter Recognition (*Oo, Pp, Qq, Rr, Ss*) _____ / __10__
High-Frequency Words (*the, little*) _____ / __2__

MONITOR PROGRESS
- Letters *Oo, Pp, Qq, Rr, Ss*
- High-frequency words

Name _____

Sequence

Put the events from "The Little Red Hen" in order.

Note to Teacher: Have children cut out the pictures. Have them glue the pictures to another sheet of paper in order to show what happens first, next, and last in "The Little Red Hen."

MONITOR PROGRESS • Sequence

Name _____

Name the Letters

T v W y u

U Y x z t

Z w V y X

Read the Words

little ☐

the ☐

Note to Teacher: Children name each letter. Children read words.

Scoring for Name the Letters and Read the Words: Score 1 point for each correct letter/word.

Letter Recognition (*Tt, Uu, Vv, Ww, Xx, Yy, Zz*) _____ /__15__
High-Frequency Words (*little, the*) _____ /__2__

MONITOR PROGRESS
- Letters *Tt, Uu, Vv, Ww, Xx, Yy, Zz*
- High-frequency words

407

Name _____

Classify and Categorize

Sort these items into "tools" and "ingredients."

Note to Teacher: Have children cut out the pictures and sort them into two groups: "Tools for Baking" and "Ingredients for Baking." Children should glue the groups of pictures onto another piece of paper.

MONITOR PROGRESS   • Classify and Categorize   411

Name _____

Name the Sound

Read the Words

a   ☐

to   ☐

Note to Teacher: Children listen for and identify initial /m/. Children read the words.

Scoring for Name the Sound/Read the Words: Score 1 point for each correct sound/word.

Name the Sound (*mop, mouse, map, man, mitten*) _____ /__5__

High-Frequency Words *i* (*a, to*) _____ /__2__

MONITOR PROGRESS
- /m/ Spelled *Mm*
- High-frequency words

Name _____

Character

Cut out the characters from "Sam Sings."

Note to Teacher: Have children cut out the characters from the story and glue them to another sheet of paper. Have them color the pictures.

MONITOR PROGRESS • Character

Name _____

Name the Sounds

Read the Words

to ☐

a ☐

Note to Teacher: Children listen for and identify initial /t/. Children read each word.

Scoring for Name the Sounds/Read the Words: Score 1 point for each correct sound/word.

Name the Sounds (*taxi, ten, tire, tiger*) _____ /__4__

High-Frequency Words (*to, a*) _____ /__2__

MONITOR PROGRESS
- /t/ Spelled *Tt*
- High-frequency words

Name _____

Classify and Categorize

Note to Teacher: Distribute another sheet of paper folded in half. Children copy "Red" on one column and "Yellow" on the other. Cut out objects and glue red objects under "Red" and yellow objects under "Yellow." Color the pictures red or yellow.

MONITOR PROGRESS   • Classify and Categorize

Name _____

Read the Words

Tam	☐		at	☐
mat	☐		am	☐
have	☐		is	☐

Read the Sentences

1. I have a mat.

2. The mat is little.

3. I have a little mat.

4. Is Tam little?

Note to Teacher: Children read each word. Children read two sentences.

Scoring for Read the Words: Score 1 point for each correct word.

Short *a* (*Tam, mat, at, am*) _____ / ___4___

High-Frequency Words (*have, is*) _____ / ___2___

Copyright © by Pearson Education, Inc., or its affiliates. All rights reserved.

MONITOR PROGRESS
- /a/ Spelled Aa
- High-frequency words

Flowers • 95

Name _____

Compare and Contrast

Circle the two that are alike.

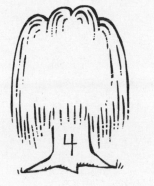  

Put an X through the one that is different.

Note to Teacher: Have children circle the two that are alike in the first row. Have them put an *X* on the one that is different in the second row.

• Compare and Contrast

Name _____

Read the Words

is   ☐   have   ☐

sat   ☐   Sam   ☐

mats   ☐

Read the Sentences

1. Is Sam little?

2. Sam is little.

3. I have the mats.

4. I have little mats.

Note to Teacher: Children read each word. Children read two sentences.

Scoring for Read the Words: Score 1 point for each correct word.

/s/Ss (*sat, mats, Sam*) _____ /___3___

High-Frequency Words (*is, have*) _____ /___2___

- /s/ Spelled *Ss*
- High-frequency words

Name _____

Setting

Draw where the story happens. Then draw the animals.

Note to Teacher: Have children draw where "The Mitten" takes place. Then have them draw the animals from the story.

MONITOR PROGRESS

• Setting

Name _____

Read the Words

pat ☐   sap ☐

Pam ☐   map ☐

we ☐   like ☐

my ☐   tap ☐

Read the Sentences

1. I have my map.

2. I like to tap.

3. We have little Pat.

4. We have the map.

Note to Teacher Children read each word. Children read two sentences.

Scoring for Read the Words: Score 1 point for each correct word.
/p/*Pp* (*pat, Pam, sap, map, tap*) _____ /__5__
High-Frequency Words (*we, my, like*) _____ /__3__

MONITOR PROGRESS
• /p/ Spelled *Pp*
• High-frequency words

295

Name _____

Main Idea

Color the picture that shows what the story is about.

Note to Teacher: Have children color the picture that shows what "All Night Near the Water" is all about.

MONITOR PROGRESS   • Main Idea   299

Name _____

Read the Words

cat ☐   caps ☐
like ☐   Cam ☐
cap ☐   we ☐
my ☐   cats ☐

Read the Sentences

1. Sam is my little cat.

2. I like the little cap.

3. We have a cat.

4. Cam is at my mat.

Note to Teacher: Children read each word. Children read two sentences.

Scoring for Read the Words: Score 1 point for each correct word.
/k/ Cc (*cat, cap, caps, Cam, cats*) _____ /___5___
High-Frequency Words (*like, my, we*) _____ /___3___

MONITOR PROGRESS
• /k/ Spelled *Cc*
• High-frequency words

Name _____

Realism and Fantasy

Color the make-believe bear.

Note to Teacher: Have children color the make-believe bear.

Name _____

Read the Words

sip ☐   tip ☐
he ☐   for ☐
Tim ☐   sit ☐
Sis ☐   pit ☐

Read the Sentences

1. I have a map for Sis.

2. He likes to sit.

3. He likes Tim.

4. I have a cat for Tip.

Note to Teacher: Children read each word. Children read two sentences.

Scoring for Read the Words: Score 1 point for each correct word.

Short i (*sip, Tim, Sis, tip, sit, pit*) _____ /___6___

High-Frequency Words (*he, for*) _____ /___2___

MONITOR PROGRESS
• /i/ Spelled *Ii*
• High-frequency words

A Bed for the Winter • **497**

Copyright © by Pearson Education, Inc., or its affiliates. All rights reserved.

184

Name _____

Sequence

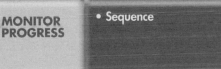

Note to Teacher: Have children cut out the three scenes and glue them to another sheet of paper in the correct order.

MONITOR PROGRESS • Sequence

Name _____

Read the Words

sip	☐		Tim	☐
for	☐		he	☐
pit	☐		tip	☐
sit	☐		Sis	☐

Read the Sentences

1. I have a cap for Tim.

2. He tips the cap.

3. He likes little Tim.

4. Pip is a cat for Pam.

Note to Teacher: Children read each word. Children read two sentences.

Scoring for Read the Words: Score 1 point for each correct word.

Short *i* (*sip, pit, sit, Tim, tip, Sis*) _____ /___6___
High-Frequency Words (*for, he*) _____ /___2___

MONITOR PROGRESS
- Short *i*
- High-frequency words

Name _____

Realism and Fantasy

Color the make-believe pictures.
Circle the real pictures.

Note to Teacher: Have children color the pictures that are make-believe and circle the pictures that are real.

MONITOR PROGRESS • Realism and Fantasy

Name _____

Read the Words

can ☐   nap ☐
cab ☐   bin ☐
me ☐   she ☐
bat ☐   Nat ☐
with ☐   bib ☐
Nan ☐   man ☐

Read the Sentences

1. She can bat.

2. We bat with Nat.

3. The tan cab is for me.

4. She can have the little bib.

Note to Teacher: Children read each word. Children read two sentences.

Scoring for Read the Words: Score 1 point for each correct word.

/b/Bb (cab, bat, bin, bib) _____ /___4___
/n/Nn (can, Nan, nap, bin, Nat, man) _____ /___6___
High-Frequency Words (me, with, she) _____ /___3___

MONITOR PROGRESS
- /b/ Spelled *Bb*
- /n/ Spelled *Nn*
- **High-frequency words**

Little Panda • 97

Name _____

Compare and Contrast

Color the things that are alike. Draw an *X* on things that are different.

Note to Teacher: Have children compare and contrast the two pictures. Have them color things that are the same and draw *X*s on things that are different.

Name _____

Read the Words

rat	☐	rip	☐
rib	☐	rim	☐
she	☐	with	☐
ram	☐	rap	☐
ran	☐	me	☐

Read the Sentences

1. She likes the rat that can sit.

2. She likes the ribs.

3. I ran with Tim.

4. Nat did a rap for me.

Note to Teacher: Children read each word. Children read two sentences.

Scoring for Read the Words: Score 1 point for each correct word.

/r/Rr (rat, rib, ram, ran, rip, rim, rap) _____ /__7__
High-Frequency Words (she, with, me) _____ /__3__

MONITOR PROGRESS
- /r/ Spelled Rr
- High-frequency words

Little Quack • 197

Name _____

Plot

Put these pictures in order to show the plot of
"The Ugly Duckling."

Note to Teacher: Have children cut out the boxes and glue them onto another sheet of paper in the correct order of the story.

Name _____

Read the Words

kid	☐	sad	☐
Kim	☐	did	☐
mad	☐	look	☐
see	☐	bad	☐
dip	☐	dab	☐
kit	☐	Dan	☐

Read the Sentences

1. Kim can see Dad.

2. Little Dan can look in the kit.

3. We did look for Kim.

4. I see that Kip is sad.

Note to Teacher: Children read each word. Children read two sentences.

Scoring for Read the Words: Score 1 point for each correct word.

/d/Dd (*kid, mad, dip, sad, did, bad, dab, Dan*) _____ /__8__

/k/Kk (*kid, Kim, kit*) _____ /__3__

High-Frequency Words (*see, look*) _____ /__2__

MONITOR PROGRESS
- /d/Dd
- High-frequency words
- /k/Kk

Name _____

Cause and Effect

Cut out the pictures. Glue them in the right box.

Note to Teacher: Have children cut out pictures and glue them in the correct box.

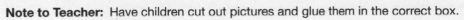

MONITOR PROGRESS • Cause and Effect

Name _____

Read the Words

fan	☐	fad	☐
fit	☐	fat	☐
if	☐	see	☐
look	☐	fib	☐
fab	☐	fin	☐

Read the Sentences

1. We see the little fin.

2. Look at the fat cat.

3. I see the fat cat nap.

4. We like to look at the fan.

Note to Teacher: Children read each word. Children read two sentences.

Scoring for Read the Words: Score 1 point for each correct word.
/f/Ff (fan, fit, if, fab, fad, fat, fib, fin) _____ /___8___
High-Frequency Words (look, see) _____ /___2___

MONITOR PROGRESS
• /f/ Spelled Ff
• High-frequency words

Farfallina and Marcel • **395**

Name _____

Plot

Put these events from "Otis" in order.

Note to Teacher: Have children cut out the scenes and glue them in the correct order on a separate sheet of paper.

MONITOR PROGRESS

• Plot

Farfallina and Marcel • 399

Name _____

Read the Words

top	☐		dot	☐
on	☐		mom	☐
they	☐		mop	☐
cot	☐		of	☐
you	☐		pop	☐

Read the Sentences

1. Ron sat on the mat with you.

2. We have a lot of pots.

3. Did you see the cat on top?

4. They got a mop for Dad.

Note to Teacher: Children read each word. Children read two sentences.

Scoring for Read the Words: Score 1 point for each correct word.

Short o (*top, on, cot, dot, mom, mop, pop*) _____ /__7__
High-Frequency Words (*they, you, of*) _____ /__3__

MONITOR PROGRESS
• /o/ Spelled Oo
• High-frequency words

Name _____

Draw Conclusions

Draw conclusions about what Zack might do next.

Note to Teacher: Review the illustrations with children. Have children decide and draw what they think Zack might do next.

MONITOR PROGRESS • Draw Conclusions

Then and Now **497**

Name _____

Read the Words

dot ☐   not ☐

pop ☐   Ron ☐

they ☐   of ☐

you ☐   Tom ☐

pot ☐   nod ☐

Read the Sentences

1. Tom sees you with the mop.

2. They can pop the top.

3. You can not see the dot.

4. He sat on top of the bin.

Note to Teacher: Children read each word. Children read two sentences.

Scoring for Read the Words: Score 1 point for each correct word.

Short o (*dot, Ron, pop, not, nod, pot, Tom*) _____ /___7___
High-Frequency Words (*of, you, they*) _____ /___3___

MONITOR PROGRESS
- /o/ Spelled *Oo*
- High-frequency words

Name _____

Main Idea

Color the picture that shows the main idea of "Cartwheels and Butterflies."

Note to Teacher: Have children identify and color the main idea of the story.

Name _____

Read the Words

hip	☐	ham	☐
hot	☐	that	☐
hop	☐	hid	☐
had	☐	hit	☐
are	☐	do	☐
hat	☐	him	☐

Read the Sentences

1. Hap can see that dot.

2. Are you hot?

3. That man is Hal.

4. We are with him.

5. Do not hit the cab.

Note to Teacher: Children read each word. Children read two sentences.

Scoring for Read the Words: Score 1 point for each correct word.

/h/Hh (hip, hot, hop, had, hat, ham, hid, hit, him) _____ /__9__
High-Frequency Words (are, that, do) _____ /__3__

MONITOR PROGRESS
- /h/Hh
- High-frequency words

93

Name _____

Sequence

Put these events from "A Day Like Every Other Day" in order.

Note to Teacher: Have children cut out the scenes and glue them in the correct order onto another sheet of paper.

MONITOR PROGRESS   • Sequence   97

Name _____

Read the Words

lip	☐	that	☐
lad	☐	hill	☐
do	☐	lit	☐
lap	☐	are	☐
lid	☐	doll	☐
fill	☐	Bill	☐

Read the Sentences

1. That little lad is sad.

2. That is my doll.

3. Are you Bill?

4. Do they have a doll?

5. Are they in the lab?

Note to Teacher: Children read each word. Children read two sentences.

Scoring for Read the Words: Score 1 point for each correct word.

/l/Ll (lip, lad, lap, lid, fill, hill, lit, doll, Bill) _____ / __9__
High-Frequency Words (do, that, are) _____ / __3__

MONITOR PROGRESS
- /l/ Spelled Ll
- High-frequency words

Name _____

Cause and Effect

Look at the top picture. Choose and color another
picture that caused it to happen.

Note to Teacher: Have children look at the top picture. Then have them choose and color another
picture that caused the top picture to happen.

Name _____

Read the Words

one ☐	trap ☐
spot ☐	four ☐
two ☐	hand ☐
crib ☐	five ☐
three ☐	mask ☐
flat ☐	clap ☐

Read the Sentences

1. I have one raft.

2. We can see three drops.

3. Two fast cats are with me.

4. Five masks are a lot.

5. Look at the four plants.

Note to Teacher: Children read each word. Children read two sentences.

Scoring for Read the Words: Score 1 point for each correct word.

Consonant Blends (*spot, crib, flat, trap, hand, mask, clap*) _____ /___7___
High-Frequency Words (*one, two, three, four, five*) _____ /___5___

MONITOR PROGRESS
- Consonant blends
- High-frequency words

One Little Mouse • 295

Name _____

Sequence

Put events from "The Tale of Peter Rabbit" in order.

Note to Teacher: Have children cut out the scenes from the story and glue them onto another paper in sequential order. Have them label the sequence 1–3.

MONITOR PROGRESS   • Sequence

Name _____

Read the Words

got	☐	four	☐	
three	☐	dog	☐	
gas	☐	one	☐	
five	☐	grin	☐	
dig	☐	glad	☐	
log	☐	two	☐	

Read the Sentences

1. I see one pig.

2. The two tots grab the cat.

3. The three dogs are with me.

4. I have four little flags.

5. Look at the five logs.

Note to Teacher: Children read each word. Children read two sentences.

Scoring for Read the Words: Score 1 point for each correct word.

/g/Gg (*got, gas, dig, log, dog, grin, glad*) _____ /___7___

High-Frequency Words (*three, five, four, one, two*) _____ /___5___

MONITOR PROGRESS
- /g/Spelled *Gg*
- High-frequency words

397

Name _____

Character

Draw the characters from "A Canary's Song."

Huey
The Canary

Note to Teacher: Have children draw the two characters from "A Canary's Song" in the appropriate boxes.

Name _____

Read the Words

hen ☐   pet ☐
left ☐   beg ☐
here ☐   from ☐
pen ☐   dress ☐
go ☐   sent ☐
egg ☐   lend ☐

Read the Sentences

1. Ben is here in the den.

2. I see the dress from Peg.

3. Ken can go to the pen.

4. I got my little hen from Meg.

5. Len and I go to the tent.

Note to Teacher: Children read each word. Children read two sentences.

Scoring for Read the Words: Score 1 point for each correct word.

Short e (*hen, left, pen, egg, pet, beg, dress, sent, lend*) _____ / __9__
High-Frequency Words (*from, here, go*) _____ / __3__

MONITOR PROGRESS
• Short e
• High-frequency words

Name _____

Classify and Categorize

Cut out the pictures and glue them on the correct side of the chart.

At Snow Hill	At the Ocean

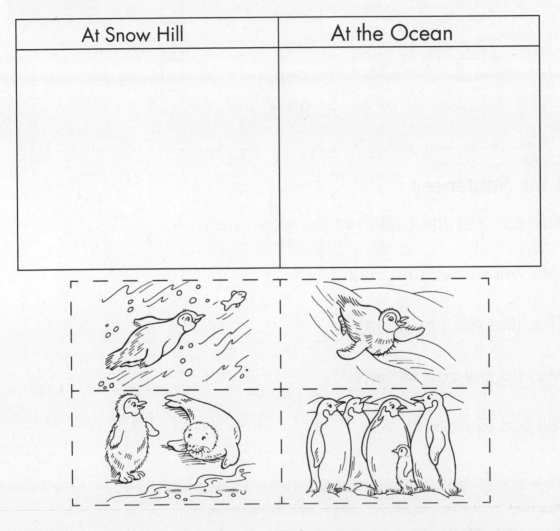

Note to Teacher: Have children cut out pictures and glue them on the appropriate side of the T-chart.

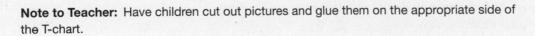

MONITOR PROGRESS • Classify and Categorize

Name _____

Read the Words

Ted	☐	here	☐
from	☐	spend	☐
sled	☐	melt	☐
leg	☐	help	☐
send	☐	step	☐
bell	☐	go	☐

Read the Sentences

1. You can see the bell from the step.

2. We will go with Ned and Ted.

3. The little red hen is here.

4. My red pet can sit here.

5. Tell Ted to go with you.

Note to Teacher: Children read each word. Children read two sentences.

Scoring for Read the Words: Score 1 point for each correct word.

Short e (*Ted, sled, leg, send, bell, spend, melt, help, step*) _____ /__9__
High-Frequency Words (*from, here, go*) _____ /__3__

MONITOR PROGRESS
• Short e
• High-frequency words

Abuela • 597

Name _____

Setting

Draw where each part of the story happens.

Polly and her parents wait for Gran at the airport.

Gran and Polly take a walk.

Gran and Polly have a tea party.

Note to Teacher: Have children fill in the setting in each picture by drawing the background for each of the three scenes.

MONITOR PROGRESS • Setting

Name _____

Read the Words

wet ☐   will ☐

jet ☐   Jill ☐

yellow ☐   went ☐

win ☐   blue ☐

job ☐   jig ☐

green ☐   web ☐

Read the Sentences

1. Wes sat in the little blue jet.

2. Did Jeff win the green hat?

3. Jill went to get a yellow bag.

4. The blue jet went fast.

5. Jan will get the green cap.

Note to Teacher: Children read each word. Children read two sentences.

Scoring for Read the Words: Score 1 point for each correct word.

/w/ Ww (wet, win, will, went, web) _____ / __5__
/j/ Jj (jet, job, jill, jig) _____ / __4__
High-Frequency Words (yellow, green, blue) _____ / __3__

MONITOR PROGRESS
• /w/ Spelled Ww and /j/ Spelled Jj
• High-frequency words

Name _____

Realism and Fantasy

Color the make-believe picture.

Note to Teacher: Have children color the scene that is make-believe.

MONITOR PROGRESS

• **Realism and Fantasy**

Name _____

Read the Words

fox ☐   green ☐
wax ☐   box ☐
blue ☐   Max ☐
fix ☐   yellow ☐
Rex ☐   tax ☐
mix ☐   six ☐

Read the Sentences

1. I have six green pens.

2. Jan can wax the yellow bin.

3. They will go next on the blue jet.

4. Rex and I look in the little green cup.

5. Will the blue hat fit Max?

Note to Teacher: Children read each word. Children read two sentences.

Scoring for Read the Words: Score 1 point for each correct word.

/ks/Xx (*fox, wax, fix, Rex, mix, box, Max, tax, six*) _____ /__9__
High-Frequency Words (*blue, green, yellow*) _____ /__3__

MONITOR PROGRESS
• /ks/Spelled *Xx*
• High-frequency words

Name _____

Cause and Effect

Color the picture that shows what happens in "The Mysteries of Flight." Then color the picture that shows why it happens.

What happened?

Why did it happen?

Note to Teacher: Have children color the large picture of what happens in the story. Then have them choose and color the picture showing why it happens.

MONITOR PROGRESS   • Cause and Effect

Name _____

Read the Words

up ☐   jump ☐

rug ☐   drum ☐

what ☐   was ☐

tub ☐   club ☐

said ☐   dust ☐

cup ☐   plum ☐

Read the Sentences

1. Bud said he will hug Mom.

2. Was that a bump in the rug?

3. What will Bud do in the tub?

4. She said, "Mud is fun."

5. What bug will jump?

Note to Teacher: Children read each word. Children read two sentences.

Scoring for Read the Words: Score 1 point for each correct word.

Short *u* (*up, rug, tub, cup, jump, drum, club, dust, plum*) _____ /__9__

High-Frequency Words (*what, said, was*) _____ /__3__

MONITOR PROGRESS
- /u/ Spelled *Uu*
- High-frequency words

Trucks Roll! • **301**

Name _____

Compare and Contrast

Color the things that are alike in the two pictures.
Cross out the things that are different.

Note to Teacher: Have children practice comparing and contrasting by coloring things that are the same and crossing out things that are different in the two pictures.

Name _____

Read the Words

mug	☐	club	☐
cub	☐	what	☐
was	☐	rub	☐
nut	☐	plus	☐
said	☐	drum	☐
bug	☐	dust	☐

Read the Sentences

1. What is in the cup, Gus?

2. He said, "I dug in the mud."

3. Was a bug on the rug?

4. Was the pup a gift for Russ?

5. Dad said, "I can see dust on the drum."

Note to Teacher: Children read each word. Children read two sentences.

Scoring for Read the Words: Score 1 point for each correct word.

/u/Uu (*mug, cub, nut, bug, club, rub, plus, drum, dust*) _____ /__9__
High-Frequency Words (*was, said, what*) _____ /__3__

MONITOR PROGRESS
- /u/ spelled *Uu*
- High-frequency words

405

Name _____

Plot

Color the boy in his bed. Then color the picture that shows what he finds out in the middle of the story.

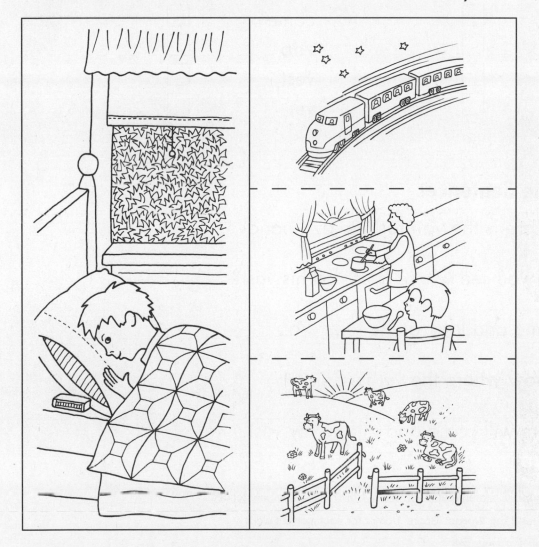

Note to Teacher: Have children color the picture of the boy and what he discovers in the middle of the story.

MONITOR PROGRESS • Plot

409

Name _____

Read the Words

zip	☐	frizz	☐
van	☐	Val	☐
where	☐	come	☐
jazz	☐	zap	☐
Bev	☐	vest	☐
buzz	☐	vet	☐

Read the Sentences

1. Where is the van for the jazz band?

2. Did you see where Buzz left his vest?

3. Come and look at the fuzz, Val.

4. I know where the vet is, Zak.

5. Mom will come and zip up my vest.

Note to Teacher: Children read each word. Children read two sentences.

Scoring for Read the Words: Score 1 point for each correct word.

/v/Vv (*van, Bev, Val, vest, vet*) _____ /__5__
/z/Zz (*zip, jazz, buzz, frizz, zap*) _____ /__5__
High-Frequency Words (*where, come*) _____ /__2__

MONITOR PROGRESS
• /v/Vv
• /z/Zz
• High-frequency words

On the Move! • 503

Name _____

Main Idea

Color the picture that shows the main idea of "Man on the Moon."

Note to Teacher: Have children color the picture that shows the correct main idea.

MONITOR PROGRESS   • Main Idea

Name _____

Read the Words

quit	☐	yam	☐
yell	☐	Quinn	☐
quiz	☐	where	☐
yak	☐	yet	☐
come	☐	quill	☐
quilt	☐	yes	☐

Read the Sentences

1. Yes, you can come and see the quilt.

2. Quinn, where is the yam?

3. Yes, I like where the quiz is.

4. Come and see the yak with a quill.

5. Come and see that Dad will not quit yet.

Note to Teacher: Children read each word. Children read two sentences.

Scoring for Read the Words: Score 1 point for each correct word.

/y/Yy (*yell, yak, yam, yet, yes*) _____ /__5__
/kw/*qu* (*quit, quiz, quilt, Quinn, quill*) _____ /__5__
High-Frequency Words (*come, where*) _____ /__2__

MONITOR PROGRESS
• /y/ Spelled *Yy*
• /kw/ Spelled *qu*
• High-frequency words

607

Name _____

Draw Conclusions

Draw conclusions about what might happen next.

Note to Teacher: Review the illustrations with children. Have the children decide and draw what might happen next.

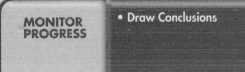

MONITOR PROGRESS   • Draw Conclusions

Name _____

Read the Words

pat	☐	sad	☐
hid	☐	spin	☐
me	☐	you	☐
rip	☐	snap	☐
lap	☐	see	☐
are	☐	quit	☐

Read the Sentences

1. I hid my bat from Gus.

2. We are sad that Jeff quit.

3. Can you spin the green top?

4. Did you see the red van?

5. I like my big hat.

Note to Teacher: Children read each word. Children read two sentences.

Scoring for Read the Words: Score 1 point for each correct word.

Short a (pat, lap, sad, snap) _____ /__4__
Short i (hid, rip, spin, quit) _____ /__4__
High-Frequency Words (my, are, you, see) _____ /__4__

MONITOR PROGRESS
• Review short *a*
• Review short *i*
• Review high-frequency words

Building with Dad • 97

Name _____

Compare and Contrast

Sort these pictures. Which belong at the construction site? Which do not belong there?

At the Construction Site   **Not at the Construction Site**

Note to Teacher: Have children color the pictures, cut them out, and paste each picture in the correct circle.

MONITOR PROGRESS • Compare and Contrast

Building with Dad • 101

Name _____

Read the Words

do	☐	jog	☐
lot	☐	frog	☐
fox	☐	stop	☐
hot	☐	like	☐
pot	☐	drop	☐
to	☐	he	☐

Read the Sentences

1. I can see the frog hop.

2. Sam will run to the shop with Don.

3. I am with my Mom and Pop.

4. We pet the dog that Tim got.

5. He will see Bob at the bus stop.

Note to Teacher: Children read each word. Children read two sentences.

Scoring for Read the Words: Score 1 point for each correct word.

Short o (*lot, fox, hot, pot, jog, frog, stop, drop*) _____ / 8

High-Frequency Words (*go, where, come, that*) _____ / 4

MONITOR PROGRESS
- Short o
- High-frequency words

195

Name _____

Character

Color the characters from "The Elves and the Shoemaker."

Note to Teacher: Have children color the characters from "The Elves and the Shoemaker."

Name _____

Read the Words

have	☐	kept	☐
pet	☐	for	☐
nest	☐	step	☐
little	☐	next	☐
hen	☐	two	☐
bend	☐	rest	☐

Read the Sentences

1. We have a pet hen.

2. A little rest will help you.

3. Mom kept one pen for Dad and me.

4. Where are two red jets?

5. Fred sat next to the little pup.

Note to Teacher: Children read each word. Children read two sentences.

Scoring for Read the Words: Score 1 point for each correct word.

/e/Ee (*pet, nest, hen, bend, kept, step, next, rest*) _____/__8__

High-Frequency Words (*have, little, for, two*) _____/__4__

MONITOR PROGRESS
• /e/ Spelled *Ee*
• High-frequency words

Name _____

Main Idea

Color the picture that shows what "Robin's Nest" is all about.

Note to Teacher: Have children color the picture that shows the main idea of the story.

Name _____

Read the Words

bump	☐	said	☐
sun	☐	drum	☐
look	☐	must	☐
hut	☐	club	☐
rug	☐	with	☐
green	☐	bun	☐

Read the Sentences

1. Nat must go to the club.

2. They sat on the rug with Bud.

3. "I did not bump the hut," said Bill.

4. Go and have fun in the sun.

5. She just got a bib for Gus.

Note to Teacher: Children read each word. Children read two sentences.

Scoring for Read the Words: Score 1 point for each correct word.

Short *u* (*bump, sun, hut, rug, drum, must, club, bun*) _____ /__8__
High-Frequency Words (*look, green, said, with*) _____ /__4__

MONITOR PROGRESS
- /u/ Spelled *Uu*
- High-Frequency Words

Alistair and Kip's Great Adventure! **397**

Name _____

Plot

Show the beginning, middle, and end of "Night in the Country."

Note to Teacher: Have children cut out the boxes and glue them onto another sheet of paper in the correct story order.

MONITOR PROGRESS

• Plot

401

Name _____

Read the Words

bug   ☐   went   ☐

here   ☐   trip   ☐

log   ☐   last   ☐

zip   ☐   four   ☐

she   ☐   jug   ☐

end   ☐   they   ☐

Read the Sentences

1. Here is a red bug.

2. They see the ant hop.

3. Come to where Meg skips.

4. The little mug is hot.

5. I hid my box here.

Note to Teacher: Children read each word. Children read two sentences.

Scoring for Read the Words: Score 1 point for each correct word.

Short Vowels *a, e, i, o, u* (*bug, log, zip, end, went, trip, last, jug*) _____ / __8__
High-Frequency Words (*here, she, four, they*) _____ / __4__

MONITOR PROGRESS
- **Short Vowels**
- **High-Frequency Words**

Name _____

Setting

Color the picture that shows "A House by the Sea."

Note to Teacher: Have children color the picture that is an appropriate setting for the story.

MONITOR PROGRESS   • Setting

497

Name _____

Read the Words

wax	☐	bug	☐
six	☐	pens	☐
jog	☐	was	☐
what	☐	stop	☐
met	☐	glad	☐
blue	☐	where	☐

Read the Sentences

1. We see six bugs here.

2. The nuts are from Pat.

3. Is that mask from Tom?

4. We jog to that end.

5. She said Fred looks fit.

Note to Teacher: Children read each word. Children read two sentences.

Scoring for Read the Words: Score 1 point for each correct word.

Short Vowels a, e, i, o, u (wax, six, jog, met, bug, pens, stop, glad) _____ /_8_
High-Frequency Words (what, blue, come, where) _____ /_4_

MONITOR PROGRESS
• Review short vowels
• Review high-frequency words

Name _____

Draw Conclusions

Look at the machines, tools, and parts. What is made using all of these items? Color the picture.

Note to Teacher: Have children use the information in the text to color the correct building that was made using the items shown.

Assessment Charts and Student Progress Report
from
First Stop Kindergarten

Name _____

Letter/Word Reading Chart

S = Satisfactory
N = Needs practice

	Letter Recognition		High-Frequency		Comprehension		Reteach	Reassess: Number Correct
	Total Letters	Letters Correct	Total Words	Words Correct	S ✔	N ✔	✔	
Week 1 *The Little School Bus*								
Aa, Bb, Cc, Dd, Ee	10							
High-Frequency Words			2					
Character								
Week 2 *We Are So Proud*								
Ff, Gg, Hh, Ii, Jj, Kk, Ll, Mm, Nn	18							
High-Frequency Words			2					
Setting								
Week 3 *Plaidypus Lost*								
Oo, Pp, Qq, Rr, Ss	10							
High-Frequency Words			2					
Sequence								
Week 4 *Miss Bindergarten*								
Tt, Uu, Vv, Ww, Xx, Yy, Zz	15							
High-Frequency Words			2					
Classify and Categorize								
Week 5 *Smash! Crash!*								
/m/Mm	5							
High-Frequency Words			2					
Character and Setting								
Week 6 *Dig Dig Digging*								
/t/Tt	4							
High-Frequency Words			2					
Classify and Categorize								
Unit Scores	62		12					

- **RECORD SCORES** Use this chart to record scores for the Day 5 Letter/Word Reading Assessment.
- **RETEACH SKILLS** If the child is unable to successfully complete the assessments, use the Reteach lessons in *First Stop*.
- **PRACTICE HIGH-FREQUENCY WORDS** If the child is unable to read all the tested high-frequency words, then provide additional practice for the week's words. Use Routine Card 5 for Nondecodable Words.

Name _____

Word/Sentence Reading Chart

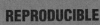

USE WITH GRADE K UNIT 2

S = Satisfactory
N = Needs practice

	Phonics		High-Frequency		Comprehension		Reteach	Reassess: Words Correct
	Total Words	Words Correct	Total Words	Words Correct	S ✔	N ✔	✔	
Week 1 *Flowers*								
Short *a*	6							
High-Frequency Words			4					
Compare and Contrast								
Week 2 *Nature Spy*								
/s/Ss	5							
High-Frequency Words			4					
Setting								
Week 3 *Animal Babies in Grasslands*								
/p/Pp	7							
High-Frequency Words			5					
Main Idea								
Week 4 *Bear Snores On*								
/k/Cc	7							
High-Frequency Words			5					
Realism and Fantasy								
Week 5 *A Bed for the Winter*								
Short *i*	8							
High-Frequency Words			4					
Sequence								
Week 6 *Jack and the Beanstalk*								
Short *i*	8							
High-Frequency Words			4					
Realism and Fantasy								
Unit Scores	41		26					

- **RECORD SCORES** Use this chart to record scores for the Day 5 Word Reading Assessment.

- **RETEACH SKILLS** If the child is unable to successfully complete the assessments, use the Reteach lessons in *First Stop*.

- **PRACTICE HIGH-FREQUENCY WORDS** If the child is unable to read all the tested high-frequency words, then provide additional practice for the week's words. Use Routine Card 5 for Nondecodable Words.

- **REASSESS** Use two different sentences for reassessment.

Name _____

Word/Sentence Reading Chart

USE WITH GRADE K UNIT 3

S = Satisfactory
N = Needs practice

| | Phonics | | High-Frequency | | Comprehension | | Reteach | Reassess: |
	Total Words	Words Correct	Total Words	Words Correct	S ✔	N ✔	✔	Words Correct
Week 1 *Little Panda*								
/b/Bb; /n/Nn	14							
High-Frequency Words			5					
Compare and Contrast								
Week 2 *Little Quack*								
/r/Rr	9							
High-Frequency Words			5					
Plot								
Week 3 *George Washington Visits*								
/d/Dd; /k/Kk	15							
High-Frequency Words			4					
Cause and Effect								
Week 4 *Farfallina and Marcel*								
/f/Ff	10							
High-Frequency Words			4					
Plot								
Week 5 *Then and Now*								
Short o	11							
High-Frequency Words			5					
Draw Conclusions								
Week 6 *The Lion and the Mouse*								
Short o	11							
High-Frequency Words			5					
Main Idea								
Unit Scores	70		28					

- **RECORD SCORES** Use this chart to record scores for the Day 5 Letter/Word Reading Assessment.

- **RETEACH SKILLS** If the child is unable to successfully complete the assessments, use the Reteach lessons in *First Stop.*

- **PRACTICE HIGH-FREQUENCY WORDS** If the child is unable to read all the tested high-frequency words, then provide additional practice for the week's words. Use Routine Card 5 for Nondecodable Words.

- **REASSESS** Use two different sentences for reassessment.

Name _____

Word/Sentence Reading Chart

USE WITH GRADE K UNIT 4

S = Satisfactory
N = Needs practice

| | Phonics | | High-Frequency | | Comprehension | | Reteach | Reassess: Words Correct |
	Total Words	Words Correct	Total Words	Words Correct	S ✔	N ✔	✔	
Week 1 *Rooster's Off to See the World*								
/h/Hh	11							
High-Frequency Words			5					
Sequence								
Week 2 *My Lucky Day*								
/l/Ll	11							
High-Frequency Words			5					
Cause and Effect								
Week 3 *One Little Mouse*								
Consonant Blends	9							
High-Frequency Words			7					
Sequence								
Week 4 *Goldilocks*								
/g/Gg	9							
High-Frequency Words			7					
Character, Setting, Plot								
Week 5 *If You Could Go to Antarctica*								
Short e	13							
High-Frequency Words			5					
Classify and Categorize								
Week 6 *Abuela*								
Short e	13							
High-Frequency Words			5					
Setting								
Unit Scores	66		34					

Copyright: © by Pearson Education, Inc., or its affiliates. All Rights Reserved.

- **RECORD SCORES** Use this chart to record scores for the Day 5 Word/Sentence Reading Assessment.

- **RETEACH SKILLS** If the child is unable to successfully complete the assessments, use the Reteach lessons in *First Stop*.

- **PRACTICE HIGH-FREQUENCY WORDS** If the child is unable to read all the tested high-frequency words, then provide additional practice for the week's words. Use Routine Card 5 for Nondecodable Words.

- **REASSESS** Use two different sentences for reassessment.

241

Name _____

Word/Sentence Reading Chart

USE WITH GRADE K UNIT 5

S = Satisfactory
N = Needs practice

	Phonics		High-Frequency		Comprehension		Reteach	Reassess: Words Correct
	Total Words	Words Correct	Total Words	Words Correct	S ✔	N ✔	✔	
Week 1 *Max Takes the Train*								
/w/Ww; /j/Jj	11							
High-Frequency Words			5					
Realism and Fantasy								
Week 2 *Mayday! Mayday!*								
/ks/Xx	11							
High-Frequency Words			5					
Cause and Effect								
Week 3 *Trucks Roll!*								
/u/Uu	13							
High-Frequency Words			5					
Compare and Contrast								
Week 4 *The Little Engine*								
/u/Uu	13							
High-Frequency Words			5					
Plot								
Week 5 *On the Move!*								
/v/Vv; /z/Zz	14							
High-Frequency Words			4					
Main Idea								
Week 6 *This Is the Way We Go to School*								
/y/Yy; /kw/Qq	14							
High-Frequency Words			4					
Draw Conclusions								
Unit Scores	76		28					

- **RECORD SCORES** Use this chart to record scores for the Day 5 Word/Sentence Reading Assessment.

- **RETEACH SKILLS** If the child is unable to successfully complete the assessments, use the Reteach lessons in *First Stop*.

- **PRACTICE HIGH-FREQUENCY WORDS** If the child is unable to read all the tested high-frequency words, then provide additional practice for the week's words. Use Routine Card 5 for Nondecodable Words.

- **REASSESS** Use two different sentences for reassessment.

Name _____

Word/Sentence Reading Chart

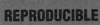

S = Satisfactory
N = Needs practice

	Phonics		High-Frequency		Comprehension		Reteach	Reassess: Words Correct
	Total Words	Words Correct	Total Words	Words Correct	S ✔	N ✔	✔	
Week 1 *Building With Dad*								
Short *a;* Short *i*	12							
High-Frequency Words			10					
Compare and Contrast								
Week 2 *Old MacDonald*								
Short *o*	12							
High-Frequency Words			10					
Character								
Week 3 *Building Beavers*								
Short *e*	12							
High-Frequency Words			10					
Main Idea								
Week 4 *Alistair and Kip's Great Adventure*								
Short *u*	12							
High-Frequency Words			10					
Plot								
Week 5 *The House That Tony Lives In*								
Short vowels *a, e, i, o, u*	12							
High-Frequency Words			10					
Setting								
Week 6 *Ants and Their Nests*								
Short vowels *a, e, i, o, u*	12							
High-Frequency Words			10					
Draw Conclusions								
Unit Scores	72		60					

- **RECORD SCORES** Use this chart to record scores for the Day 5 Word/Sentence Reading Assessment.

- **RETEACH SKILLS** If the child is unable to successfully complete the assessments, use the Reteach lessons in *First Stop.*

- **PRACTICE HIGH-FREQUENCY WORDS** If the child is unable to read all the tested high-frequency words, then provide additional practice for the week's words. Use Routine Card 5 for Nondecodable Words.

- **REASSESS** Use two different sentences for reassessment.

Student Progress Report: Grade K

Name _____

This chart lists the skills taught in this program. Record each student's progress toward mastery of the skills covered during this school year. Use this chart to track the coverage of these skills.

Literature Standards	Date	Date	Date
Key Ideas and Details			
With prompting and support, ask and answer questions about key details in a text.			
With prompting and support, retell familiar stories, including key details.			
With prompting and support, identify characters, settings, and major events in a story.			
Craft and Structure			
Ask and answer questions about unknown words in a text.			
Recognize common types of texts (e.g., storybooks, poems).			
With prompting and support, name the author and illustrator of a story and define the role of each in telling the story.			
Integration of Knowledge and Ideas			
With prompting and support, describe the relationship between illustrations and the story in which they appear (e.g., what moment in a story an illustration depicts).			
With prompting and support, compare and contrast the adventures and experiences of characters in familiar stories.			
Range of Reading and Level of Text Complexity			
Actively engage in group reading activities with purpose and understanding.			

Informational Text Standards	Date	Date	Date
Key Ideas and Details			
With prompting and support, ask and answer questions about key details in a text.			

Informational Text Standards	Date	Date	Date
With prompting and support, identify the main topic and retell key details of a text.			
With prompting and support, describe the connection between two individuals, events, ideas, or pieces of information in a text.			
Craft and Structure			
With prompting and support, ask and answer questions about unknown words in a text.			
Identify the front cover, back cover, and title page of a book.			
Name the author and illustrator of a text and define the role of each in presenting the ideas or information in a text.			
Integration of Knowledge and Ideas			
With prompting and support, describe the relationship between illustrations and the text in which they appear (e.g., what person, place, thing, or idea in the text an illustration depicts).			
With prompting and support, identify the reasons an author gives to support points in a text.			
With prompting and support, identify basic similarities in and differences between two texts on the same topic (e.g., in illustrations, descriptions, or procedures).			
Range of Reading and Level of Text Complexity			
Actively engage in group reading activities with purpose and understanding.			

Foundational Skills Standards	Date	Date	Date
Print Concepts			
Demonstrate understanding of the organization and basic features of print.			
Follow words from left to right, top to bottom, and page-by-page.			
Recognize that spoken words are represented in written language by specific sequences of letters.			

Foundational Skills Standards	Date	Date	Date
Print Concepts *continued*			
Understand that words are separated by spaces in print.			
Recognize and name all upper- and lowercase letters of the alphabet.			
Phonological Awareness			
Demonstrate understanding of spoken words, syllables, and sounds (phonemes).			
Recognize and produce rhyming words.			
Count, pronounce, blend, and segment syllables in spoken words.			
Blend and segment onsets and rimes of single-syllable spoken words.			
Isolate and pronounce the initial, medial vowel, and final sounds (phonemes) in three-phoneme (CVC) words.			
Add or substitute individual sounds (phonemes) in simple, one-syllable words to make new words.			
Phonics and Word Recognition			
Know and apply grade-level phonics and word analysis skills in decoding words.			
Demonstrate basic knowledge of one-to-one letter-sound correspondences by producing the primary or many of the most frequent sounds for each consonant.			
Associate the long and short sounds with the common spellings (graphemes) for the five major vowels.			
Read common high-frequency words by sight (e.g., *the, of, to, you, she, my, is, are, do, does*).			
Distinguish between similarly spelled words by identifying the sounds of the letters that differ.			
Fluency			
Read emergent-reader texts with purpose and understanding.			

Writing Standards	Date	Date	Date
Text Types and Purposes			
Use a combination of drawing, dictating, and writing to compose opinion pieces in which students tell a reader the topic or the name of the book they are writing about and state an opinion or preference about the topic or book (e.g., *My favorite book is . . .*).			
Use a combination of drawing, dictating, and writing to compose informative/explanatory texts in which students name what they are writing about and supply some information about the topic.			
Use a combination of drawing, dictating, and writing to narrate a single event or several loosely linked events, tell about the events in the order in which they occurred, and provide a reaction to what happened.			
Production and Distribution of Writing			
With guidance and support from adults, respond to questions and suggestions from peers and add details to strengthen writing as needed.			
With guidance and support from adults, explore a variety of digital tools to produce and publish writing, including in collaboration with peers.			
Research to Build and Present Knowledge			
Participate in shared research and writing projects (e.g., explore a number of books by a favorite author and express opinions about them).			
With guidance and support from adults, recall information from experiences or gather information from provided sources to answer a question.			

Speaking and Listening Standards	Date	Date	Date
Comprehension and Collaboration			
Participate in collaborative conversations with diverse partners about kindergarten topics and texts with peers and adults in small and larger groups.			

Speaking and Listening Standards	Date	Date	Date
Comprehension and Collaboration *continued*			
Follow agreed-upon rules for discussions (e.g., listening to others and taking turns speaking about the topics and texts under discussion).			
Continue a conversation through multiple exchanges.			
Confirm understanding of a text read aloud or information presented orally or through media by asking and answering questions about key details and requesting clarification if something is not understood.			
Ask and answer questions in order to seek help, get information, or clarify something that is not understood.			
Presentation of Knowledge and Ideas			
Describe familiar people, places, things, and events and, with prompting and support, provide additional detail.			
Add drawings or other visual displays to descriptions as desired to provide additional detail.			
Speak audibly and express thoughts, feelings, and ideas clearly.			

Language Standards	Date	Date	Date
Conventions of Standard English			
Demonstrate command of the conventions of standard English grammar and usage when writing or speaking.			
Print many upper- and lowercase letters.			
Use frequently occurring nouns and verbs.			
Form regular plural nouns orally by adding /s/ or /es/ (e.g., *dog, dogs; wish, wishes*).			
Understand and use question words (interrogatives) (e.g., *who, what, where, when, why, how*).			
Use the most frequently occurring prepositions (e.g., *to, from, in, out, on, off, for, of, by, with*).			

Language Standards	Date	Date	Date
Produce and expand complete sentences in shared language activities.			
Demonstrate command of the conventions of standard English capitalization, punctuation, and spelling when writing.			
Capitalize the first word in a sentence and the pronoun *I*.			
Recognize and name end punctuation.			
Write a letter or letters for most consonant and short-vowel sounds (phonemes).			
Spell simple words phonetically, drawing on knowledge of sound-letter relationships.			

Vocabulary Acquisition and Use

	Date	Date	Date
Determine or clarify the meaning of unknown and multiple-meaning words and phrases based on kindergarten reading and content.			
Identify new meanings for familiar words and apply them accurately (e.g., knowing *duck* as a bird and learning the verb *to duck*).			
Use the most frequently occurring inflections and affixes (e.g., *-ed, -s, re-, un-, pre-, -ful, -less*) as a clue to the meaning of an unknown word.			
With guidance and support from adults, explore word relationships and nuances in word meanings.			
Sort common objects into categories (e.g., shapes, foods) to gain a sense of the concepts the categories represent.			
Demonstrate understanding of frequently occurring verbs and adjectives by relating them to their opposites (antonyms).			
Identify real-life connections between words and their use (e.g., note places at school that are *colorful*).			
Distinguish shades of meaning among verbs describing the same general action (e.g., *walk, march, strut, prance*) by acting out the meanings.			
Use words and phrases acquired through conversations, reading and being read to, and responding to texts.			

First Grade Formal Assessment Tools

First Grade Forms from Baseline Group Test Teacher's Manual

Name _____ Date _____

Phonemic Awareness Scoring Sheet

Directions: Follow the instructions for scoring as given for each section below. Record notes and observations in the box at the bottom. Count up the total number correct, and record the results of this assessment on the Evaluation Chart for Grade 1 on page T46.

Element	Points
Initial and Final Sounds:	Underline each correct sound/blend that the child says. Each correct sound/blend is worth 1 point. (Maximum: 7 points)
1. /b/	
2. /s/	
3. /p/	
4. /g/	
5. /g/ /r/	
6. /n/ /d/	
7. /s/ /k/	
Segmenting Words:	Underline each correct sound. All sounds in a word must be identified correctly to score 1 point for each word. (Maximum: 4 points)
1. /w/ /i/ /g/	
2. /r/ /u/ /b/	
3. /m/ /o/ /p/	
4. /p/ /e/ /t/	
Blending Words:	Underline each word said correctly. Each word is worth 1 point. (Maximum: 4 points)
1. lip	
2. bed	
3. fox	
4. run	
PHONEMIC AWARENESS TOTAL: _____ (Maximum: 15 points)	
Notes and Observations:	

Grade 1 Baseline Test Evaluation Chart

Child's Name _____ Date _____

Teacher's Name _____ Class _____

SUBTEST Skills/Item Numbers			Subtest Percentages	SUBTEST Skills/Item Numbers			Subtest Percentages
Letter Recognition				**Word Recognition**			
_____/12 Correct				_____/7 Correct			
1.	0	1	1=8%	1.	0	1	1=14%
2.	0	1	2=16%	2.	0	1	2=29%
3.	0	1	3=25%	3.	0	1	3=43%
4.	0	1	4=34%	4.	0	1	4=57%
5.	0	1	5=42%	5.	0	1	5=71%
6.	0	1	6=50%	6.	0	1	6=86%
7.	0	1	7=58%	7.	0	1	7=100%
8.	0	1	8=66%				
9.	0	1	9=75%				
10.	0	1	10=83%				
11.	0	1	11=91%				
12.	0	1	12=100%				
Phonics				**Listening Comprehension**			
_____/14 Correct				_____/12 Correct			
1.	0	1	1=7%	1.	0	1	1=8%
2.	0	1	2=14%	2.	0	1	2=16%
3.	0	1	3=21%	3.	0	1	3=25%
4.	0	1	4=29%	4.	0	1	4=34%
5.	0	1	5=36%	5	0	1	5=42%
6.	0	1	6=43%	6.	0	1	6=50%
7.	0	1	7=50%	7.	0	1	7=58%
8.	0	1	8=57%	8.	0	1	8=66%
9.	0	1	9=64%	9.	0	1	9=75%
10.	0	1	10=71%	10.	0	1	10=83%
11.	0	1	11=79%	11.	0	1	11=91%
12.	0	1	12=86%	12.	0	1	12=100%
13.	0	1	13=93%	**Phonemic Awareness**			
14.	0	1	14=100%	_____/15 Correct			
				Total Test _____/60 Correct			
				Fluency _____			
				Alternate Baseline Test _____/61 Correct			

Total # Correct	Total Percentage	Total # Correct	Total Percentage	Total # Correct	Total Percentage	Total # Correct	Total Percentage
1	2%	16	27%	31	52%	46	77%
2	3%	17	28%	32	53%	47	78%
3	5%	18	30%	33	55%	48	80%
4	7%	19	32%	34	57%	49	82%
5	8%	20	33%	35	58%	50	83%
6	10%	21	35%	36	60%	51	85%
7	12%	22	37%	37	62%	52	87%
8	13%	23	38%	38	63%	53	88%
9	15%	24	40%	39	65%	54	90%
10	17%	25	42%	40	67%	55	92%
11	18%	26	43%	41	68%	56	93%
12	20%	27	45%	42	70%	57	95%
13	22%	28	47%	43	72%	58	97%
14	23%	29	48%	44	73%	59	98%
15	25%	30	50%	45	75%	60	100%

Fluency Forms

Class Fluency Progress Chart

Child's Name	Unit R		Unit 1		Unit 2		Unit 3		Unit 4		Unit 5	
	Date	WCPM	Date	WCPM	Date	WCPM	Date	WCPM	Date	WCPM	Date	WCPM
1.												
2.												
3.												
4.												
5.												
6.												
7.												
8.												
9.												
10.												
11.												
12.												
13.												
14.												
15.												
16.												
17.												
18.												
19.												
20.												
21.												
22.												
23.												
24.												
25.												
26.												
27.												
28.												
29.												
30.												
31.												
32.												
33.												
34.												
35.												

Fluency Progress Chart, Grade 1

Name _____

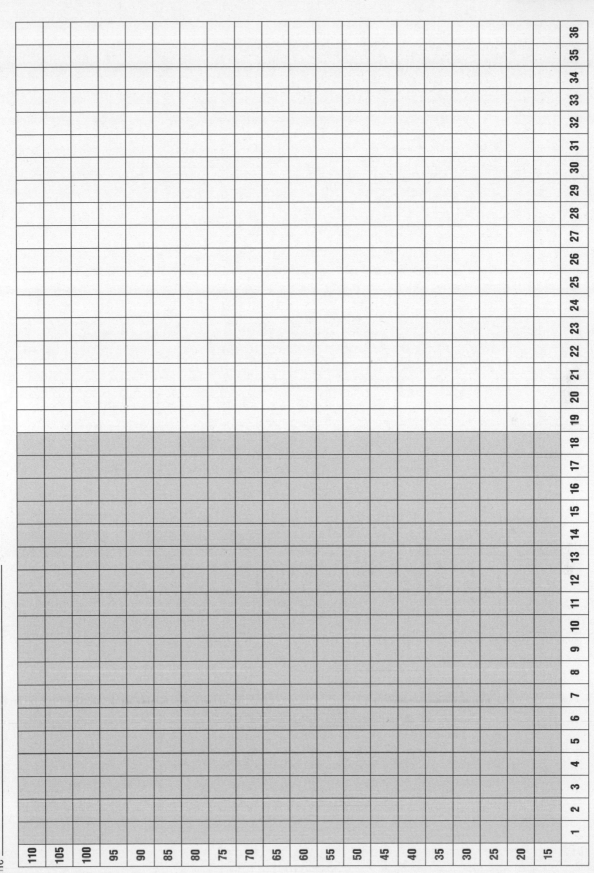

WCPM

Timed Reading/Week

Forms from First Grade Weekly Tests Teacher's Manual

Scott Foresman *Reading Street*
Student Weekly Test Progress Chart—Grade 1

Name: _____

Test	High-Frequency Words	Word Reading/ Phonics	Comprehension	Multiple-Choice Total	Writing	TOTAL
Weekly Test R1	/5	/5	/5	/20		
Weekly Test R2	/5	/5	/5	/20		
Weekly Test R3	/5	/5	/5	/20		
Weekly Test R4	/5	/5	/5	/20		
Weekly Test R5	/5	/5	/5	/15		
Weekly Test R6	/5	/5	/5	/15		
Weekly Test 1	/5	/5	/5	/15		
Weekly Test 2	/5	/5	/5	/15		
Weekly Test 3	/5	/5	/5	/15		
Weekly Test 4	/5	/5	/5	/15		
Weekly Test 5	/5	/5	/5	/15		
Weekly Test 6	/5	/5	/5	/15		
Weekly Test 7	/5	/5	/5	/15		
Weekly Test 8	/5	/5	/5	/15		
Weekly Test 9	/5	/5	/5	/15		
Weekly Test 10	/5	/5	/5	/15		
Weekly Test 11	/5	/5	/5	/15		
Weekly Test 12	/5	/5	/5	/15		
Weekly Test 13	/5	/5	/5	/15		
Weekly Test 14	/5	/5	/5	/15		
Weekly Test 15	/5	/5	/5	/15		
Weekly Test 16	/5	/5	/5	/15		
Weekly Test 17	/5	/5	/5	/15		
Weekly Test 18	/5	/5	/5	/15		
Weekly Test 19	/5	/5	/5	/15		
Weekly Test 20	/5	/5	/5	/15		
Weekly Test 21	/5	/5	/5	/15		
Weekly Test 22	/5	/5	/5	/15		
Weekly Test 23	/5	/5	/5	/15		
Weekly Test 24	/5	/5	/5	/15		
Weekly Test 25	/5	/5	/5	/15		
Weekly Test 26	/5	/5	/5	/15		
Weekly Test 27	/5	/5	/5	/15		
Weekly Test 28	/5	/5	/5	/15		
Weekly Test 29	/5	/5	/5	/15		
Weekly Test 30	/5	/5	/5	/15		

Scott Foresman *Reading Street*
Class Weekly Test Progress Chart—Grade 1

Teacher's Name: _____

Weekly Test Total Score

Child's Name	R1	R2	R3	R4	R5	R6	1	2	3	4	5	6	7	8	9	10	11	12	13	14	15	16	17	18	19	20	21	22	23	24	25	26	27	28	29	30
1																																				
2																																				
3																																				
4																																				
5																																				
6																																				
7																																				
8																																				
9																																				
10																																				
11																																				
12																																				
13																																				
14																																				
15																																				
16																																				
17																																				
18																																				
19																																				
20																																				
21																																				
22																																				
23																																				
24																																				
25																																				
26																																				
27																																				
28																																				
29																																				
30																																				

Comprehension Target Skill Coverage

How can the Weekly Tests predict student success on Unit Benchmark Tests?

Each Unit Benchmark Test, as well as assessing overall student reading ability, concentrates on two skills taught and/or reviewed during the unit by including several questions on those skills. In order to ensure that comprehension target skill can be accurately learned and then tested, students learn each target skill through a combination of being taught and reviewing the skill multiple times before testing occurs. The charts below show the units/weeks where the target comprehension skills are taught and where they are tested on Weekly Tests. Based on the student's number of correct answers for each tested target skill, the teacher will know whether a student has gained the necessary skill knowledge before the Unit Test is given. A low score on the Weekly Tests probably indicates a need for closer review of the student's performance and perhaps additional instruction. It is important to understand that these tests provide only one look at the student's progress and should be interpreted in conjunction with other assessments and the teacher's observation.

Using the Comprehension Target Skill Coverage Chart

To score target skill knowledge, use the Comprehension Target Skill Coverage Chart.

1. Make a copy of the appropriate Comprehension Target Skill Coverage chart for each student.

2. To score, circle the number of correct answers the student had for that skill on the appropriate Weekly Test.

3. Using the total number of correct answers for a skill, check the appropriate box under *Student Trend* to indicate whether or not the student has acquired the target skill knowledge. We recommend 90% correct as the criterion for skill acquisition at this level. Add any notes or observations that may be helpful to you and the student in later instruction.

GRADE 1 — COMPREHENSION TARGET SKILL COVERAGE CHART

Student Name _____

Unit R Tested Skills	Weekly Test Locations	Number Correct	Student Trend
Literary Element: Plot **Common Core State Standards** Literature 3., Literature 7.	Weekly Test R3	0 1 2 3 4 5	_____ Skill knowledge acquired
	Weekly Test R5	0 1 2 3 4 5	_____ Skill needs further review
Realism and Fantasy **Common Core State Standards** Literature 5., Literature 7.	Weekly Test R4	0 1 2 3 4 5	_____ Skill knowledge acquired
	Weekly Test R6	0 1 2 3 4 5	_____ Skill needs further review

Unit 1 Tested Skills	Weekly Test Locations	Number Correct	Student Trend
Literary Elements: Character/Setting **Common Core State Standards** Literature 3., Literature 7.	Weekly Test R1	0 1 2 3 4 5	
	Weekly Test R2	0 1 2 3 4 5	_____ Skill knowledge acquired
	Weekly Test 1	0 1 2 3 4 5	
	Weekly Test 3	0 1 2 3 4 5	_____ Skill needs further review
Main Idea and Details **Common Core State Standards** Literature 2.; Informational Text 2.	Weekly Test 4	0 1 2 3 4 5	_____ Skill knowledge acquired
	Weekly Test 5	0 1 2 3 4 5	_____ Skill needs further review

GRADE 1 — COMPREHENSION TARGET SKILL COVERAGE CHART

Student Name _____

Unit 2 Tested Skills	Weekly Test Locations	Number Correct	Student Trend
Cause and Effect **Common Core State Standards** Literature 1., Literature 3.	Weekly Test 6	0 1 2 3 4 5	_____ Skill knowledge acquired
	Weekly Test 8	0 1 2 3 4 5	_____ Skill needs further review
Author's Purpose **Common Core State Standards** Literature 1.; Informational Text 8.	Weekly Test 9	0 1 2 3 4 5	_____ Skill knowledge acquired
	Weekly Test 11	0 1 2 3 4 5	_____ Skill needs further review

Unit 3 Tested Skills	Weekly Test Locations	Number Correct	Student Trend
Sequence **Common Core State Standards** Literature 3.; Informational Text 1.	Weekly Test 7	0 1 2 3 4 5	_____ Skill knowledge acquired
	Weekly Test 10	0 1 2 3 4 5	
	Weekly Test 13	0 1 2 3 4 5	_____ Skill needs further review
Compare and Contrast **Common Core State Standards** Literature 9.; Informational Text 3.	Weekly Test 12	0 1 2 3 4 5	_____ Skill knowledge acquired
	Weekly Test 14	0 1 2 3 4 5	_____ Skill needs further review

GRADE 1 — COMPREHENSION TARGET SKILL COVERAGE CHART

Student Name _____

Unit 4 Tested Skills	Weekly Test Locations	Number Correct	Student Trend
Fact and Opinion **Common Core State Standards** Informational Text 1.	Weekly Test 15	0 1 2 3 4 5	_____ Skill knowledge acquired
	Weekly Test 17	0 1 2 3 4 5	_____ Skill needs further review
Draw Conclusions **Common Core State Standards** Literature 1., Literature 3.	Weekly Test 18	0 1 2 3 4 5	_____ Skill knowledge acquired
	Wcckly Test 19	0 1 2 3 4 5	_____ Skill needs further review

Unit 5 Tested Skills	Weekly Test Locations	Number Correct	Student Trend
Literary Element: Theme **Common Core State Standards** Literature 2.	Weekly Test 20	0 1 2 3 4 5	_____ Skill knowledge acquired
	Weekly Test 23	0 1 2 3 4 5	
	Weekly Test 30	0 1 2 3 4 5	_____ Skill needs further review
Facts and Details **Common Core State Standards** Informational Text 1., Informational Text 2.	Weekly Test 21	0 1 2 3 4 5	_____ Skill knowledge acquired
	Weekly Test 22	0 1 2 3 4 5	_____ Skill needs further review

Weekly Test Item Analysis—Grade 1

TEST	SECTION	ITEMS	SKILL	COMMON CORE STATE STANDARD
Weekly Test R1	**High-Frequency Words**	1–5	Understand and use new vocabulary	Foundational Skills 3.g.
	Word Reading	6–10	Consonants *m* /m/; *s, ss* /s/; *t* /t/; Short *a*	Foundational Skills 3.b.
	Comprehension	11–15	◎ Character	Literature 7.
	Written Response	Look Back and Write	Respond to literature	Literature 7. (Also Literature 1., Language 1., 2.)
Weekly Test R2	**High-Frequency Words**	1–5	Understand and use new vocabulary	Foundational Skills 3.g.
	Word Reading	6–10	Consonants *c* /k/; *p* /p/, *n* /n/	Foundational Skills 3.b.
	Comprehension	11–15	◎ Setting	Literature 7.
	Written Response	Look Back and Write	Respond to literature	Literature 7. (Also Literature 1., 3., Language 1., 2.)
Weekly Test R3	**High-Frequency Words**	1–5	Understand and use new vocabulary	Foundational Skills 3.g.
	Word Reading	6–10	Consonants *f, ff* /f/; *b* /b/; *g* /g/; Short *i*	Foundational Skills 3.b.
	Comprehension	11–15	◎ Plot	Literature 7.
	Written Response	Look Back and Write	Respond to literature	Literature 7. (Also Literature 1., 3., Language 1., 2.)
Weekly Test R4	**High-Frequency Words**	1–5	Understand and use new vocabulary	Foundational Skills 3.g.
	Word Reading	6–10	Consonants *d* /d/; *l, ll* /l/; *h* /h/; Short *o*	Foundational Skills 3.b.
	Comprehension	11–15	◎ Realism and fantasy	Literature 7.
	Written Response	Look Back and Write	Respond to literature	Literature 7. (Also Literature 1., 3., Language 1., 2.)

Weekly Test Item Analysis—Grade 1

TEST	SECTION	ITEMS	SKILL	COMMON CORE STATE STANDARD
Weekly Test R5	**High-Frequency Words**	1–5	Understand and use new vocabulary	Foundational Skills 3.g.
	Word Reading	6–10	Consonants *r* /r/; *w* /w/; *j* /j/; *k* /k/; Short *e*	Foundational Skills 3.b.
	Comprehension	11–15	◉ Plot	Literature 3.
	Written Response	Look Back and Write	Respond to literature	Literature 7. (Also Literature 1., 3., Language 1., 2.)
Weekly Test R6	**High-Frequency Words**	1–5	Understand and use new vocabulary	Foundational Skills 3.g.
	Word Reading	6–10	Consonants *v* /v/; *y* /y/; *z, zz* /z/; *qu* /kw/ Short *u*	Foundational Skills 3.b.
	Comprehension	11–15	◉ Realism and fantasy	Literature 5.
	Written Response	Look Back and Write	Respond to literature	Literature 7. (Also Literature 1., 3., Language 1., 2.)
Weekly Test 1	**High-Frequency Words**	1–5	Understand and use new vocabulary	Foundational Skills 3.g.
	Phonics	6–10	Short *a*, Consonant pattern -*ck*	Foundational Skills 3.b.
	Comprehension	11–15	◉ Character and setting	Literature 3.
	Written Response	Look Back and Write	Respond to literature	Literature 7. (Also Literature 1., 3., Language 1., 2.)
Weekly Test 2	**High-Frequency Words**	1–5	Understand and use new vocabulary	Foundational Skills 3.g.
	Phonics	6–10	Short *i;* Consonant *x* /ks/	Foundational Skills 3.b.
	Comprehension	11–15	◉ Plot	Literature 3.
	Written Response	Look Back and Write	Respond to literature	Literature 7. (Also Literature 1., 3., Language 1., 2.)

Weekly Test Item Analysis—Grade 1

TEST	SECTION	ITEMS	SKILL	COMMON CORE STATE STANDARD
Weekly Test 3	**High-Frequency Words**	1–5	Understand and use new vocabulary	Foundational Skills 3.g.
	Phonics	6–10	Short *o;* Plural *-s;* Consonant *s/z/*	Foundational Skills 3.b.
	Comprehension	11–15	◉ Character	Literature 3.
	Written Response	Look Back and Write	Respond to literature	Literature 7. (Also Literature 1., 3., Language 1., 2.)
Weekly Test 4	**High-Frequency Words**	1–5	Understand and use new vocabulary	Foundational Skills 3.g.
	Phonics	6–10	Inflected ending *-s;* Inflected ending *-ing*	Foundational Skills 3.f
	Comprehension	11–15	◉ Main idea and details	Informational Text 2.
	Written Response	Look Back and Write	Respond to literature	Informational Text 3. (Also Informational Text 2., 7., Writing 2., Language 1., 2.)
Weekly Test 5	**High-Frequency Words**	1–5	Understand and use new vocabulary	Foundational Skills 3.g.
	Phonics	6–10	Short *e;* Initial consonant blends	Foundational Skills 3.b.
	Comprehension	11–15	◉ Main idea and details	Literature 2.
	Written Response	Look Back and Write	Respond to literature	Literature 3. (Also Literature 1., 7., Language 1., 2.)
Weekly Test 6	**High-Frequency Words**	1–5	Understand and use new vocabulary	Foundational Skills 3.g.
	Phonics	6–10	Short *u;* Final Consonant blends	Foundational Skills 3.b.
	Comprehension	11–15	◉ Cause and effect	Literature 1.
	Written Response	Look Back and Write	Respond to literature	Writing 2. (Also Informational Text 6., Informational Text 7., Language 1., 2.)

Weekly Test Item Analysis—Grade 1

TEST	SECTION	ITEMS	SKILL	COMMON CORE STATE STANDARD
Weekly Test 7	**High-Frequency Words**	1–5	Understand and use new vocabulary	Foundational Skills 3.g.
	Phonics	6–10	Consonant digraphs *sh, th;* Vowel sound in *ball: a, al*	6–8: Foundational Skills 3.a. 9–10: Foundational Skills 3.
	Comprehension	11–15	◉ Sequence	Literature 3.
	Written Response	Look Back and Write	Respond to literature	Writing 2. (Also Language 1., 2.)
Weekly Test 8	**High-Frequency Words**	1–5	Understand and use new vocabulary	Foundational Skills 3.g.
	Phonics	6–10	Long *a;* Consonants *c* /s/; *g* /j/	6–9: Foundational Skills 3.c. 10: Foundational Skills 3.
	Comprehension	11–15	◉ Cause and effect	Literature 1.
	Written Response	Look Back and Write	Respond to literature	Writing 2. (Also Language 1., 2.)
Weekly Test 9	**High-Frequency Words**	1–5	Understand and use new vocabulary	Foundational Skills 3.g.
	Phonics	6–10	Long *i;* Consonant digraphs *wh, ch, tch, ph*	6–7: Foundational Skills 3.c. 8–10: Foundational Skills 3.
	Comprehension	11–15	◉ Author's purpose	11–14: Literature 3. 15: Literature 1.
	Written Response	Look Back and Write	Respond to literature	Writing 2. (Also Language 1., 2.)
Weekly Test 10	**High-Frequency Words**	1–5	Understand and use new vocabulary	Foundational Skills 3.g.
	Phonics	6–10	Long *o;* Contractions	6–7: Foundational Skills 3.c. 8–10. Foundational Skills 3.
	Comprehension	11–15	◉ Sequence	Literature 3.
	Written Response	Look Back and Write	Respond to literature	Writing 2. (Also Language 1., 2.)

Weekly Test Item Analysis—Grade 1

TEST	SECTION	ITEMS	SKILL	COMMON CORE STATE STANDARD
Weekly Test 11	High-Frequency Words	1–5	Understand and use new vocabulary	Foundational Skills 3.g.
	Phonics	6–10	Long *u*, long *e*; Inflected ending -*ed*	6–7: Foundational Skills 3.c. 8–10: Foundational Skills 3.f.
	Comprehension	11–15	◉ Author's purpose	11–14: Informational Text 2. 15: Informational Text 8.
	Written Response	Look Back and Write	Respond to literature	Writing 2. (Also Language 1., 2.)
Weekly Test 12	High-Frequency Words	1–5	Understand and use new vocabulary	Foundational Skills 3.g.
	Phonics	6–10	Long *e*; Syllables VC/CV	6–7: Foundational Skills 3.c. 8–10: Foundational Skills 3.d.
	Comprehension	11–15	◉ Compare and contrast	11: Informational Text 8. 12–15: Informational Text 3.
	Written Response	Look Back and Write	Respond to literature	Writing 2. (Also Language 1., 2.)
Weekly Test 13	High-Frequency Words	1–5	Understand and use new vocabulary	Foundational Skills 3.g.
	Phonics	6–10	Vowel sound of *y*; Syllable pattern CV	Foundational Skills 3.
	Comprehension	11–15	◉ Sequence	Informational Text 1.
	Written Response	Look Back and Write	Respond to literature	Writing 2. (Also Language 1., 2.)
Weekly Test 14	High-Frequency Words	1–5	Understand and use new vocabulary	Foundational Skills 3.g.
	Phonics	6–10	Consonant patterns *ng*, *nk*; Compound words	Foundational Skills 3.
	Comprehension	11–15	◉ Compare and contrast	Literature 9.
	Written Response	Look Back and Write	Respond to literature	Writing 3. (Also Literature 7., Language 1., 2.)

Weekly Test Item Analysis—Grade 1

TEST	SECTION	ITEMS	SKILL	COMMON CORE STATE STANDARD
Weekly Test 15	**High-Frequency Words**	1–5	Understand and use new vocabulary	Foundational Skills 3.g.
	Phonics	6–10	Ending *es;* Vowel: *r*-controlled *or, ore*	6–7: Foundational Skills 3. 8–10: Foundational Skills 3.f.
	Comprehension	11–15	⊙ Fact and opinion	Informational Text 1.
	Written Response	Look Back and Write	Respond to literature	Writing 2. (Also Language 1., 2.)
Weekly Test 16	**High-Frequency Words**	1–5	Understand and use new vocabulary	Foundational Skills 3.g.
	Phonics	6–10	Adding endings: Vowel: *r*-controlled *ar*	6–7: Foundational Skills 3. 8–10: Foundational Skills 3.f.
	Comprehension	11–15	⊙ Author's purpose	Informational Text 8.
	Written Response	Look Back and Write	Respond to literature	Writing 2. (Also Language 1., 2.)
Weekly Test 17	**High-Frequency Words**	1–5	Understand and use new vocabulary	Foundational Skills 3.g.
	Phonics	6–10	Vowel: *r*-controlled *er, ir, ur;* Contractions	Foundational Skills 3.
	Comprehension	11–15	⊙ Fact and opinion	Informational Text 1.
	Written Response	Look Back and Write	Respond to literature	Writing 2. (Also Informational Text 3., Writing 5., Language 1., 2.)
Weekly Test 18	**High-Frequency Words**	1–5	Understand and use new vocabulary	Foundational Skills 3.g.
	Phonics	6–10	Comparative endings -*er*, -*est*, Consonant pattern -*dge*	Foundational Skills 3.
	Comprehension	11–15	⊙ Draw conclusions	Literature 1.
	Written Response	Look Back and Write	Respond to literature	Writing 2. (Also Language 1., 2.)

Weekly Test Item Analysis—Grade 1

TEST	SECTION	ITEMS	SKILL	COMMON CORE STATE STANDARD
Weekly Test 19	**High-Frequency Words**	1–5	Understand and use new vocabulary	Foundational Skills 3.g.
	Phonics	6–10	Vowel digraphs *ai, ay;* Singular and plural possessives	6–8: Foundational Skills 3.c. 9–10: Foundational Skills 3.
	Comprehension	11–15	◉ Draw conclusions	Literature 1.
	Written Response	Look Back and Write	Respond to literature	Literature 3. (Also Literature 1., 7., Language 1., 2.)
Weekly Test 20	**High-Frequency Words**	1–5	Understand and use new vocabulary	Foundational Skills 3.g.
	Phonics	6–10	Vowel digraphs *ea;* Adding endings	6–7: Foundational Skills 3.c. 8–10: Foundational Skills 3.f.
	Comprehension	11–15	◉ Theme	Literature 2.
	Written Response	Look Back and Write	Respond to literature	Literature 3. (Also Literature 1., 4., 7., Language 1., 2.)
Weekly Test 21	**High-Frequency Words**	1–5	Understand and use new vocabulary	Foundational Skills 3.g.
	Phonics	6–10	Vowel digraphs *oa, ow;* Three-letter consonant blends	6–8: Foundational Skills 3.c. 9–10: Foundational Skills 3.
	Comprehension	11–15	◉ Facts and details	Informational Text 2.
	Written Response	Look Back and Write	Respond to literature	Writing 2. (Also Informational Text 7., Language 1., 2.)
Weekly Test 22	**High-Frequency Words**	1–5	Understand and use new vocabulary	Foundational Skills 3.g.
	Phonics	6–10	Vowel digraphs *ie, igh;* Consonant patterns *kn, wr*	6–8: Foundational Skills 3.c. 9–10: Foundational Skills 3.
	Comprehension	11–15	◉ Facts and details	Informational Text 1.
	Written Response	Look Back and Write	Respond to literature	Writing 2. (Also Informational Text 7., Language 1., 2.)

Weekly Test Item Analysis—Grade 1

TEST	SECTION	ITEMS	SKILL	COMMON CORE STATE STANDARD
Weekly Test 23	**High-Frequency Words**	1–5	Understand and use new vocabulary	Foundational Skills 3.g.
	Phonics	6 10	Compound words; Vowel digraphs *ue, ew, ui*	6–8: Foundational Skills 3. 9–10: Foundational Skills 3.e.
	Comprehension	11–15	◉ Theme	11: Literature 2. 12–15: Literature 3.
	Written Response	Look Back and Write	Respond to literature	Literature 3. (Also Literature 1., 7., Language 1., 2.)
Weekly Test 24	**High-Frequency Words**	1–5	Understand and use new vocabulary	Foundational Skills 3.g.
	Phonics	6–10	Vowel sound in *moon: oo;* Suffixes *-ly, -ful*	Foundational Skills 3.
	Comprehension	11–15	◉ Cause and effect	Literature 3.
	Written Response	Look Back and Write	Respond to literature	Literature 3. (Also Literature 1., 7., Language 1., 2.)
Weekly Test 25	**High-Frequency Words**	1–5	Understand and use new vocabulary	Foundational Skills 3.g.
	Phonics	6–10	Diphthongs *ow, ou;* Final syllable *-le*	6–7: Foundational Skills 3. 8–10: Foundational Skills 3.e.
	Comprehension	11–15	◉ Character, setting and plot	Literature 3.
	Written Response	Look Back and Write	Respond to literature	Literature 3. (Also Literature 1., 7., Language 1., 2.)
Weekly Test 26	**High-Frequency Words**	1–5	Understand and use new vocabulary	Foundational Skills 3.g.
	Phonics	6 10	Vowel patterns *ow, ou;* Syllables V/CV, VC/V	6–7: Foundational Skills 3. 8–10: Foundational Skills 3.e.
	Comprehension	11–15	◉ Draw conclusions	Literature 3.
	Written Response	Look Back and Write	Respond to literature	Literature 3. (Also Literature 1., 7., Language 1., 2.)

Weekly Test Item Analysis—Grade 1

TEST	SECTION	ITEMS	SKILL	COMMON CORE STATE STANDARD
Weekly Test 27	**High-Frequency Words**	1–5	Understand and use new vocabulary	Foundational Skills 3.g.
	Phonics	6–10	Vowel sound in *foot: oo;* Adding endings	6–7: Foundational Skills 3. 8–10: Foundational Skills 3.f.
	Comprehension	11–15	◉ Compare and contrast	Informational Text 3.
	Written Response	Look Back and Write	Respond to literature	Informational Text 7. (Also Informational Text 1., Writing 2., Language 1., 2.)
Weekly Test 28	**High-Frequency Words**	1–5	Understand and use new vocabulary	Foundational Skills 3.g.
	Phonics	6–10	Diphthongs *oi, oy;* Suffixes *-er, -or*	Foundational Skills 3.
	Comprehension	11–15	◉ Main idea and details	Informational Text 2.
	Written Response	Look Back and Write	Respond to literature	Informational Text 7. (Also Information Text 1., Language 1., 2.)
Weekly Test 29	**High-Frequency Words**	1–5	Understand and use new vocabulary	Foundational Skills 3.g.
	Phonics	6–10	Vowel sound in *ball: aw, au;* Syllable patterns: Vowel digraphs and diphthongs	6–7: Foundational Skills 3.e. 8–10: Foundational Skills 3.
	Comprehension	11–15	◉ Sequence	Informational Text 1.
	Written Response	Look Back and Write	Respond to literature	Writing 2. (Also Informational Text 1., Language 1., 2.)
Weekly Test 30	**High-Frequency Words**	1–5	Understand and use new vocabulary	Foundational Skills 3.g.
	Phonics	6–10	Prefixes *un- re-;* Long *o,* long *i*	Foundational Skills 3.
	Comprehension	11–15	◉ Theme	Literature 2.
	Written Response	Look Back and Write	Respond to literature	Writing 2. (Also Literature 1., 2., 3., Language 1., 2.)

Forms from Grade 1 Unit and End-of-Year Benchmark Tests Teacher's Manual

CLASS RECORD CHART

Grade 1 Unit Benchmark Tests

Teacher Name _____ Class _____

Student Name	Unit R		Unit 1		Unit 2		Unit 3		Unit 4		Unit 5	
	Pt 1–5	Pt 6	Pt 1–4	Pt 5	Pt 1–4	Pt 5	Pt 1–4	Pt 5	Pt 1–4	Pt 5	Pt 1–4	Pt 5
1.												
2.												
3.												
4.												
5.												
6.												
7.												
8.												
9.												
10.												
11.												
12.												
13.												
14.												
15.												
16.												
17.												
18.												
19.												
20.												
21.												
22.												
23.												
24.												
25.												
26.												
27.												
28.												
29.												
30.												

Evaluation Chart: Grade 1 – Unit R Benchmark Test

Student Name _____ **Date** _____

Item	Tested Skill	Common Core State Standard	Score (circle one)
Reading – Parts 1–5			
Reading – Part 1: Phonemic Awareness			
1. [square]	Initial /m/	Foundational Skills 2.c	0 1
2. [circle]	Initial /y/	Foundational Skills 2.c	0 1
3. [triangle]	Initial /s/	Foundational Skills 2.c	0 1
4. [heart]	Final /p/	Foundational Skills 2.c	0 1
5. [square]	Final /t/	Foundational Skills 2.c	0 1
6. [circle]	Final /g/	Foundational Skills 2.c	0 1
7. [triangle]	Final /r/	Foundational Skills 2.c	0 1
8. [square]	Short *u* (CVC)	Foundational Skills 2.a.	0 1
9. [circle]	Short *i* (CVC)	Foundational Skills 2.a.	0 1
10. [triangle]	Short *e* (CVC)	Foundational Skills 2.a.	0 1
Reading – Part 2: Phonics			
11. [square]	Initial *p*	Foundational Skills 2.c.	0 1
12. [circle]	Initial *w*	Foundational Skills 2.c.	0 1
13. [triangle]	Initial *b*	Foundational Skills 2.c.	0 1
14. [heart]	Initial *qu*	Foundational Skills 2.c.	0 1
15. [rectangle]	Initial *j*	Foundational Skills 2.c.	0 1
16. [square]	Final *l*	Foundational Skills 2.c.	0 1
17. [circle]	Final *f*	Foundational Skills 2.c.	0 1
18. [triangle]	Final *r*	Foundational Skills 2.c.	0 1
19. [heart]	Final *x*	Foundational Skills 2.c.	0 1
20. [rectangle]	Final *d*	Foundational Skills 2.c.	0 1
Reading – Part 3: Word Reading			
21. [square]	CVC	Foundational Skills 3.c.	0 1
22. [circle]	CVC	Foundational Skills 3.c.	0 1
23. [triangle]	CVCC	Foundational Skills 3.c.	0 1
24. [heart]	CVC	Foundational Skills 3.c.	0 1
25. [rectangle]	CVC	Foundational Skills 3.c.	0 1
26. [square]	CVC	Foundational Skills 3.c.	0 1
27. [circle]	CVC	Foundational Skills 3.c.	0 1
28. [triangle]	CVCC	Foundational Skills 3.c.	0 1
29. [heart]	CVC	Foundational Skills 3.c.	0 1
30. [rectangle]	CVCC	Foundational Skills 3.c.	0 1

Reading – Part 4: Word Knowledge				
31. [square]	High-frequency words	Foundational Skills 3.g.	0	1
32. [circle]	High-frequency words	Foundational Skills 3.g.	0	1
33. [triangle]	High-frequency words	Foundational Skills 3.g.	0	1
34. [heart]	High-frequency words	Foundational Skills 3.g.	0	1
35. [rectangle]	High-frequency words	Foundational Skills 3.g.	0	1
36. [square]	High-frequency words	Foundational Skills 3.g.	0	1
37. [circle]	High-frequency words	Foundational Skills 3.g.	0	1
38. [triangle]	High-frequency words	Foundational Skills 3.g.	0	1
39. [heart]	High-frequency words	Foundational Skills 3.g.	0	1
40. [rectangle]	High-frequency words	Foundational Skills 3.g.	0	1
Reading – Part 5: Comprehension				
41. [square]	Literary elements: character	Literature 3.	0	1
42. [circle]	Literary elements: setting	Literature 3.	0	1
43. [triangle]	Realism/fantasy	Literature 5.	0	1
44. [heart]	Literary elements: plot	Literature 3.	0	1
45. [rectangle]	Realism/fantasy	Literature 5.	0	1
46. [square]	Literary elements: setting	Literature 3.	0	1
47. [triangle]	Main ideas and details	Literature 2.	0	1
48. [heart]	Literary elements: character	Literature 3.	0	1
49. [circle]	Literary elements: plot	Literature 3.	0	1
50. [rectangle]	Literary elements: plot	Literature 3.	0	1
Student's Reading Total Score/Total Possible Score _____**/50**				

Reading percentage score: _____ ÷ 50 = _____ × 100 = _____%

        (student's total score)   (percentage score)

Written Composition – Part 6	
Writing Score (Complete one.) _____/6 _____/5 _____/4 _____/3	**Common Core State Standards**
Notes/Observations:	Writing 3. Writing 5. Language 1. Language 2.

Evaluation Chart: Grade 1 – Unit 1 Benchmark Test

Student Name _____ **Date** _____

	Reading – Parts 1–4			
Item	**Tested Skill**	**Item Type***	**Common Core State Standard**	**Score** (circle one)
Reading – Part 1: Comprehension				
1.	Literary elements: character	L	Literature 7.	0 1
2.	Literary elements: setting	L	Literature 3.	0 1
3.	Realism/fantasy	I	Literature 5.	0 1
4.	Main idea	L	Literature 2.	0 1
5.	Setting	L	Literature 3.	0 1
6.	Genre (realism/fantasy)	I	Literature 3.	0 1
7.	Draw conclusions	I	Literature 2.	0 1
8.	Setting	L	Literature 1.	0 1
9.	Main idea	L	Literature 5.	0 1
10.	Main idea	I	Literature 2.	0 1
11.	Literary elements: character	I	Literature 3.	0 1
12.	Literary elements: character	I	Literature 3.	0 1
13.	Literary elements: character	I	Literature 3.	0 1
14.	Sequence	I	Literature 1.	0 1
Reading – Part 2: High-Frequency Words				
15.	High-frequency words		Foundational Skills 3.g.	0 1
16.	High-frequency words		Foundational Skills 3.g.	0 1
17.	High-frequency words		Foundational Skills 3.g.	0 1
18.	High-frequency words		Foundational Skills 3.g.	0 1
19.	High-frequency words		Foundational Skills 3.g.	0 1
20.	High-frequency words		Foundational Skills 3.g.	0 1
Reading – Part 3: Phonics				
21.	Short *a*		Foundational Skills 3.b.	0 1
22.	Short *o*/ck/ final consonant blend		Foundational Skills 3.b.	0 1
23.	Short *o*/x/		Foundational Skills 3.b.	0 1
24.	Short *e*		Foundational Skills 3.b.	0 1
25.	Short *o*		Foundational Skills 3.b.	0 1
26.	Plural *-s*		Foundational Skills 3.f.	0 1
27.	Inflected ending *-ing*		Foundational Skills 3.f.	0 1
28.	Short *i*		Foundational Skills 3.b.	0 1
29.	Initial consonant blend		Foundational Skills 3.b.	0 1
30.	Short *u*		Foundational Skills 3.b.	0 1

Reading – Part 3: Phonics (continued)				
31.	Final consonant cluster	Foundational Skills 3.b.	0	1
32.	Inflected ending -s	Foundational Skills 3.f.	0	1
33.	Short e/ final consonant cluster	Foundational Skills 3.b.	0	1
34.	Short i	Foundational Skills 3.b.	0	1
Student's Regrouping Multiple-Choice Score/Total Possible Score			**/34**	
Reading – Part 4: Writing Conventions				
35.	Sentences	Language 1.	0	1
36.	Sentences	Language 1.c.	0	1
37.	Sentences	Language 1.c.	0	1
38.	Sentences	Language 1.	0	1
39.	Sentences	Language 2.b.	0	1
40.	Sentences	Language 2.b.	0	1
Student's Reading Total Score/Total Possible Score			**/40**	

*L = literal   I = inferential   C = critical analysis

Regrouping (Reading – Parts 1–3) percentage: _____ ÷ 34 = _____ × 100 = _____%
                                            (student's score)   (percentage score)

Reading – Parts 1–4 percentage score: _____ ÷ 40 = _____ × 100 = _____%
                                     (student's total score)   (percentage score)

Writing – Part 5	**Common Core State Standards**
Writing Score (Complete one.) ____/6 ____/5 ____/4 ____/3	
Notes/Observations:	Writing 3. Writing 5. Language 1. Language 2.

Evaluation Chart: Grade 1 – Unit 2 Benchmark Test

Student Name _____ **Date** _____

Reading – Parts 1–4					
Item	**Tested Skill**	**Item Type***	**Common Core State Standard**	**Score** (circle one)	
Reading – Part 1: Comprehension					
1.	Cause and effect	L	Literature 1.	0	1
2.	Main idea	I	Literature 2.	0	1
3.	Cause and effect	I	Literature 1.	0	1
4.	Sequence	L	Literature 1.	0	1
5.	Author's purpose	I	Literature 1.	0	1
6.	Main idea	I	Literature 2.	0	1
7.	Cause and effect	I	Literature 1.	0	1
8.	Main idea	I	Literature 2.	0	1
9.	Author's purpose	I	Literature 1.	0	1
10.	Genre (realism/fantasy)	I	Literature 5.	0	1
11.	Sequence	I	Literature 1.	0	1
12.	Author's purpose	I	Literature 1.	0	1
13.	Literary elements: setting	I	Literature 3.	0	1
14.	Literary elements: character	I	Literature 3.	0	1
Reading – Part 2: High-Frequency Words					
15.	High-frequency words		Foundational Skills 3.g.	0	1
16.	High-frequency words		Foundational Skills 3.g.	0	1
17.	High-frequency words		Foundational Skills 3.g.	0	1
18.	High-frequency words		Foundational Skills 3.g.	0	1
19.	High-frequency words		Foundational Skills 3.g.	0	1
20.	High-frequency words		Foundational Skills 3.g.	0	1
Reading – Part 3: Phonics					
21	-sh Digraph		Foundational Skills 3.a.	0	1
22.	a sound in ball; -ed inflectional ending		Foundational Skills 3.b., 3.f.	0	1
23.	-th Digraph		Foundational Skills 3.a.	0	1
24.	Long a (CVCe)		Foundational Skills 3.c.	0	1
25.	Long i (CVCe)		Foundational Skills 3.c.	0	1
26.	c/s/		Foundational Skills 3.	0	1
27.	ch Digraph		Foundational Skills 3.a.	0	1
28.	g/j/		Foundational Skills 3.	0	1
29.	tch Digraph		Foundational Skills 3.a.	0	1
30.	Contraction 'll		Foundational Skills 3.	0	1

Reading – Part 3: Phonics (continued)

31.	*th* Digraph	Foundational Skills 3.a.	0	1
32.	Long *e*	Foundational Skills 3.c.	0	1
33.	Long *o* (CVCe)	Foundational Skills 3.c.	0	1
34.	Syllables VCCV	Foundational Skills 3.d.	0	1

Student's Regrouping Multiple-Choice Score/Total Possible Score _____/34

Reading – Part 4: Writing Conventions

35.	Nouns	Language 1.b.	0	1
36.	Nouns	Language 1.b.	0	1
37.	Nouns	Language 2.a.	0	1
38.	Nouns	Language 2.a.	0	1
39.	Nouns	Language 2.a.	0	1
40.	Nouns	Language 2.a.	0	1

Student's Reading Total Score/Total Possible Score _____/40

*L = literal   I = inferential   C = critical analysis

Regrouping (Reading – Parts 1–3) percentage: _____ ÷ 34 = _____ × 100 = _____%

(student's score)   (percentage score)

Reading – Parts 1–4 percentage score: _____ ÷ 40 = _____ × 100 = _____%

(student's total score)   (percentage score)

Writing – Part 5	
Writing Score (Complete one.) _____/6 _____/5 _____/4 _____/3	**Common Core State Standards**
Notes/Observations:	Writing 2. Writing 5. Language 1. Language 2.

Evaluation Chart: Grade 1 – Unit 3 Benchmark Test

Student Name _____ **Date** _____

Item	Tested Skill	Item Type*	Common Core State Standard	Score (circle one)
Reading – Part 1: Comprehension				
1.	Literary elements: plot	L	Literature 3.	0 1
2.	Compare/contrast	I	Literature 9.	0 1
3.	Compare/contrast	I	Literature 9.	0 1
4.	Sequence	L	Literature 1.	0 1
5.	Draw conclusions	I	Literature 1.	0 1
6.	Genre (realism/fantasy)	I	Literature 5.	0 1
7.	Author's purpose	I	Literature 1.	0 1
A.	Constructed-response text-to-self connection		Writing 1.	0 1 2
8.	Literary elements: plot	I	Literature 3.	0 1
9.	Sequence	L	Literature 1.	0 1
10.	Draw conclusions	I	Literature 1.	0 1
11.	Literary elements: theme	I	Literature 2.	0 1
12.	Sequence	L	Literature 1.	0 1
13.	Literary elements: plot	I	Literature 3.	0 1
14.	Compare/contrast	I	Literature 3.	0 1
B.	Constructed-response text-to-text connection		Literature 9.	0 1 2
Reading – Part 2: High-Frequency Words				
15.	High-frequency words		Foundational Skills 3.g.	0 1
16.	High-frequency words		Foundational Skills 3.g.	0 1
17.	High-frequency words		Foundational Skills 3.g.	0 1
18.	High-frequency words		Foundational Skills 3.g.	0 1
19.	High-frequency words		Foundational Skills 3.g.	0 1
20.	High-frequency words		Foundational Skills 3.g.	0 1
Reading – Part 3: Phonics				
21.	Long *i* vowel sound of *y*		Foundational Skills 3.c.	0 1
22.	Long *e* vowel sound of *y*		Foundational Skills 3.c.	0 1
23.	Long vowel pattern CV		Foundational Skills 3.c.	0 1
24.	Compound word		Foundational Skills 3.	0 1
25.	Word family *ng*		Foundational Skills 3.	0 1
26.	Long vowel pattern CV		Foundational Skills 3.c.	0 1
27.	*-es* Plural		Foundational Skills 3.f.	0 1
28.	Word family *nk*		Foundational Skills 3.	0 1

Reading – Part 3: Phonics (continued)

29.	r-Controlled *ore*	Foundational Skills 3.	0	1
30.	Contraction *'s*	Foundational Skills 3.	0	1
31.	Comparative *-est*	Foundational Skills 3.	0	1
32.	r-Controlled *ar*	Foundational Skills 3.	0	1
33.	Inflected ending *-ed* with double final consonant	Foundational Skills 3.f.	0	1
34.	Contraction *'ve*	Foundational Skills 3.	0	1
Student's Regrouping Multiple-Choice Score/Total Possible Score			**_____ /34**	

Reading – Part 4: Writing Conventions

35.	Verbs	Language 1.	0	1
36.	Verbs	Language 1.c.	0	1
37.	Verbs	Language 1.c.	0	1
38.	Verbs	Language 1.e.	0	1
39.	Verbs	Language 1.e.	0	1
40.	Verbs	Language 2.	0	1
Student's Reading Total Score/Total Possible Score			**_____ /44**	

*L = literal   I = inferential   C = critical analysis

Regrouping (Reading – Parts 1–3) percentage: _____ ÷ 34 = _____ × 100 = _____%

$\quad$ (student's score) $\qquad\qquad\qquad\qquad$ (percentage score)

Reading – Parts 1–4 percentage score: _____ ÷ 44 = _____ × 100 = _____%

$\quad$ (student's total score) $\qquad\qquad\qquad$ (percentage score)

Writing – Part 5

Writing – Part 5	Common Core State Standards
Writing Score (Complete one.) _____/6 _____/5 _____/4 _____/3	
Notes/Observations:	Writing 2. Writing 5. Language 1. Language 2.

Evaluation Chart: Grade 1 – Unit 4 Benchmark Test

Student Name _____ Date _____

Item	Tested Skill	Item Type*	Common Core State Standard	Score (circle one)
Reading – Parts 1–4				
Reading – Part 1: Comprehension				
1.	Cause and effect	L	Literature 1.	0 1
2.	Author's purpose	I	Literature 1.	0 1
3.	Draw conclusions	I	Literature 1.	0 1
4.	Draw conclusions	I	Literature 1.	0 1
5.	Literary elements: theme	I	Literature 2.	0 1
6.	Draw conclusions	I	Literature 1.	0 1
7.	Literary elements: plot	I	Literature 3.	0 1
A.	Constructed-response text-to-self connection		Writing 3.	0 1 2
8.	Sequence	L	Informational Text 1.	0 1
9.	Main idea	I	Informational Text 2.	0 1
10.	Fact and opinion	I	Informational Text 1.	0 1
11.	Author's purpose	I	Informational Text 8.	0 1
12.	Cause and effect	L	Informational Text 1.	0 1
13.	Cause and effect	L	Informational Text 1.	0 1
14.	Fact and opinion	I	Informational Text 1.	0 1
B.	Constructed-response text-to-text connection		Literature 9.	0 1 2
Reading – Part 2: High-Frequency Words				
15.	High-frequency words		Foundational Skills 3.g.	0 1
16.	High-frequency words		Foundational Skills 3.g.	0 1
17.	High-frequency words		Foundational Skills 3.g.	0 1
18.	High-frequency words		Foundational Skills 3.g.	0 1
19.	High-frequency words		Foundational Skills 3.g.	0 1
20.	High-frequency words		Foundational Skills 3.g.	0 1
Reading – Part 3: Phonics				
21.	Long *a: ay*		Foundational Skills 3.c.	0 1
22.	Long *o: ow, oa*		Foundational Skills 3.c.	0 1
23.	Long *e: ea*		Foundational Skills 3.c.	0 1
24.	Long *i: igh*		Foundational Skills 3.c.	0 1
25.	Vowels *oo, ui*		Foundational Skills 3.c.	0 1
26.	Consonant sound *wr/r/*		Foundational Skills 3.c.	0 1
27.	Possessives		Foundational Skills 3.	0 1
28.	Suffix *-ful*		Foundational Skills 3.	0 1

Reading – Part 3: Phonics (continued)				
29.	Vowels *ew, ue*	Foundational Skills 3.c.	0	1
30.	Consonant sound *kn*/n/	Foundational Skills 3.	0	1
31.	Compound words	Foundational Skills 3.	0	1
32.	Short *e: ea*	Foundational Skills 3.	0	1
33.	Long *a: ai*	Foundational Skills 3.c.	0	1
34.	Suffix *-ly*	Foundational Skills 3.	0	1
Student's Regrouping Multiple-Choice Score/Total Possible Score			**/34**	
Reading – Part 4: Writing Conventions				
35.	Adjectives	Language 1.f.	0	1
36.	Adjectives	Language 1.f.	0	1
37.	Adjectives	Language 1.f.	0	1
38.	Adjectives	Language 1.f.	0	1
39.	Adjectives	Language 1.f.	0	1
40.	Adjectives	Language 1.f.	0	1
Student's Reading Total Score/Total Possible Score			**/44**	

*L = literal   I = inferential   C = critical analysis

Regrouping (Reading – Parts 1–3) percentage: _____ ÷ 34 = _____ × 100 = _____%

                                        (student's score)   (percentage score)

Reading – Parts 1–4 percentage score: _____ ÷ 44 = _____ × 100 = _____%

                               (student's total score)   (percentage score)

Writing – Part 5	Common Core State Standards
Writing Score (Complete one.) _____/6 _____/5 _____/4 _____/3	
Notes/Observations:	Writing 1. Writing 5. Language 1. Language 2.

Evaluation Chart: Grade 1 – Unit 5 Benchmark Test

Student Name _____ Date _____

Reading – Parts 1–4

Item	Tested Skill	Item Type*	Common Core State Standards	Score (circle one)
Reading – Part 1: Comprehension				
1.	Literary elements: setting	L	Literature 3.	0 1
2.	Literary elements: theme	I	Literature 2.	0 1
3.	Cause and effect	L	Literature 1.	0 1
4.	Literary elements: theme	I	Literature 2.	0 1
5.	Literary elements: plot	I	Literature 3.	0 1
6.	Main idea	I	Literature 2.	0 1
7.	Literary elements: character	I	Literature 3.	0 1
A.	Constructed-response text-to-self connection		Writing 3.	0 1 2
8.	Facts and details	L	Informational Text 1.	0 1
9.	Compare/contrast	I	Informational Text 3.	0 1
10.	Author's purpose	I	Informational Text 8.	0 1
11.	Facts and details	L	Informational Text 1.	0 1
12.	Main idea	I	Informational Text 2.	0 1
13.	Facts and details	I	Informational Text 1.	0 1
14.	Draw conclusions	I	Informational Text 1.	0 1
B.	Constructed-response text-to-text connection		Writing 1.	0 1 2
Reading – Part 2: High-Frequency Words				
15.	High-frequency words		Foundational Skills 3.g.	0 1
16.	High-frequency words		Foundational Skills 3.g.	0 1
17.	High-frequency words		Foundational Skills 3.g.	0 1
18.	High-frequency words		Foundational Skills 3.g.	0 1
19.	High-frequency words		Foundational Skills 3.g.	0 1
20.	High-frequency words		Foundational Skills 3.g.	0 1
Reading – Part 3: Phonics				
21.	Syllables V/CV		Foundational Skills 3.e.	0 1
22.	Vowel diphthong *ou*		Foundational Skills 3.	0 1
23.	Prefix *un-*		Language 4.b.	0 1
24.	Vowel diphthong *oy*		Foundational Skills 3.	0 1
25.	Vowel diphthong *aw*		Foundational Skills 3.	0 1
26.	Inflected ending *-ed* (drop *e* before *-ed*)		Foundational Skills 3.f.	0 1
27.	Inflected ending *-ing* (drop *e* before *-ing*)		Foundational Skills 3.f.	0 1
28.	Long vowel pattern *i (nd)*		Foundational Skills 3.	0 1

Reading – Part 3: Phonics (continued)				
29.	Suffix -er (agent)	Language 4.b.	0	1
30.	Compound words	Foundational Skills 3.	0	1
31.	Vowel diphthong -ow	Foundational Skills 3.	0	1
32.	Final syllable -le	Foundational Skills 3.c.	0	1
33.	Long vowel pattern o (st)	Foundational Skills 3.c.	0	1
34.	Vowels: oo as in foot	Foundational Skills 3.c.	0	1
Student's Regrouping Multiple-Choice Score/Total Possible Score			_____/34	
Reading – Part 4: Writing Conventions				
35.	Pronouns	Language 1.d.	0	1
36.	Pronouns	Language 1.d.	0	1
37.	Adverbs	Language 1.	0	1
38.	Pronouns	Language 1.d.	0	1
39.	Pronouns	Language 1.d.	0	1
40.	Sentences	Language 1.	0	1
Student's Reading Total Score/Total Possible Score			_____/44	

*L = literal   I = inferential   C = critical analysis

Regrouping (Reading – Parts 1–3) percentage: _____ ÷ 34 = _____ × 100 = _____%
                                       (student's score)   (percentage score)

Reading – Parts 1–4 percentage score: _____ ÷ 44 = _____ × 100 = _____%
                                       (student's total score)   (percentage score)

Writing – Part 5	
Writing Score (Complete one.) _____/6 _____/5 _____/4 _____/3	**Common Core State Standards**
Notes/Observations:	Writing 3. Writing 5. Language 1. Language 2.

Evaluation Chart: Grade 1 – End-of-Year Benchmark Test

Student Name _____ Date _____

Reading – Parts 1–4

Item	Tested Skill	Item Type*	Common Core State Standard	Score (circle one)
1.	Literary elements: setting	I	Literature 3.	0 1
2.	Draw conclusions	I	Literature 1.	0 1
3.	Realism/fantasy	I	Literature 5.	0 1
4.	Main idea (fiction)	I	Literature 2.	0 1
5.	Facts and details	I	Literature 1.	0 1
6.	Literary elements: character	I	Literature 3.	0 1
7.	Literary elements: plot	L	Literature 3.	0 1
8.	Sequence	L	Literature 1.	0 1
9.	Literary elements: character	I	Literature 3.	0 1
10.	Draw conclusions	I	Literature 1.	0 1
11.	Main idea (fiction)	I	Literature 2.	0 1
12.	Author's purpose	I	Literature 1.	0 1
13.	Facts and details	L	Literature 1.	0 1
14.	Literary elements: theme	I	Literature 2.	0 1
A.	Contructed-response item – text-to-text connection		Writing 2.	0 1 2
15.	Fact and opinion	I	Informational Text 1.	0 1
16.	Sequence	I	Informational Text 3.	0 1
17.	Compare/contrast	I	Informational Text 3.	0 1
18.	Cause and effect	I	Informational Text 3.	0 1
19.	Compare/contrast	I	Informational Text 3.	0 1
20.	Sequence	L	Informational Text 3.	0 1
21.	Author's purpose	I	Informational Text 8.	0 1
B.	Constructed-response item – text-to-text connection		Writing 1.	0 1 2
22.	High-frequency words		Foundational Skills 3.g.	0 1
23.	High-frequency words		Foundational Skills 3.g.	0 1
24.	High-frequency words		Foundational Skills 3.g.	0 1
25.	High-frequency words		Foundational Skills 3.g.	0 1
26.	High-frequency words		Foundational Skills 3.g.	0 1
27.	High-frequency words		Foundational Skills 3.g.	0 1
28.	High-frequency words		Foundational Skills 3.g.	0 1
29.	High-frequency words		Foundational Skills 3.g.	0 1
30.	High-frequency words		Foundational Skills 3.g.	0 1
31.	Vowel diphthong oy, oi/oi/		Foundational Skills 3.	0 1
32.	Inflected ending -ing		Foundational Skills 3.f.	0 1
33.	Long a: CVCe; c/s/		Foundational Skills 3.c.	0 1
34.	Contraction n't		Foundational Skills 3.	0 1
35.	Long e: ea, ee		Foundational Skills 3.c.	0 1

Reading – Parts 1–4 (continued)

36.	Syllables V/CV	Foundational Skills 3.e.	0	1
37.	Compound words	Foundational Skills 3.	0	1
38.	Vowel pattern *ew, ue*	Foundational Skills 3.	0	1
39.	Comparative ending *-est*	Language 4.b.	0	1
40.	Vowels *oo* as in *moon*	Foundational Skills 3.	0	1
41.	Vowel diphthong *ow, ou*/ou/	Foundational Skills 3.	0	1
42.	Long *a: ai, ay*	Foundational Skills 3.c.	0	1
43.	Suffix *-ful*	Language 4.b.	0	1
44.	Consonant sound *kn*/n/	Foundational Skills 3.	0	1
45.	Long *i: igh*	Foundational Skills 3.	0	1
46.	Long *o: ow*	Foundational Skills 3.	0	1
47.	Suffix *-er* (agent)	Language 4.b.	0	1
48.	Short *e: ea*	Foundational Skills 3.	0	1
49.	Comparative ending *-er*	Language 4.b.	0	1
50.	Vowels *oo* as in *book*	Foundational Skills 3.	0	1
51.	Long vowel pattern *o (ld)*	Foundational Skills 3.	0	1
52.	Sentences	Language 1.	0	1
53.	Nouns	Language 1.b.	0	1
54.	Verbs	Language 1.e.	0	1
55.	Adjectives	Language 1.f.	0	1
56.	Pronouns	Language 1.d.	0	1
57.	Verbs	Language 1.e.	0	1
58.	Pronouns	Language 1.d.	0	1
59.	Nouns	Language 1.b.	0	1
60.	Verbs	Language 1.	0	1
	Student's Reading Total Score/Total Possible Score _____ **/64**			

*L = literal   I = inferential   C = critical analysis

Reading – Parts 1–4 percentage score: _____ ÷ 64 = _____ × 100 = _____%
(student's total score)   (percentage score)

Writing – Part 5

Writing Score (Complete one.) _____/6 _____/5 _____/4 _____/3	**Common Core State Standards**
Notes/Observations:	Writing 3. Writing 5. Language 1. Language 2.

Monitor Progress Pages
from
First Grade Teacher's Editions

Name _____

Read the Words

am	I
see	Sam
at	green
a	sat
mat	Tam

MONITOR PROGRESS

- Consonants *m/m/*, *s/s/, t/t/*
- Short *a*
- High-Frequency Words

Sam **35c**

My Cat Sam

My pet is Sam. Sam is my tan cat. Sam is not a sad cat! I take care of Sam. Can you take care of a cat?

Hold up a hat. Sam will stand on his back legs. He will hit it with a paw. That is how Sam plays. A cat has a box with sand. You can put the sand in it. A cat must eat. You can give the cat food. Take the cat to a vet. The vet will help it. Sam goes to the vet with me. Sam will not get sick much.

Sam will nap on a mat in his bed. But he hops into my bed too. It is fun to take care of Sam!

Advanced Selection R1 **Vocabulary:** tan, vet

Sam **35g**

Name _____

Read the Words

can	one
cap	cat
like	we
man	map
the	sat
pan	tan
pat	tap

Read the Sentences

1. We can nap.

2. Tap the cap.

3. One can tap.

4. I like a tan cap.

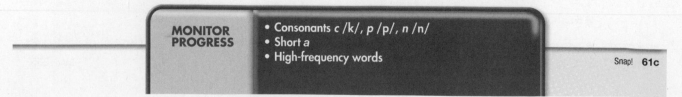

MONITOR PROGRESS
- Consonants c /k/, p /p/, n /n/
- Short a
- High-frequency words

Snap! **61c**

Nan Can Help!

Nan has a new brother! His name is Pat. Pat is little. He takes lots of naps. He gets lots of gifts. Nan is sad. She does not have a gift for Pat.

Then Aunt Pam gives Nan a new book.

"This book will help you. You can read it, Nan," says Aunt Pam.

"It tells how to help Pat!" says Nan. She reads it all. Now Nan makes a plan. Nan picks up a pink pen. She makes a nice card.

"This card is my gift for Pat!" says Nan. Then she puts the card by Pat.

My Plan to Help Pat
by Nan

I can run to get the milk.
I can help take Pat to the park.
I can put a cap on Pat to keep the sun away.

Advanced Selection R2 **Vocabulary:** gift, aunt

Name _____

Read the Words

bag	big
fan	fib
look	was
in	sit
pin	gas
do	yellow
fit	you

Read the Sentences

1. The fib was big.

2. You see a fit pig.

3. Sis was a big fan.

4. Look at the big pig.

MONITOR PROGRESS
- Consonants f/f/, b/b/, g/g/
- Short i
- High-Frequency Words

Tip and Tam **87c**

Bill and His Pals

Three pals played a fun game.

"I will count. I will find you. Then I will tag you!" said Bill.

"I will run and hide," said Tiff.

"Bill, you will not get me," said Meg.

Tiff and Meg looked. Tiff saw a hill with tall grass. Could she sit in the grass? Would Bill find her? Tiff ran up the hill and hid in the grass.

"Six, seven," yelled Bill.

Meg saw a little house. It was for Gip. Gip was a dog. Could she fit in Gip's house?

"I am too big. I must get another spot," Meg said.

"Nine," yelled Bill.

Could she dig a hole? No, she did not have time to dig. Then Meg saw a big log by the fence. That log was big! Meg hid.

"Bill will not find me by this big log!" said Meg.

"Ten!" Bill yelled. Then he ran to find and tag his pals. The game in the yard was fun!

Advanced Selection R3   **Vocabulary:** spot, log

Tip and Tam **87g**

297

Name _____

Read the Words

hop	hog
lot	are
that	cod
dog	have
two	log
Don	hot
they	doll

Read the Sentences

1. That dog was hot.

2. You have a hot dog.

3. They see the doll hop.

4. We are in the dog lot.

MONITOR PROGRESS
- Consonants d/d/, l/l/, h/h/
- Short o
- High-Frequency Words

The Big Top **113c**

Hat Day on Lot Hill

What kind of party was fun? The Hat Day Party was fun! It was on top of Lot Hill. Pals played games. They ate good food. They looked at hats. They stayed all day long.

Rob asked Mom for her hat. It was a hard hat for work. Hal wore Dad's floppy hat. It had spots. Miss Dodd had a big red hat with large white dots.

"I like your red hat, Miss Dodd," said Hal.

"I am glad you like it, Hal. That hat looks good on you," Miss Dodd said.

Some hats were tall. Some hats were long. One hat had duck ears!

Then a strong wind came. Hats flew off. It looked like the end of Hat Day.

"Look! A dog with a hat!" said Hal and Rob. The hat was tied on with string. That hat did not fly off! Hal and Rob ran. They got string. They gave it to all their pals. It was not the end of Hat Day. The pals stayed all day long!

Advanced Selection R4   **Vocabulary:** pal, floppy

The Big Top   **113g**

Name _____

Read the Words

red	he
wet	Ken
is	three
Jeff	jet
to	with
pen	kit
jot	well

Read the Sentences

1. Jeff is with Ken.

2. Is he in the red jet?

3. Wet Jed is with him.

4. Three can hop to the red well.

MONITOR PROGRESS
- Consonants r/r/, w/w/, j/j/, k/k/
- Short e
- High-Frequency Words

School Day **139c**

The Best Pet

Pets are fun. Some kids have pets at home. Some kids have pets at school.

A fish can be a class pet. Fish must live in water. They do not need a bed. They just swim in a tank. They eat just a little. But you must feed fish. You must clean the fish tank. Can you get a fish from a tank? You must use a net. You must put a fish back fast. Fish must stay wet. Does your class have a fish tank?

Can a bug be a pet? Bugs can live in small jars. Your class may have ten bugs in a jar. But you cannot pet a bug. Can a pig be a pet? You can pet a pig. Pigs are big. A pig will not stay on a rug. It will run around the room. Most pigs live in a pen.

A skunk can make a bad smell. A duck likes a pond. A robin likes a nest. They will not be good class pets.

What pet is in your school? Is it a good class pet?

Advanced Selection R5   **Vocabulary:** tank, pen

Name _____

Read the Words

van	yet
yum	for
here	go
buzz	quiz
where	me
zip	hum
yes	but

Read the Sentences

1. Here is a fun quiz.

2. But where is the van?

3. Go to the vet with Pug.

4. Hum with me, Quinn.

MONITOR PROGRESS
- Consonants v/v/, y/y/, z/z/, qu/kw/
- Short *u*
- High-Frequency Words

Farmers Market **165c**

A Yard for Bugs and Ducks

Vin put on his tan vest. It was time to work in the yard. Vin liked his yard. "My yard is good for plants," he said.

He planted yams. He planted flowers. Some were mums. He got water. He put water on the young plants in his yard. He got mud on his hands. He got mud on his vest. Vin worked very hard. The sun was very hot.

It was time for a quick nap, so Vin rested in the sun. But a little bug landed on his chin. "A bug! I must brush it away," said Vin.

Buzz! Buzz! He saw a bee zip by his nose. "A bee! I must brush it away," he said.

Quack! Quack! A duck walked up from the pond. The duck came very close to Vin. The bug and the bee came back. Vin got up.

"They will not quit!" he said. His yard was good for bugs and ducks. It was good for yams and mums. "My yard is not good for naps!" said Vin.

Advanced Selection R6   **Vocabulary:** yams, mums

Farmers Market   **165i**

Name _____

Read the Words

1. cat

2. my

3. tap

4. back

5. way

6. man

7. in

8. sack

9. come

10. pack

11. jam

12. on

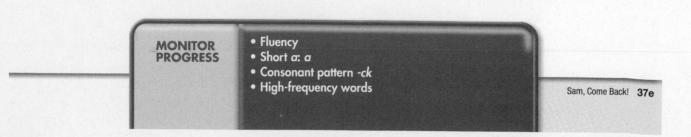

MONITOR PROGRESS
- Fluency
- Short a: a
- Consonant pattern -ck
- High-frequency words

Sam, Come Back! **37e**

Name _____

Read the Sentences

1. Mack sat on the mat.

2. Zack had my cap.

3. Come pat the cat, Jack.

4. Pam ran back that way.

5. Pack one hat in the bag.

MONITOR PROGRESS
- Fluency
- Short *a: a*
- Consonant Pattern *-ck*
- High-Frequency Words

Name _____

Read the Words

1. she

2. mix

3. fix

4. up

5. in

6. take

7. six

8. what

9. Max

10. sit

11. did

12. wig

MONITOR PROGRESS

- Short *i*: *i*
- Consonant *x*/ks/
- High-frequency words

Pig in a Wig   **65e**

Name _____

Read the Sentences

1. Tim can take the mix.

2. What did Sam mix?

3. Take the mix, Jim.

4. She can mix it.

5. What can Kim fix?

6. You can fix it up.

65f   Animals, Tame and Wild • Unit 1 • Week 2

MONITOR PROGRESS
- Fluency
- Short *i*: *i*
- Consonant x/ks/
- High-Frequency Words

Name _____

Read the Words

1. from
2. pop
3. hot
4. mom
5. logs
6. jobs

7. little
8. get
9. fox
10. help
11. use
12. blue

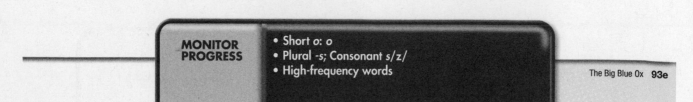

MONITOR PROGRESS
- Short *o*: *o*
- Plural -*s*; Consonant *s/z/*
- High-frequency words

The Big Blue Ox **93e**

Name _____

Read the Sentences

1. Pop can get the pots.

2. The blue pots are hot.

3. Are the rocks from the box?

4. I have little pots for Mom.

5. Use a box for the rocks.

6. Mom can help fix the rocks.

MONITOR PROGRESS

- Fluency
- Short o: o
- Plural -s; Consonant s/z/
- High-Frequency Words

Name _____

Read the Words

1. hops
2. four
3. taps
4. eat
5. her
6. kicking
7. naps

8. five
9. packing
10. picking
11. rocking
12. sits
13. this
14. too

MONITOR PROGRESS
- Ending *-s*
- Ending *-ing*
- High-frequency words

Name _____

Read the Sentences

1. Tim hops and Mom is packing this bag.

2. Jack sits packing mix to eat.

3. The cat sits licking mix too.

4. Dad stops the four men he is passing.

5. The fox is rocking her kit that naps.

MONITOR PROGRESS
- Fluency
- Inflected Ending -s
- Inflected Ending -ing
- High-Frequency Words

Name _____

Read the Words

1. bed
2. Ben
3. small
4. frog
5. traps
6. net
7. saw
8. sled
9. spot
10. tree
11. wet
12. your

MONITOR PROGRESS

- Short *e: e*
- Initial Consonant Blends
- High-Frequency Words

Get the Egg! **145e**

Name _____

Read the Sentences

1. Pop saw ten blocks.

2. Brad, look at your net.

3. The small frog is wet.

4. Meg saw a green spot.

5. We met Fran at the tree.

6. Ted, come and see your frog.

MONITOR PROGRESS
- Fluency
- Short e: e
- Initial Consonant Blends
- High-Frequency Words

Name _____

Read the Words

1. home

2. bus

3. into

4. rest

5. jump

6. many

7. pond

8. hugs

9. stump

10. mud

11. them

12. slug

MONITOR PROGRESS

- Short *u: u*
- **Final Consonant Blends**
- **High-Frequency Words**

Animal Park **171e**

Name _____

Read the Sentences

1. Pop runs into the pond.

2. Russ saw them in the sand.

3. Gus is home to rest.

4. The pups hop into the nest.

5. I see many buds on the plant.

6. He went to get many hugs from Mom.

MONITOR PROGRESS
- Fluency
- Short *u: u*
- Final Consonant Blends
- High-Frequency Words

Name _____

Read the Words

1. good
2. dash
3. shop
4. no
5. path
6. small
7. want

8. this
9. catch
10. said
11. walk
12. put
13. fall
14. talk

MONITOR PROGRESS
- Consonant Digraphs *sh, th*
- Vowel Sound in *ball: a, al*
- High-Frequency Words

A Big Fish for Max **43e**

Name _____

Read the Sentences

1. That was a good walk.

2. A small slug has no shell.

3. Put the salt on the shelf.

4. Pam can catch the ball with me.

5. I want all the fish.

6. Max said he can walk with Ted.

43f Communities • Unit 2 • Week 1

MONITOR PROGRESS
- Fluency
- Consonant Digraphs *sh, th*
- Vowel Sound in *ball: a, al*
- High-Frequency Words

Name _____

Read the Words

1.	name	**7.**	stage
2.	could	**8.**	cent
3.	page	**9.**	horse
4.	paper	**10.**	rake
5.	of	**11.**	old
6.	be	**12.**	trace

MONITOR PROGRESS
- Long *a: a_e*
- Consonants *c/s/, g/j/*
- High-Frequency Words

The Farmer in the Hat **77e**

Name _____

Read the Sentences

1. The tame horse can race.

2. Place the paper plate.

3. A game will be on stage.

4. We had an old cage for sale.

5. Beth made a hat of lace.

6. Don could make a face.

MONITOR PROGRESS
- Fluency
- Long *a*: *a_e*
- Consonants c/s/, g/j/
- High-Frequency Words

Name _____

Read the Words

1.	people	**8.**	smile
2.	chip	**9.**	patch
3.	work	**10.**	out
4.	nine	**11.**	when
5.	live	**12.**	lunch
6.	nice	**13.**	bite
7.	who	**14.**	graph

MONITOR PROGRESS
- Long *i: i_e*
- Consonant Digraphs *wh, ch, tch, ph*
- High-Frequency Words

Who Works Here? **103e**

Name _____

Read the Sentences

1. People like to see Phil.

2. When will it be time to go out?

3. Who can patch my kite?

4. I work at lunch all the time.

5. They live on a fine ranch.

6. A cat went out to catch the mice.

MONITOR PROGRESS

- Fluency
- Long *i: i_e*
- Consonant Digraphs *wh, ch, tch, ph*
- High-Frequency Words

103f   Communities • Unit 2 • Week 3

Name _____

Read the Words

1. down

2. I'm

3. note

4. together

5. we'll

6. broke

7. can't

8. home

9. inside

10. there

11. bone

12. now

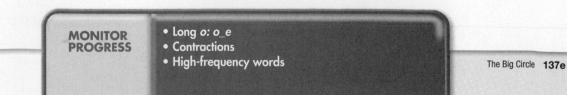

MONITOR PROGRESS

- Long *o: o_e*
- Contractions
- High-frequency words

The Big Circle **137e**

Name _____

Read the Sentences

1. Ants can't fall down a hole.

2. I'm inside my home.

3. We'll ride home together.

4. There isn't a note for Jim.

5. I broke my bike and now I'm sad.

6. He'll dig down for a bone.

MONITOR PROGRESS
- Fluency
- Long *o: o_e*
- Contractions
- High-Frequency Words

Name _____

Read the Words

1. huge   8. Pete

2. hunted   9. grow

3. cute   10. find

4. camped   11. around

5. tube   12. kicked

6. Steve   13. water

7. food   14. under

MONITOR PROGRESS

- Long *u: u_e;* Long *e: e_e*
- Inflected Ending *-ed*
- High-Frequency Words

Life in the Forest **169e**

Name _____

Read the Sentences

1. A huge fox hunted for food.

2. Steve camped where pines grow.

3. We wanted to find a cute pup.

4. Pete walked around the block.

5. The mule kicked the water dish.

6. Sam crushed a tube under a rock.

MONITOR PROGRESS
- Fluency
- Long *u: u_e;* Long *e: e_e*
- Inflected Ending *-ed*
- High-Frequency Words

Name _____

Read the Words

1.	she	**8.**	magnet
2.	family	**9.**	some
3.	button	**10.**	new
4.	feet	**11.**	basket
5.	their	**12.**	be
6.	keep	**13.**	other
7.	also	**14.**	rabbit

MONITOR PROGRESS

• Long *e: e, ee*
• Syllables VC/CV
• High-Frequency Words

Honey Bees **201e**

Name _____

Read the Sentences

1. She and her family pick up napkins.

2. We saw some cute kittens.

3. They have seeds in their baskets.

4. He has my other mitten.

5. Jan keeps rabbits and also sells them.

MONITOR PROGRESS
- Fluency
- Long *e: e, ee*
- Syllables VC/CV
- High-Frequency Words

Name _____

Read the Sentences

1. We wish for a sunny day.

2. Pam saw nothing go by.

3. She tells jokes that are always so funny.

4. No planes will fly on that day next week.

5. We will try to stack things on the shelf.

6. The puppy will be fine if it stays here.

7. He made everything in the shop muddy.

8. He knows it is windy, but nothing should blow away.

9. The shy girl always smiles at me in school.

10. The sly fox stays so far away that I can't take its picture.

MONITOR PROGRESS
• Vowel Sounds of *y*
• Syllable Pattern CV
• High-Frequency Words

A Place to Play **43e**

Name _____

Read the Story

A Happy Trip

Do you like to take trips? Jo likes to go on　11
trips. She gets her things together. Then she　19
packs her three bags. When she has left, she　28
likes to stop and look at the big green hills.　38
When Jo has looked at all the hills she drives　48
to her last stop. She wants to get gifts for her　59
pals. She has a lot of fun! She stays for five　70
days. Then, it is time to go home. She drives　80
past a lot of bikes, buses, and trucks. She　89
sees sheep on the grass. The last thing she　98
does is go inside her home so she can take　108
a nap!　110

MONITOR
PROGRESS
• Check Fluency
• Sequence

Name _____

Read the Sentences

1. Did you ever skate at an outside rink?

2. Frank made his treehouse big enough.

3. There were some pinecones by the swings.

4. Sandy put her own things in her backpack.

5. We will bring any homework we need.

6. My family sang every day last weekend.

7. Hank sure ate that pancake fast.

MONITOR PROGRESS
- Fluency
- Consonant patterns *ng, nk*
- Compound words
- High-frequency words

Ruby in Her Own Time **83e**

Name _____

Read the Story

Cupcake and Link

Last weekend, Frank gave his dog Cupcake 7
a bath. He filled the bathtub with water. Then Frank 17
picked up Cupcake. He put Cupcake into the bathtub. 26
Plunk! Cupcake sat inside the bathtub. Frank sang 34
a song. Everything was fine. Cupcake got her bath. 43

Frank also gave his cat Link a bath. The bathtub 53
was too big. So, Frank filled the sink with water. He put 65
Link in the sink. Link flung water all around. Then he 76
yanked himself from Frank's hands and jumped out. 84

Link sure did not like the bath. How could Frank 94
keep Link in the sink? He had to think of something. 105
Frank looked inside his backpack. He got a little 114
ball. When Link had the ball, he did not jump out 125
of the sink. So, Link got his bath, too. 134

MONITOR PROGRESS
• Fluency
• Compare and Contrast

Name _____

Read the Sentences

1. Jan fixes very good pork.

2. More buses came to the school.

3. His house has two benches on the porch.

4. Her friends put corn on the dishes.

5. Sam fishes in the water away from the shore.

6. The old car passes the store on the way home.

7. Dave made a fort with boxes in his house.

8. Our friends wore hats with blue patches on them.

9. A very bad storm made the red foxes hide.

10. Liz watches Ann sort the math papers at school.

MONITOR PROGRESS
- Ending -*es*; Plural -*es*
- Vowels: *r*-Controlled *or, ore*
- High-Frequency Words

The Class Pet **117e**

Name _____

Read the Story

Morning Chores

Cole and Jess met on Vic's porch one morning. "Can   10
you play ball with us?" asked Cole.   17

"I have chores for this morning," said Vic. "I must   27
pick corn. I must sort my toys. I also have dishes to dry.   40
Next, I must stack boxes. Then I must pick up branches."   51

"We can help," said Jess. "We can help with all   61
those jobs, Vic. Then we can play ball."   69

Vic's mom watched Cole, Jess, and Vic as she   78
fixed lunch for them. "Vic is so lucky to have such   89
fine pals," she said.   93

In no time at all, no more jobs were left. Now they   105
could play ball.   108

MONITOR PROGRESS
- Fluency
- Fact and Opinion

Name _____

Read the Sentences

1. Kim dropped a few cards.

2. Soon Bill jogged to the barn.

3. Meg is getting to be afraid in this dark cave.

4. How well is Mark hitting the ball?

5. Luke napped as Jack read in the yard.

6. We met Liz running in this park at lunch time again.

7. We will read the beginning part.

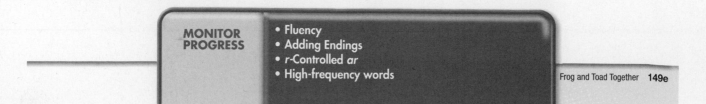

MONITOR PROGRESS
- Fluency
- Adding Endings
- *r*-Controlled *ar*
- High-frequency words

Frog and Toad Together **149e**

Name _____

Read the Story

How to Fix Up a Yard

Try these five ways to make a yard nice.	9
One way is by planting plenty of trees. Trees make	19
spots of shade, so you can rest if the sun is hot. Pine	32
trees have a nice fresh smell.	38
Make flower beds in lots of places. I planted pink	48
and red roses on all sides of my yard. Roses smell so	60
sweet!	61
Be wise and cut the grass as it starts to get tall, or it	75
will soon look messy. Cutting it again in a week or so	87
will keep it short.	91
Get rid of weeds! Weeds grow fast in summer and	101
make a yard look bad. It can be hard to dig them up,	114
but you will be glad you did.	121
Did you do all these jobs? Then it is time for the last	134
task. Set a bench under a tree so you can sit and chat	147
with pals. That is the best part of keeping a fine yard!	159

MONITOR PROGRESS
- Check Fluency
- Author's Purpose

Name _____

Read the Sentences

1. He's done with his first chore.

2. You've got to wait in line for that clerk.

3. This nurse will know if we're getting sick.

4. They're going to visit places by the shore to surf.

5. I've asked that girl to help me push this cart uphill.

6. I know I got a big fish if it's jerking my fishing rod.

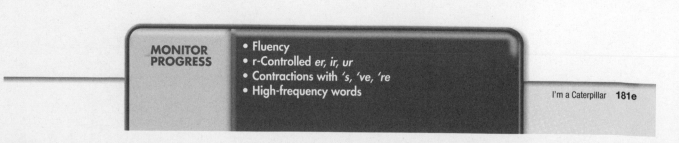

MONITOR PROGRESS
- Fluency
- r-Controlled *er, ir, ur*
- Contractions with *'s, 've, 're*
- High-frequency words

I'm a Caterpillar **181e**

Name _____

Read the Story

My Bird Pete

    Birds make the best pets. My bird Pete is green. At   11
times, he sits in his cage. He just naps or eats. Then he   24
hops out and flaps his wings. It's fun to see him fly in my   38
room. He lands on my desk or my lamp. If I sit still, he   52
perches on my head!   56

    It's not hard to take care of birds. You feed them   67
seeds and water in cups. Pete takes baths all by himself   78
in his small pink tub. That is so cute! He splashes me a   91
lot with his wings.   95

    Pete can talk. He can say "Snack time! Snack time!"   105
If I feed him a bit of grape, he yells "Sweet! Sweet!" No   118
other pet is as smart and funny as my Pete.   128

MONITOR PROGRESS
- Fluency
- Fact and Opinion

Name _____

Read the Sentences

1. Cut this grass before you trim the thickest hedge.

2. That taller judge waved good-bye to us.

3. My shortest horse won't trot to the edge of this cliff.

4. Oh, he just made the smudge on his shirt bigger!

5. Does Tad like my sweetest fudge?

6. Set this darker vase on the right side of that ledge.

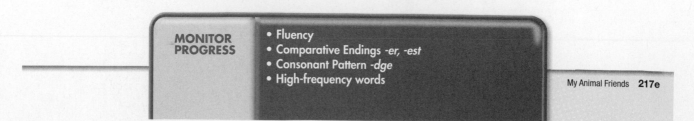

MONITOR PROGRESS
- Fluency
- Comparative Endings *-er, -est*
- Consonant Pattern *-dge*
- High-frequency words

My Animal Friends **217e**

Name _____

Read the Story

    Clark had a horse named Star. Star was his fastest   10
horse. Clark wanted Star to jump, but Star didn't jump.   20
If she came to a fence or hedge, she just stopped. She   32
didn't budge.   34

    Every day Clark went to the barn. He rode Star all   45
morning. Clark patted Star's neck and spoke to her.   54
"Won't you try jumping?" he asked.   60

    One day Clark was humming as he ate figs. "Figs!   70
That is it!" he said.   75

    Clark grabbed a bunch of figs. He let Star try one.   86
Then he let Star see him put the figs on the far side of   100
the fence. Star ran faster than ever before. She ran right   111
to the fence and jumped over it!   118

    Clark hugged Star. "Oh, what a brave girl!" he said   128
as he fed her a fig.   134

MONITOR PROGRESS
- Check Fluency
- Draw Conclusions

Name _____

Read the Sentences

1. Nell's mom was surprised that it rained.

2. Would Ben's train be late?

3. The workers would like to plant grain in the farmer's field.

4. Jane's main worry was her dog.

5. Nan gives us hay from the farmer's barn.

6. Nate's book is about a snail.

7. Did you enjoy Jed's play?

8. Would you wait for Pat's call?

9. The students' teacher told them to wait until noon for a surprise.

10. Mom pays for the family's groceries while Jane gives the bags to Dan.

MONITOR PROGRESS
- Vowel Digraphs *ai, ay*
- Singular and Plural Possessives
- High-Frequency Words

Mama's Birthday Present **51e**

Name _____

Read the Story

Gail's Dog Plays

    Rex's tail wagged as he waited for the ball. Gail   10
tossed it to him. Rex liked playing this game, so he   21
ran after the ball. That was fun for a while. But then   33
Rex saw three jays in a nest. The birds' nest was up   45
in a tall tree. Rex started barking. Then he ran after   56
the birds.   58

    Rex ran and ran. He went on a trail by the pond.   70
Then he ran into Miss May's yard.   77

    "Oh, no," Gail said. "Where did my dog go? This   87
is quite a day!"   91

    "My dog's name is Rex. Did you see him?" she   101
asked Miss May. Gail and Miss May looked around.   110
Then they spotted Rex. This time he was having fun   120
running after a skunk.   124

    Gail hid her eyes. "I hope that skunk isn't going to   135
spray him!" she said. Rex just looked at her and   145
barked.   146

MONITOR PROGRESS
- Fluency
- Draw conclusions

Name _____

Read the Sentences

1. The beads had the prettiest colors.

2. Mike drew the silliest beak on the bird.

3. We hurried over to the beach.

4. The sign said they had fried fish and bread.

5. Please show us how you pried the lid off the box.

6. Ron spied the box and we each saw the great gift.

7. Jen carried the cream to show us she would not spill it.

8. I cried each time I drew a picture of our lost dog.

9. Steve worried that the waves could be over his head.

10. Draw a picture of the funniest dream you have ever had.

MONITOR PROGRESS
- Vowel Digraph *ea*
- Adding Endings
- High-Frequency Words

Cinderella **87e**

Name _____

Read the Story

Fun at the Beach

"Mom, may we please go to the beach?" asked   9
Jean.   10

"I wish I could go, but I have so much work I must   23
do at home first."   27

"I can help," Jean said with a smile.   35

Jean worked hard. She dusted. She dried the   43
dishes. She cleaned the dirtiest sink. She helped lift   52
three heavy boxes.   55

Everything got finished quickly. "That was so much   63
easier with a helper!" said Jean's mom.   70

Jean and her mom went to the beach. They walked   80
on the hot sand. Jean picked up shells, feathers, and   90
sea glass. She even spied a cute seal.   98

Jean had so much fun. It was one of the happiest   109
days in her life.   113

MONITOR PROGRESS
- Check Fluency
- Theme

Name _____

Read the Sentences

1. Don painted wild stripes on the bowl.

2. I found a crow scratching in the dirt.

3. Joan put a bit of squash in her mouth.

4. Ted had to scrape the toast before he took a bite.

5. Show me where Kate found the string.

6. Mark may spray the box a wild color to make it glow.

7. An animal in the oak tree screeched once.

8. Tad took the box and tied it with his own string.

9. In the spring the logs will flow to the mouth of the river.

10. Once Zack split a load of wood.

MONITOR PROGRESS
- Vowel Digraphs *oa, ow*
- Three-Letter Consonant Blends
- High-Frequency Words

A Trip to Washington, D.C. **119e**

Name _____

Read the Story

Frogs, Toads, and Spring

    I like the spring. My mom and I take walks. Once   11

she took me to see big oak trees. We saw yellow   22

leaves blow in the wind. We took wild yellow roses   32

home with us.   35

    We go to a little stream too. It is down the street   47

from my house. The stream has lots of wild frogs   57

and toads. I like to watch the toads splash in the   68

water. The frogs croak a lot too.   75

    Once I saw some fish in a stream. I wanted to   86

show them to my mom. We slowed down to see   96

them. One wild fish splashed water on my new   105

coat.   106

MONITOR PROGRESS
- Fluency
- Facts and Details

Name _____

Read the Sentences

1. Eight wrens soared over the field.

2. Do not touch the pie or the knife.

3. The big knot in the tie made me laugh.

4. Jan will knit eight bright hats.

5. I know the fries are too hot to touch.

6. Sue will write about a flight to the moon.

7. Do not laugh at the sight of my wreath.

8. The right knob is above the shelf.

9. The chief was wrapped in a blanket under the moon.

10. The wrenches lie on a shelf above the three hammers.

MONITOR PROGRESS
- Vowel Digraphs *ie, igh*
- Consonant Patterns *kn, wr*
- High-Frequency Words

A Southern Ranch **153e**

Name _____

Read the Story

Wren Writes Songs

"I like to write songs," said Wren.   7

She wrote a long song. Then she sang her song for   18
Ben. Wren had a knack for singing.   25

This song was about a girl called Jen. Her dog ran   36
far away. Jen missed her dog. Jen cried and cried.   46

"That song is sad," whispered Ben.   52

"I know," said Wren, sighing.   57

"Can you write a funny song?" asked Ben.   65

"I think I can," said Wren.   71

Wren wrote about a sneaky thief. This thief stole   80
pies. Then he tried to hide in a field. The moon shone   92
bright. He could not hide in that light. That sneaky thief   103
was a billy goat! The billy goat had a nice white coat.   115

"That song makes me laugh," said Ben.   122

"I will sing it one more time!" cried Wren.   131

MONITOR PROGRESS
- Check Fluency
- Facts and Details

Name _____

Read the Sentences

1. Jay's blue backpack is in his room.

2. Ned stood on this new racetrack.

3. That picture with Sue in the baseball cap is cute.

4. I thought three blackbirds just flew by.

5. Remember that fresh fruit is in this lunchbag.

MONITOR PROGRESS
- Compound Words
- Vowel Digraphs *ue, ew, ui*
- High-Frequency Words

Peter's Chair **189e**

Name _____

Read the Story

Sue Goes Camping

Sue's family went on a camping trip. They had 9
new blue tents. Sue liked camping with Mom and Dad. 19

One day, Dad and Sue went for a walk. Sue wished 30
to see a fox. They spotted three bluebirds in oak trees. 41
They spotted five rabbits and a few snakes in tall grass. 52
But they did not see a fox. Sue felt sad. 62

Back at the campfire, Dad and Sue ate stew and 72
fruit. Then they had snacks. Mom left bags of chips on 83
a big stone bench. 87

The next day, those chips were missing. Who had 96
the chips? Then Sue spied clues. She spied tracks in 106
sand. Sue knew these were fox tracks. But she did not 117
see the fox. "Maybe next time," Sue thought. 125

MONITOR
PROGRESS

- Fluency
- Theme

Name _____

Read the Sentences

1. Kate swam across the pool quickly.

2. We were thankful the dance was in a cool hall.

3. The tool is useful because it is small.

4. You can be graceful in shoes or boots.

5. She quickly opened the gift and showed me the smooth silk.

6. Rick told us he would gladly be here at noon.

7. The brightly colored bird flew across the room.

8. I enjoy my weekly visit to dance school.

9. We will now have our troop meetings only once a month instead of weekly.

10. The snoop opened the letter slowly.

MONITOR PROGRESS
- Suffixes *-ly, -ful*
- Vowel Sound in *moon: oo*
- High-Frequency Words

Henry and Mudge **227e**

Name _____

Read the Story

Penny's Messy Room

"This room is a mess!" said Penny's mom.   8
Penny liked to be helpful. She got a broom and   18
started sweeping. She slowly swept up a big pile   27
of dust and dirt. She kept sweeping and sweeping.   36
The pile grew higher and higher.   42

Then the phone rang. Penny went to the phone.   51
She talked for a long time. When she hung up, the   62
phone rang again. This time, she talked longer.   70
Was Penny forgetful? Yes! She forgot about all that   79
dust and dirt.   82

Penny's dog Scooter was in the backyard. He barked   91
to come in. Penny let him in. Scooter ran in quickly.   102
He zoomed to the pile of dust and dirt. His feet slid   114
and skidded. Dust and dirt flew all over. Soon Penny's   124
room was messier than before!   129

MONITOR PROGRESS
• Check Fluency
• Cause and Effect

Name _____

Read the Sentences

1. The dog had little brown eyes.

2. Now the turtle is behind the tree.

3. My uncle drove toward town.

4. A single cow walked along the path.

5. The clown with the big eyes can juggle.

6. The dogs pulling the sled made a circle and started to howl.

7. Jill walked out toward the puddle.

8. The girl in the middle never made a sound.

9. Please hang the purple towel behind the door.

10. Jenna saw a mouse wiggle along the ledge.

MONITOR PROGRESS
- Diphthongs *ow, ou*
- Final Syllable *-le*
- High-Frequency Words

Tippy-Toe Chick, Go! **51e**

Name _____

Read the Story

My Uncle's Ranch

My Uncle Jud owns a cattle ranch. I stayed with him   11
for a week last summer.   16

I rode a brown horse. Her name was Apple. Uncle   26
Jud had a new saddle just for me. I helped Uncle Jud on   39
the ranch.   41

One day we went out to check on the cattle. A cow   53
was missing. We checked behind rocks. We looked   61
along a line of trees. But we did not see the cow.   73

At last we found her. That little cow had gotten stuck   84
in a mud puddle. Uncle Jud pulled her out with a rope.   96

The cow made a loud sound but she had happy   106
eyes. She seemed glad to be free!   113

I hope I can spend next summer on Uncle Jud's   123
ranch.   124

MONITOR PROGRESS
- Check Fluency
- Character, Setting, and Plot

Name _____

Read the Sentences

1. My dad should know that tigers are cats.

2. Even Annie sat at that wood counter.

3. Ned planted tulips out by the back door.

4. Tom and I loved to sail south on the rapids.

5. A total of three plants grow in a wood pot.

6. You should not eat the lemon.

7. Amy loved eating sprouts on her salad.

MONITOR PROGRESS

- Vowel Patterns *ow, ou*
- Syllables V/CV, VC/V
- High-Frequency Words

Mole and the Baby Bird **89e**

Name _____

Read the Story

Pout and His Pals

There was a tiger named Pout. He lived in a cave. 11

When he came out of his cave, he would shout at 22
all of his pals. 26

"Ouch!" said his pal, Hippo, rubbing his ear. "Pout 35
is so loud!" 38

"I know!" cried his pal, Cow. "He may blow his top!" 49

Hippo and Cow ran away. That made Pout sad. 58

A little mouse saw Pout. Mouse asked, "Why are 67
you sad, Pout?" 70

Pout said, "Hippo and Cow will not play with me." 80

Mouse said, "I will show you how to fix that." 90

The next day, Pout, Hippo, Cow, and Mouse 98
played. Pout did not have a loud mouth. The pals 108
played and had fun all day. 114

MONITOR PROGRESS
• Check Fluency
• Draw Conclusions

Name _____

Read the Sentences

1. None of the wood is piled in the shed.

2. The cook is tasting another bit of food.

3. Ty hoped to get another wool scarf.

4. None of the girls took the dancing class.

5. His dancing footwork is among the best there is.

6. This book is among the three Steve traded.

7. Tess will be hiking to the brook instead of up the hill.

8. None of the dogs raced to where I stood.

9. The cat is hiding in its nook instead of eating.

10. Look for another skating champ at the rink.

MONITOR PROGRESS
- Vowel Sound in *foot: oo*
- Adding Endings
- High-Frequency Words

Dot & Jabber and the Great Acorn Mystery **129e**

Name _____

Read the Story

A Good Idea

"It might be fun to get a fish tank in this   11
classroom," stated Brook.   14

"That will cost a lot," said Miss Woods.   22

"This is how we can do it. We can pay for the tank   35
by selling cupcakes and cookies," said Mark.   42

So the class started making baked goods. The girls   51
baked cupcakes with white icing. The boys baked   59
cookies with green icing. Then they tasted the   67
cupcakes and cookies. Yum! It was all quite good!   76
The boys and girls liked it all.   83

Miss Woods's class got the fish tank they   91
had hoped for. The girls added plants. The boys   100
added fish. Brook and Mark each had a big smile.   110
Miss Woods smiled too.   114

MONITOR PROGRESS
• Fluency
• Compare and Contrast

Name _____

Read the Sentences

1. Nate will act as the boys' line leader today.

2. The gardener moved the soil against the plants.

3. An actor can use all kinds of toys on stage.

4. That driver loaded heavy coins on his truck.

5. Joy goes to visit the baker.

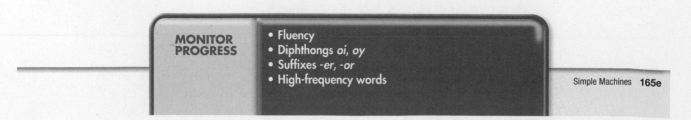

MONITOR PROGRESS
- Fluency
- Diphthongs *oi, oy*
- Suffixes *-er, -or*
- High-frequency words

Simple Machines **165e**

Name _____

Read the Story

King Troy

Troy was king in a distant land. He did not wish to   12
be king. So he tried being a sailor.   20

Troy was a good sailor. But he did not get joy at sea.   33
So he tried being a farmer.   39

He was a good farmer. But he did not like handling   50
soil. So he tried being a painter.   57

Troy was a good painter. But he got oil paint all   68
over himself. So he tried being a banker.   76

He was a good banker. But he did not like counting   87
coins each day. He did not know what to do.   97

People begged Troy, "Come back to the royal palace.   106
We need you as king."   111

So Troy went home, and he became a fine king.   121

MONITOR PROGRESS
- Check Fluency
- Main Idea and Details

Name _____

Read the Sentences

1. In science we read about hawks that live downtown.

2. Paul played football early this morning.

3. Ted will learn how to make oatmeal with fruit sauce.

4. Did he crawl through the soybean field?

5. That pig built his straw house near the railroad.

6. We saw that play to learn how seaweed grows.

7. He hauled wood when he built our sailboat.

8. Kim can draw in moonlight through the night.

9. Dawn found rainbows in her science book.

10. Austin got up early and played on his seesaw.

MONITOR PROGRESS
- Vowel Sound in *ball: aw, au*
- Vowel Digraphs and Diphthongs
- High-Frequency Words

Alexander Graham Bell **201e**

Name _____

Read the Story

Dawn's Gift

Dawn looked at her sweater. There were little   8
holes in the arms. She put the sweater in the laundry.   19

"Mom, may I have a shawl for my birthday?"   28

"We will see," said Mom.   33

Dawn went to her room. First she put on a dress   44
with rainbows on it. Next she slipped on her boots.   54
Last she put a straw hat on her head. "A shawl would   66
look good with this outfit," she said to her cat. Muffin   77
just yawned and licked her paw.   83

On her birthday, Dawn woke up at six. Then her   93
mom sang "Happy Birthday." At last Dawn opened   101
her gift. It was wrapped in gauze. Dawn saw a soft,   112
blue shawl. Her mom had knitted it.   119

"Thanks, Mom." Dawn and Mom smiled and   126
hugged each other.   129

MONITOR PROGRESS
- Check Fluency
- Sequence

Name _____

Read the Sentences

1. Ron is unable to carry that heavy gold.

2. Peg reread most of that story after she answered her door.

3. Did Ned find this poor unhappy dog?

4. That child had a different way to rewrap the box.

5. Unlock this cage and carry my wild bird.

6. I don't mind if Ann uses a different brush to repaint her wall.

7. Zack replanted different roses by that post.

MONITOR PROGRESS
- Fluency
- Prefixes *un-*, *re-*
- Long *o:o*; long *i: i*
- High-frequency words

The Stone Garden **241e**

Name _____

Read the Story
Gold

Roy was a poor man. His town was poor too. 10

One day Roy sold his house. He left home to look 21

for gold. He said he would come back and help his 32

town when he became rich. 37

Roy got a mule. He was unable to take much. 47

He walked to a stream. Roy unpacked his mule. He 57

looked but did not find gold. Roy felt unhappy. 66

A man told him that most of the gold was over the 78

next hill. He repacked his mule and went over the hill. 89

He unloaded his mule and then he slept. 97

The next day, Roy worked hard. He found the 106

most gold he had ever seen! He replaced his mule 116

with a horse and rode home. Roy was rich and 126

kind. He helped his neighbors fix up their town. 135

MONITOR PROGRESS
• Check Fluency
• Theme

Assessment Charts and Student Progress Report
from
First Stop First Grade

Fluency Progress Chart, Grade 1

Name

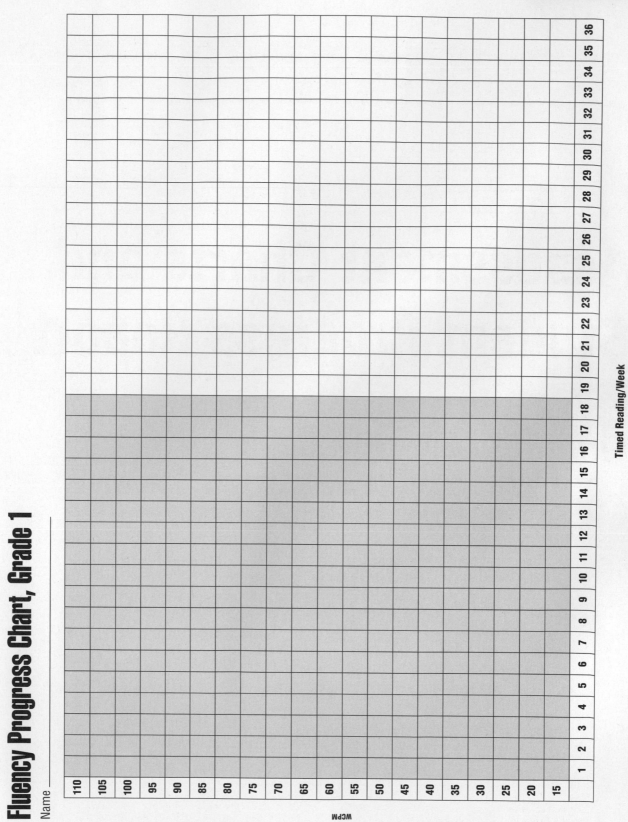

WCPM

Timed Reading/Week

Word/Sentence Reading Chart

USE WITH GRADE **1** READY, SET, READ!

	Phonics		High-Frequency		Reteach	Reassess: Words Correct
	Total Words	Words Correct	Total Words	Words Correct	✔	
Week 1 *Sam*						
Consonants /m/m; s/s/, ss; /t/t	6					
Short a	6					
High-Frequency Words			4			
Week 2 *Snap!*						
Consonants /k/c, /p/p, /n/n	13					
Short a	14					
High-Frequency Words			6			
Week 3 *Tip and Tam*						
Consonants /f/f, ff; /b/b; /g/g	8					
Short i	10					
High-Frequency Words			7			
Week 4 *The Big Top*						
Consonants /d/d; /l/l, ll; /h/h	13					
Short o	13					
High-Frequency Words			7			
Week 5 *School Day*						
Consonants /r/r, /w/w, /j/j, /k/k	12					
Short e	11					
High-Frequency Words			9			
Week 6 *Farmers Market*						
Consonants /v/v; /y/y; /z/z, zz; /kw/qu	9					
Short u	6					
High-Frequency Words			7			
Unit Scores	121		40			

- **RECORD SCORES** Use this chart to record scores for the Day 5 Word/Sentence Reading Assessment.

- **RETEACH PHONICS SKILLS** If the child is unable to read all the tested phonics words, then reteach the phonics skills using the Reteach lessons in *First Stop*.

- **PRACTICE HIGH-FREQUENCY WORDS** If the child is unable to read all the tested high-frequency words, then provide additional practice for the week's words.

- **REASSESS** Choose two different sentences for children to read.

Word/Sentence Reading Chart

USE WITH GRADE 1 UNIT 1

	Phonics		High-Frequency		Reteach	Reassess: Words Correct
	Total Words	Words Correct	Total Words	Words Correct	✔	
Week 1 *Sam, Come Back!*						
Short *a*	13					
Final *ck*	5					
High-Frequency Words			7			
Week 2 *Pig in a Wig*						
Short *i*	11					
Final *x*	6					
High-Frequency Words			6			
Week 3 *The Big Blue Ox*						
Short *o*	10					
-*s* Plurals, /z/s	4					
High-Frequency Words			8			
Week 4 *A Fox and a Kit*						
Inflected Ending -*s*	6					
Inflected Ending -*ing*	6					
High-Frequency Words			8			
Week 5 *Get the Egg!*						
Short *e*	7					
Initial Blends	6					
High-Frequency Words			6			
Week 6 *Animal Park*						
Short *u*	8					
Final Blends	6					
High-Frequency Words			6			
Unit Scores	88		41			

- **RECORD SCORES** Use this chart to record scores for the Day 5 Word/Sentence Reading Assessment.

- **RETEACH PHONICS SKILLS** If the child is unable to read all the tested phonics words, then reteach the phonics skills using the Reteach lessons in *First Stop*.

- **PRACTICE HIGH-FREQUENCY WORDS** If the child is unable to read all the tested high-frequency words, then provide additional practice for the week's words.

- **REASSESS** Choose two different sentences for children to read.

Name _____

Word/Sentence Reading Chart

USE WITH GRADE 1 UNIT 2

	Phonics		High-Frequency		Reteach	Reassess: Words Correct
	Total Words	Words Correct	Total Words	Words Correct	✔	
Week 1 *A Big Fish for Max*						
Digraphs *sh, th*	6					
Vowel Sound in *ball*	6					
High-Frequency Words			8			
Week 2 *The Farmer in the Hat*						
Long *a (a_e)*	9					
/s/*c* and /j/*g*	6					
High-Frequency Words			8			
Week 3 *Who Works Here?*						
Long *i (i_e)*	6					
Digraphs *wh, ch, tch, ph*	7					
High-Frequency Words			7			
Week 4 *The Big Circle*						
Long *o (o_e)*	6					
Contractions	5					
High-Frequency Words			7			
Week 5 *Life in a Forest*						
Long *u*, Long *e (u_e, e_e)*	7					
Inflected Ending *-ed*	5					
High-Frequency Words			8			
Week 6 *Honey Bees*						
Long *e: e, ee*	6					
Syllables VC/CV	6					
High-Frequency Words			8			
Unit Scores	75		46			

- **RECORD SCORES** Use this chart to record scores for the Day 5 Word/Sentence Reading Assessment.
- **RETEACH PHONICS SKILLS** If the child is unable to read all the tested phonics words, then reteach the phonics skills using the Reteach lessons in *First Stop*.
- **PRACTICE HIGH-FREQUENCY WORDS** If the child is unable to read all the tested high-frequency words, then provide additional practice for the week's words.
- **REASSESS** Choose two different sentences for children to read.

Copyright © by Pearson Education, Inc., or its affiliates. All Rights Reserved.

369

Sentence Reading Chart

USE WITH GRADE 1 UNIT 3

	Phonics		High-Frequency		Reteach	Reassess: Words Correct
	Total Words	Words Correct	Total Words	Words Correct	✔	
Week 1 *A Place to Play*						
Long *e* and long *i* spelled *y*	2					
Syllable Patterns CV	2					
High-Frequency Words			2			
Week 2 *Ruby in Her Own Time*						
Final *ng, nk*	2					
Compound Words	2					
High-Frequency Words			2			
Week 3 *The Class Pet*						
Ending *-es*; Plural *-es*	2					
r-Controlled *or, ore*	2					
High-Frequency Words			2			
Week 4 *Frog and Toad Together*						
Inflected Endings *-ed, -ing*	2					
r-Controlled *ar*	2					
High-Frequency Words			2			
Week 5 *I'm a Caterpillar*						
r-Controlled *er, ir, ur*	2					
Contractions *'s, 've, 're*	2					
High-Frequency Words			2			
Week 6 *Where Are My Animal Friends?*						
Comparative Endings *-er, -est*	2					
/j/*dge*	2					
High-Frequency Words			2			
Unit Scores	24		12			

- **RECORD SCORES** Use this chart to record scores for the Day 5 Sentence Reading Assessment.

- **RETEACH PHONICS SKILLS** If the child is unable to read all the tested phonics words, then reteach the phonics skills using the Reteach lessons in *First Stop*.

- **PRACTICE HIGH-FREQUENCY WORDS** If the child is unable to read all the tested high-frequency words, then provide additional practice for the week's words.

- **REASSESS** Choose two different sentences for children to read.

Sentence Reading Chart

USE WITH GRADE 1 UNIT 4

	Phonics		High-Frequency		Reteach	Reassess: Words Correct
	Total Words	Words Correct	Total Words	Words Correct	✔	
Week 1 *Mama's Birthday Present*						
Vowel Digraphs *ai, ay*	2					
Possessives	2					
High-Frequency Words			2			
Week 2 *Cinderella*						
Vowel Digraph *ea*	2					
Adding Endings	2					
High-Frequency Words			2			
Week 3 *A Trip to Washington, D.C.*						
Vowel Digraphs *oa, ow*	2					
Three-Letter Blends	2					
High-Frequency Words			2			
Week 4 *A Southern Ranch*						
Vowel Digraphs *ie, igh*	2					
/n/*kn* and /r/*wr*	2					
High-Frequency Words			2			
Week 5 *Peter's Chair*						
Compound Words	2					
Vowel Digraphs *ue, ew, ui*	2					
High-Frequency Words			2			
Week 6 *Henry and Mudge and Mrs. Hopper's House*						
Suffixes *-ly, -ful*	2					
Vowel Sound In *moon*	2					
High-Frequency Words			2			
Unit Scores	24		12			

- **RECORD SCORES** Use this chart to record scores for the Day 5 Sentence Reading Assessment.

- **RETEACH PHONICS SKILLS** If the child is unable to read all the tested phonics words, then reteach the phonics skills using the Reteach lessons in *First Stop*.

- **PRACTICE HIGH-FREQUENCY WORDS** If the child is unable to read all the tested high-frequency words, then provide additional practice for the week's words.

- **REASSESS** Choose two different sentences for children to read.

Name _____

Sentence Reading Chart

USE WITH GRADE 1 UNIT 5

	Phonics		High-Frequency		Reteach	Reassess: Words Correct
	Total Words	Words Correct	Total Words	Words Correct	✔	
Week 1 *Tippy-Toe Chick, Go!*						
Diphthongs *ow, ou*	2					
Final Syllable *le*	2					
High-Frequency Words			2			
Week 2 *Mole and the Baby Bird*						
Vowel Patterns *ow, ou*	2					
Syllables v/cv, vc/v	2					
High-Frequency Words			2			
Week 3 *Dot and Jabber and the Great Acorn Mystery*						
Vowel sound in *foot*	2					
Inflected Endings	2					
High-Frequency Words			2			
Week 4 *Simple Machines*						
Diphthongs *oi, oy*	2					
Suffixes *-er, -or*	2					
High-Frequency Words			2			
Week 5 *Alexander Graham Bell: A Great Inventor*						
Vowels *aw, au*	2					
Vowel Digraphs and Diphthongs	2					
High-Frequency Words			2			
Week 6 *The Stone Garden*						
Prefixes *un-, re-*	2					
Long *i, o*	2					
High-Frequency Words			2			
Unit Scores	24		12			

- **RECORD SCORES** Use this chart to record scores for the Day 5 Sentence Reading Assessment.

- **RETEACH PHONICS SKILLS** If the child is unable to read all the tested phonics words, then reteach the phonics skills using the Reteach lessons in *First Stop*.

- **PRACTICE HIGH-FREQUENCY WORDS** If the child is unable to read all the tested high-frequency words, then provide additional practice for the week's words.

- **REASSESS** Choose two different sentences for children to read.

Student Progress Report: Grade 1

Name _____

This chart lists the skills taught in this program. Record each student's progress toward mastery of the skills covered during this school year. Use this chart to track the coverage of these skills.

Literature Standards	Date	Date	Date
Key Ideas and Details			
Ask and answer questions about key details in a text.			
Retell stories, including key details, and demonstrate understanding of their central message or lesson.			
Describe characters, settings, and major events in a story, using key details.			
Craft and Structure			
Identify words and phrases in stories or poems that suggest feelings or appeal to the senses.			
Explain major differences between books that tell stories and books that give information, drawing on a wide reading of a range of text types.			
Identify who is telling the story at various points in a text.			
Integration of Knowledge and Ideas			
Use illustrations and details in a story to describe its characters, setting, or events.			
Compare and contrast the adventures and experiences of characters in stories.			
Range of Reading and Level of Text Complexity			
With prompting and support, read prose and poetry of appropriate complexity for grade 1.			

Informational Text Standards	Date	Date	Date
Key Ideas and Details			
Ask and answer questions about key details in a text.			
Identify the main topic and retell key details of a text.			
Describe the connection between two individuals, events, ideas, or pieces of information in a text.			
Craft and Structure			
Ask and answer questions to help determine or clarify the meaning of words and phrases in a text.			
Know and use various text features (e.g., headings, tables of contents, glossaries, electronic menus, icons) to locate key facts or information in a text.			
Distinguish between information provided by pictures or other illustrations and information provided by the words in a text.			
Integration of Knowledge and Ideas			
Use the illustrations and details in a text to describe its key ideas.			
Identify the reasons an author gives to support points in a text.			
Identify basic similarities in and differences between two texts on the same topic (e.g., in illustrations, descriptions, or procedures).			
Range of Reading and Level of Text Complexity			
With prompting and support, read informational texts appropriately complex for grade 1.			

Foundational Skills Standards	Date	Date	Date
Print Concepts			
Demonstrate understanding of the organization and basic features of print.			
Recognize the distinguishing features of a sentence (e.g., first word, capitalization, ending punctuation).			
Phonological Awareness			
Demonstrate understanding of spoken words, syllables, and sounds (phonemes).			
Distinguish long from short vowel sounds in spoken single-syllable words.			
Orally produce single-syllable words by blending sounds (phonemes), including consonant blends.			
Isolate and pronounce initial, medial vowel, and final sounds (phonemes) in spoken single-syllable words.			
Segment spoken single-syllable words into their complete sequence of individual sounds (phonemes).			
Phonics and Word Recognition			
Know and apply grade-level phonics and word analysis skills in decoding words.			
Know the spelling-sound correspondences for common consonant digraphs (two letters that represent one sound).			
Decode regularly spelled one-syllable words.			
Know final -e and common vowel team conventions for representing long vowel sounds.			
Use knowledge that every syllable must have a vowel sound to determine the number of syllables in a printed word.			
Decode two-syllable words following basic patterns by breaking the words into syllables.			
Read words with inflectional endings.			
Recognize and read grade-appropriate irregularly spelled words.			

Foundational Skills Standards	Date	Date	Date
Fluency			
Read with sufficient accuracy and fluency to support comprehension.			
Read on-level text with purpose and understanding.			
Read on-level text orally with accuracy, appropriate rate, and expression on successive readings.			
Use context to confirm or self-correct word recognition and understanding, rereading as necessary.			

Writing Standards	Date	Date	Date
Text Types and Purposes			
Write opinion pieces in which students introduce the topic or name the book they are writing about, state an opinion, supply a reason for the opinion, and provide some sense of closure.			
Write informative/explanatory texts in which students name a topic, supply some facts about the topic, and provide some sense of closure.			
Write narratives in which students recount two or more appropriately sequenced events, include some details regarding what happened, use temporal words to signal event order, and provide some sense of closure.			
Production and Distribution of Writing			
With guidance and support from adults, focus on a topic, respond to questions and suggestions from peers, and add details to strengthen writing as needed.			
With guidance and support from adults, use a variety of digital tools to produce and publish writing, including in collaboration with peers.			

Writing Standards	Date	Date	Date
Research to Build and Present Knowledge			
Participate in shared research and writing projects (e.g., explore a number of "how-to" books on a given topic and use them to write a sequence of instructions).			
With guidance and support from adults, recall information from experiences or gather information from provided sources to answer a question.			

Speaking and Listening Standards	Date	Date	Date
Comprehension and Collaboration			
Participate in collaborative conversations about grade 1 topics and texts with peers and adults in small and larger groups.			
Follow agreed-upon rules for discussions (e.g., listening to others with care, speaking one at a time about the topics and texts under discussion).			
Build on others' talk in conversations by responding to the comments of others through multiple exchanges.			
Ask questions to clear up any confusion about the topics and texts under discussion.			
Ask and answer questions about key details in a text read aloud or information presented orally or through other media.			
Ask and answer questions about what a speaker says in order to gather additional information or clarify something that is not understood.			
Presentation of Knowledge and Ideas			
Describe people, places, things, and events with relevant details, expressing ideas and feelings clearly.			
Add drawings or other visual displays to descriptions when appropriate to clarify ideas, thoughts, and feelings.			
Produce complete sentences when appropriate to task and situation.			

Language Standards	Date	Date	Date
Conventions of Standard English			
Demonstrate command of the conventions of standard English grammar and usage when writing or speaking.			
Print all upper- and lowercase letters.			
Use common, proper, and possessive nouns.			
Use singular and plural nouns with matching verbs in basic sentences (e.g., *He hops; We hop*).			
Use personal, possessive, and indefinite pronouns (e.g., *I, me, my; they, them, their, anyone, everything*).			
Use verbs to convey a sense of past, present, and future (e.g., *Yesterday I walked home; Today I walk home; Tomorrow I will walk home*).			
Use frequently occurring adjectives.			
Use frequently occurring conjunctions (e.g., *and, but, or, so, because*).			
Use determiners (e.g., articles, demonstratives).			
Use frequently occurring prepositions (e.g., *during, beyond, toward*).			
Produce and expand complete simple and compound declarative, interrogative, imperative, and exclamatory sentences in response to prompts.			
Demonstrate command of the conventions of standard English capitalization, punctuation, and spelling when writing.			
Capitalize dates and names of people.			
Use end punctuation for sentences.			
Use commas in dates and to separate single words in a series.			
Use conventional spelling for words with common spelling patterns and for frequently occurring irregular words.			
Spell untaught words phonetically, drawing on phonemic awareness and spelling conventions.			

Language Standards	Date	Date	Date
Vocabulary Acquisition and Use			
Determine or clarify the meaning of unknown and multiple-meaning words and phrases based on *grade 1 reading and content*, choosing flexibly from an array of strategies.			
Use sentence-level context as a clue to the meaning of a word or phrase.			
Use frequently occurring affixes as a clue to the meaning of a word.			
Identify frequently occurring root words (e.g., *look*) and their inflectional forms (e.g., *looks, looked, looking*).			
With guidance and support from adults, demonstrate understanding of word relationships and nuances in word meanings.			
Sort words into categories (e.g., colors, clothing) to gain a sense of the concepts the categories represent.			
Define words by category and by one or more key attributes (e.g., a *duck* is a bird that swims; a *tiger* is a large cat with stripes).			
Identify real-life connections between words and their use (e.g., note places at home that are *cozy*).			
Distinguish shades of meaning among verbs differing in manner (e.g., *look, peek, glance, stare, glare, scowl*) and adjectives differing in intensity (e.g., *large, gigantic*) by defining or choosing them or by acting out the meanings.			
Use words and phrases acquired through conversations, reading and being read to, and responding to texts, including using frequently occurring conjunctions to signal simple relationships (e.g., *I named my hamster Nibblet because she nibbles too much because she likes that*).			